MiXeD NuTS

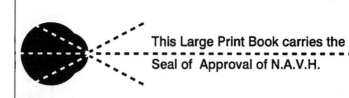

This Large Print Book carries the
Seal of Approval of N.A.V.H.

MiXeD NuTS

America's Love Affair with Comedy Teams

From Burns and Allen to Belushi and Aykroyd

Lawrence J. Epstein

Thorndike Press • Waterville, Maine

Published in 2005 by arrangement with Public Affairs, a member of Perseus Books LLC.

Thorndike Press® Large Print Americana.

The tree indicium is a trademark of Thorndike Press.

The text of this Large Print edition is unabridged. Other aspects of the book may vary from the original edition.

Set in 16 pt. Plantin by Liana M. Walker.

Printed in the United States on permanent paper.

Library of Congress Cataloging-in-Publication Data

Epstein, Lawrence J. (Lawrence Jeffrey)
    Mixed nuts : America's love affair with comedy teams from Burns and Allen to Belushi and Aykroyd / by Lawrence J. Epstein.
      p. cm. — (Thorndike Press large print Americana)
    Originally published: New York : PublicAffairs, c2004.
    ISBN 0-7862-7523-5 (lg. print : hc : alk. paper)
    1. Comedians — United States — Biography.
  2. Large type books. I. Title. II. Thorndike Press large print Americana series.
PN2285.E67 2005
  792.702′8′092273—dc22
                                      2004031060

*This book is dedicated to my team —
my wife, Sharon,
and our children,
Michael, Elana, Rachel, and Lisa.*

Trust me, I'm the straight man.

As the Founder/CEO of NAVH, the only national health agency solely devoted to those who, although not totally blind, have an eye disease which could lead to serious visual impairment, I am pleased to recognize Thorndike Press★ as one of the leading publishers in the large print field.

Founded in 1954 in San Francisco to prepare large print textbooks for partially seeing children, NAVH became the pioneer and standard setting agency in the preparation of large type.

Today, those publishers who meet our standards carry the prestigious "Seal of Approval" indicating high quality large print. We are delighted that Thorndike Press is one of the publishers whose titles meet these standards. We are also pleased to recognize the significant contribution Thorndike Press is making in this important and growing field.

Lorraine H. Marchi, L.H.D.
Founder/CEO
NAVH

★ Thorndike Press encompasses the following imprints: Thorndike, Wheeler, Walker and Large Print Press

CONTENTS

FOREWORD

When I was young, a doctor injected my brother and me with shots that later made us unable to raise our arms. Hurting and frightened, we dragged ourselves in front of the grainy television screen. The flickering images of Abbott and Costello's movie *Keep 'Em Flying* made us both laugh until we forgave the doctor.

A few years later, I sat in a darkened college classroom with other world-weary students and literally could not stop laughing at Groucho Marx's verbal charges and gallivanting stride, Harpo's angelic innocence, regularly punctured by his chasing an attractive woman, and Chico's assaults on language.

In other happy moments, I watched Lucille Ball and Vivian Vance struggling mightily against a relentless, candy-filled conveyor belt. And Laurel and Hardy dragging a piano across a narrow, swaying rope bridge, precariously perched high over a Swiss gorge, only to get halfway before encountering a gorilla.

This didn't happen where I lived.

And then, except for a few like the reliable Three Stooges, they were gone. The classic comedy teams, the teams in which members joined their professional lives together, were lifted by the cultural whirlwind of the 1960s and 1970s and set down in the land of nostalgia.

I continued to enjoy seeing the films and shows of comedy teams, and a few years ago, I began to probe the mystery of why those classic teams disappeared. I collected the comedy teams' jokes and routines and uncovered the little-known life stories of the team members. I found out how different the real Gracie Allen was from her character as she charmed and baffled George Burns, what had happened to Dean Martin and Jerry Lewis that made them stop talking for so many years after their breakup, and how Abbott and Costello, with quick talk and clever slapstick, could heal a hurting child.

Then I searched for the story of how comedy teams first began and how they changed. I discovered how the team members met and dealt with the backstage fights, the bickering over billing and wages, the egos pumped up by fame, or the tragedies in their lives, such as the death of Lou Costello's son or the suicide in a barbershop of one member of a team popular in the 1930s.

I learned about the different types of teams, like the temporary movie teams in which stars came together for a film but otherwise led separate professional lives. These temporary teams ranged from Bob Hope and Bing Crosby to those who met on *Saturday Night Live*, such as John Belushi and Dan Aykroyd, and Chris Farley and David Spade. I also learned about the comedy gangs like Monty Python.

This book is the result of my search.

When I began, I was astounded at the sheer number of comedy teams, and therefore the first problem was to find a way to fit their stories within the confines of a single volume. I decided to leave out teams that were made up of or included non-human partners. Therefore, there are no cartoon teams in the book, no Fred Flintstone and Barney Rubble, for example. Nor are there ventriloquist teams, such as the great Edgar Bergen and Charlie McCarthy. Clearly, an unabridged account of comedy teams would include the enormous talents and contributions of these teams.

Limiting comedy teams in this way

didn't entirely solve the problem, though, because there was still an amazing number of teams. I started listing all the teams in vaudeville, for example, until I realized they could fill their own encyclopedia. The teams that are included in this book are those that have made the greatest contributions to team comedy, or those with unique stories or unusual material. Because the book is a chronological account of teams in American life, I have included teams from every entertainment medium and every generation.

The popularity of comedy teams was another significant criterion in determining inclusion. At first, I thought this might mean worthy but underappreciated teams would not get their fair due, but to my astonishment, as I weighed the contributions different teams had made, I concluded that over time, the popularity of comedy teams was a fair and generally good indicator of their talent. The Marx Brothers, for example, were simply a better team than their contemporaries. Nonetheless, many teams that were popular in their own time lack an audience today. I have tried to elucidate the reasons for their original popularity, to explain their attraction, and to include as many of them as possible.

While I knew it was important to include defining personal information, I didn't want to string together a series of minibiographies of the teams, especially because there are valuable books devoted to the lives of some of the major team members.

Of course, I wanted to discuss the essence of the team and include some of their famous routines and telling anecdotes about their lives and work, including how they created their humor. But I also wanted to talk about their place in the history of comedy teams, about, for example, what teams influenced them and how they influenced future teams.

As I began writing, I quickly realized that the story of comedy teams in America was much more than simply the story of some very funny people. There was, it turned out, a deeper social history of American life embedded in their story.

I first noticed this when I turned the spotlight around from the teams and put it on us, the audience. When I looked at how we had been affected by the teams, I noticed that they had met the deepest emotional needs of American audiences and helped shape our inner lives. I considered why audience members liked some teams and not others at particular times in American life, why some teams spent only a brief moment on the cultural stage and then disappeared, while others came back over and over for performances across the decades.

The teams that attracted us reflected our emotions and simultaneously informed us about our own feelings. During times of economic deprivation and war, for example, there were Bob Hope and Bing Crosby and Abbott and Costello to give relief to the grieving and anxious, to the desperate and hungry, to those who felt unfairly trapped by fate. Audience members knew that if they could laugh they weren't dead inside. During all the eras of American life, there were comedians who charted our feelings and helped us survive the times.

The story of comedy teams is a moving picture of America's emotional life, and I wanted to project that picture from beginning to end. I wanted to understand the emotional worlds they created when, as in the case of Burns and Allen, one member of the team took us to a fantasy world, while the other member of the team helped bring us back to reality.

Finally, after tracing the rise and fall of

the teams, I concluded that the teams flourished when we most needed a communal spirit and when we most forcefully embraced the virtues of self-sacrifice. The inherent group structure of classic teams symbolized the nation's cooperation during times of national distress. The humor of the teams was vital when people faced extraordinary responsibilities, painful self-doubts, and well-founded fears. The clean humor, gentle barbs, puns, and good-natured wisecracks helped audiences accept their sacrifices and appreciate the common struggles they faced. The comedy teams were a sign of hope during such times. Members of comedy teams were not the tortured geniuses who created comedy alone, like Chaplin, but more commonly (and allowing for possible exceptions like Groucho Marx) were dispensers of deeply needed humor. The stand-up comedians who emerged in the late 1950s and 1960s reflected their own era and so, in contrast to the teams, put the emphasis more on individual authenticity and happiness than on sacrificing the self for family and social cohesion. In this sense, the story of the rise and fall of comedy teams emerges as a metaphor for the struggle Americans undergo between

17

communal responsibilities and personal desires.

Telling the story of comedy teams, it turns out, is an unexplored path to understanding what it means to be an American.

I also noticed that the seeming disappearance of the comedy teams was deceptive. The full arc of their story certainly includes their origins, their golden age, and their decline. But it also includes the uncharted course of their enduring afterlife, reflected in such forms as contemporary situation comedies.

The story of comedy teams is a long one, starting in the nineteenth century, spanning the twentieth, and with those influences, continuing on into the current century. It is a story that opens as a man and woman are headed toward a tiny room in a lavish vaudeville theater and are about to enter the breathtaking gateway to fortune and fame.

ONE

MUSTY THEATERS AND ASBESTOS CURTAINS

The Rise of Burns and Allen

Nobody had believed he would ever play the Palace.

But George Burns, in a flashy new suit and clean spats, boldly strode across Broadway toward the top theater in vaudeville. It was 1926 and he was headed for his first performance in the home of show business legends.

This show was for his mother, too sick to attend the performance, for his father, who had died so young, for Gracie, who hesitantly trailed beside him, for the nasty managers who had fired him, and for the audiences that had mocked him. And though he had loved the life, this was also to make up for all those years dragging steamer trunks on trains to Altoona or Fargo only to stay in cramped hotel rooms and cook on illegal hot plates. Soon he would belong to entertainment royalty.

The Palace was a tall, narrow building on Broadway and 47th decorated in gold and crimson. Burns and Allen strode past the sidewalk out in front, nicknamed "the beach," where vaudevillians, would-be vaudevillians, and dazzled members of the public met and mingled, discussing jokes and acts, wages and sins, and the hazards and joys of the profession.

They walked past the sign backstage that

read, "This Theater caters to Ladies and Gentlemen and Children. Vulgarity will not be tolerated," past the chalkboard where, at rehearsal that morning, they had learned their spot on the bill, and past the dressing room on the first floor reserved for headliners, who wouldn't have to climb the stairs or enter the rickety steel elevator the management deemed perfectly suitable for newcomers. Burns and Allen, though, had to ride the shaky contraption upstairs. Their dressing room was small and old-fashioned but clean. The size of the room didn't bother Burns. He felt the exuberant surge of adrenaline, the sheer fun, that only performing gave him.

Gracie was, as always, dressed in long sleeves, careful to cover her bad arm. They each put on their makeup. It took Gracie three tries before she got her lipstick on the way she wanted. They didn't speak to each other.

The show was a Monday matinee, the traditional first performance when friends and colleagues would be there for support. Burns knew Jack Benny and Archie Leach, the good-looking British guy who wanted to become an actor but for now earned $5 a week walking on his stilts at Coney Island, and the others would arrange for an usher to bring flowers to the stage after the show.

He would not let them down.

Burns stared in the mirror. His thirty-year-old face stared back.

It had never been easy being George Burns.

He and his eight brothers and sisters had slept on one mattress in a single-room tenement apartment at 95 Pitt Street in New York's predominantly Jewish Lower East Side. Three more children would eventually join the family, so they moved to a larger three-room apartment at 259 Rivington Street. It was a bustling time. The Williamsburg Bridge to Brooklyn had opened in 1903, and the first subway line began in 1904.

Burns's father, Louis, labored in a kosher butcher shop but never made enough money. Dora, his wife, seemingly fed her family from the air. Their difficult situation grew tragic when Louis, sitting by the window reading from his prayer book, slumped over and died from influenza. He was forty-seven, and young George, then still known by his real name, Nat Birnbaum, was eight. Determined to assume his father's failed place as breadwinner, the young boy might have chosen a career in crime. Meyer Lansky, for example, had arrived with his family from Russia in 1911 and grew up on the Lower East Side.

Instead, Burns worked at Rosenzweig's candy store. There, mixing cherry and chocolate syrup, Nat and two brothers sang in harmony, a common pastime in poverty-stricken immigrant homes.

One day, Lewis Farley, a postal worker determined to enter show business, came into the store and heard the boys singing. Farley urged them to add a fourth partner and form a group he offered to manage. Soon the "Peewee Quartet" was born.

Farley booked the group where he could — which meant they usually played on street corners. Burns claimed they were most successful on the Staten Island ferry; young couples paid them to sing somewhere else. Burns noted, "The only place they could go to avoid us was by jumping overboard."

By the age of ten, Nat Birnbaum had lost a long struggle with arithmetic. He could barely read or write. It was torture for him to unscramble letters and recognize words. He knew his mind was faster than those of the other students, but still he could not grasp the lessons.

So he fled school and joined a dance team called the Burns Brothers. Burns claimed he took the last name from his habit of stealing coal from the Burns Brothers Coal Yard, which may or may not have been the case.

Burns had a lifelong penchant for sweetening reality, giving it what was then called a "vaudeville shine," making it funnier than it was or permitting him to separate himself emotionally from painful memories.

It is likely that young Nat acquired the name of Burns simply by shortening Birnbaum. It was common for immigrants entering show business to alter their birth names. They didn't want to ruin their family's reputation. Most people, after all, thought that vaudevillians led neither a dignified nor a moral life.

Nat Birnbaum, though, couldn't call himself Nat Burns on stage because there was already a vaudevillian named Nat Burns who didn't want an upstart stealing his name. So Nat Birnbaum changed his first name to George. Burns's brother Izzy had chosen to call himself George, and Nat thought that sounded fine.

George Burns was born, although vaudeville didn't much notice or care. After signing Burns, managers quickly returned his pictures to him, the dreaded vaudeville signal that a performer's contract had been cancelled. He tried acts of every kind. He danced tangos. He roller-skated. It didn't matter. Nobody wanted him, or if they wanted him once, they didn't want him twice.

He had to change his stage name frequently to trick managers into rehiring him. He was Pedro Lopez or Phil Baxter, among many others. He starred — very briefly — in the act "Maurice Valenti and His Wonder Dog." The dog was somewhat less wondrous than advertised. Burns appeared with a supposedly trained seal in "Flipper and Friend." The seal didn't do much — despite its top billing.

It was difficult to earn enough money just to eat. Burns often had to pour ketchup into hot water and slurp spoonfuls of this cheap version of tomato soup. It became his lifelong habit to add ketchup to all meals.

Along the way, Burns married a partner from a ballroom dancing act. Hannah Siegel's parents supposedly wouldn't allow their daughter to go on a twenty-six-week tour with a single man, and so, Burns claimed, he married her and gave her the stage name of Hermosa (after his favorite cigar). He later suggested that the marriage lasted only as long as the tour, though this was a characteristic exaggeration.

His next act was with Billy Lorraine; the two imitated popular singers. Fifteen-year-old Milton Berle was higher on the bill than they were. Berle thought — correctly — that Burns and Lorraine's act was hopeless. Burns, already twenty-seven, found himself married to a woman who was no longer his partner in any sense of the word, poor, with few prospects and a pathetically weak act. He had plenty of drive and ambition, he was happy, but he knew he needed something else.

Burns's life changed at a final booking in Union City, New Jersey, during the late autumn of 1923. Rena Arnold, another performer on the bill, had invited her roommates, Mary Kelly and Gracie Allen, backstage. Arnold told Gracie that Burns and Lorraine were splitting up and each was looking for a woman partner. Arnold strongly suggested that Gracie should team up with Billy Lorraine. Gracie went with the intention of meeting him but ended up chatting with Burns. The two met again a few days later at a rehearsal room in a song publisher's office.

There was no romance at first. Burns remained nominally married to Hannah Siegel, and Gracie, just seventeen, was in love with Benny Ryan, a big, handsome Irish song-and-dance man. Ryan was familiar territory for Gracie. Her father, George Allen, was a big, handsome Irish song-and-dance man, but one who had abandoned his family, pausing, before he left, to teach five-year-old Gracie the steps of an Irish jig. She began her entertainment career doing the dance at a church social.

Gracie would later become famous for a line about her childhood: "When I was born, I was so surprised I couldn't talk for a year and a half." It was more poignant than audiences realized. At exactly the age of a year and a half, the infant Gracie had grabbed a pot off the stove and spilled boiling liquid on her arm and shoulder, scalding herself terribly. The accident left permanent scars. She took to covering up the arm, so that there are no pictures of Gracie Allen with the arm bare.

Gracie entered show business with her sisters in a singing quartet. When one sister left the act, the remaining three joined another, but it didn't do well. Discouraged, Gracie quit and went to stenography school. But she detested it and longed to return to show business.

She was, therefore, ready when George Burns, then still calling himself Nat Birnbaum, came along. They were prepared for their first performance three weeks after they met. Originally, she was billed as "Grace Allen." The nickname would come later when cops, taxi drivers, and newsboys began to call her "Gracie."

Burns was convinced that he should be the comic and Gracie the "talking woman" (the female version of "the straight man"). He wanted to be the one getting the laughs, even if he lifted the material from joke books.

The new team started out at a theater in Boonton, New Jersey, in late 1922. They were booked for one night and were paid $10. By one account, the manager wanted to know what kind of an act they did. Burns replied, "Dialogue."

"Okay," the manager answered. "But whatever you do, just cut out the talk."

The manager's son standing nearby added, "If there's anything my dad hates, it's talk."

Burns couldn't cut out the talk. He and Gracie were a "patter team," getting laughs just by talking, not by odd makeup or zany slapstick, although he knew that clothes were an important laugh prompt for the audience. Burns wore new clothes, but he wanted them to scream "funny." He therefore shortened his pants and turned up the brim of his hat. The two went out on stage with Burns prepared not only to talk but also to be hilarious doing it.

He talked all right in his rolled-up pants, but he wasn't in the least bit hilarious.

Later in life, he savored his retelling of that night's performance, making it and its consequences mythic. The audience, he claimed, adding a vaudeville shine to the story, laughed at Gracie's straight lines but didn't laugh at his supposedly funny lines. So, right after the first show he knew he had to change roles. At the very next performance, he related, he became the feeder, the straight man, and Gracie became the comedian.

In reality, George Burns was extremely reluctant to give up his role. Burns and Allen were reviewed in *Variety* twice the next year, in April and June, and both reviewers identified Burns as the wisecracking comic.

During that time, Burns and Allen were relegated to a seemingly permanent status as a "disappointment act." Such acts were used when another act cancelled, usually due to illness or drunkenness. New shows opened on Mondays and Thursdays. On these days, George and Gracie would stay in their hotel, waiting for a call about a cancellation. The couple would then hop a train to wherever the original act had been scheduled to appear.

It was painful for Burns, but he gradually came to the conclusion that he would have to relinquish his role as comic. Gracie was funny; he was not. Audiences loved her. They loved her voice. They loved the sincerity with which she spoke. They loved her twinkling eyes and porcelain skin, her dainty figure and curly hair.

His decision made, Burns struggled with how to define Gracie's role. Always extremely sensitive to audience reactions, Burns noticed that they didn't like it if Gracie was sarcastic. Burns enjoyed what he would eventually call "illogical logic," explanations that made sense, but only on their own terms. Part of this came from his mother. "My mother didn't know she was funny. She once said 'I know I'm going to die . . . and Uncle Frank is going to come to the funeral. . . . Make sure the coffee is hot . . . because if the coffee isn't hot . . .

he won't go.'" Burns thought he and Gracie could do a flirtation act, a man and a woman discussing male-female relationships, in which Gracie could perform that crazy logic. It was an idea that challenged vaudeville tradition because although there were many mixed acts, the woman's role in almost all of them was to be the "Dumb Dora," a dizzy and empty-headed woman.

One typical act, for example, was "Dialogue Between Master of Ceremonies and a Dumb Dora," by a vaudevillian with the improbable name of James Madison. Here's how it began:

Master of Ceremonies: If you do well this week, I may hold you over.
Dumb Dora: Hold me over what?
Master of Ceremonies: I mean I'll renew your engagement.
Dumb Dora: Has it been broken?
Master of Ceremonies: Has what been broken?
Dumb Dora: Our engagement.
Master of Ceremonies: We're not engaged. Getting married is foreign to my thoughts.
Dumb Dora: That's all right. I'm a foreigner.
Master of Ceremonies: You intrigue me.

31

Dumb Dora: What's that?

Master of Ceremonies: I said, "You intrigue me."

Dumb Dora: Not while all these people
are watching.

Essentially the Dumb Dora acts consisted of one joke — the woman's misun-
derstanding replayed in various ways.
Burns knew audiences wanted more from
Gracie because they cared for her. And so
he gave her the mercurial brilliance of his
mother's illogical logic. He created a new
kind of woman partner, a woman who, at
least within her own world, was not at all
dumb. Burns's conception would give
Gracie the punch lines and the profundity,
and, in one stroke, turn vaudeville tradition on its head.

He began writing especially for her. He
knew the Gracie character he wanted to
create, and he brilliantly integrated events
from their real lives — Gracie's relatives
and their crowded homes, for example.
Crucially, Burns then hired talented
writers to develop the character that made
Gracie famous:

Gracie: All great singers have their
trials. Look at Caruso. Thirty years

on a desert island with all those cannibals.

George: You've got the wrong man.

Gracie: No. You're the man for me.

George: But they say I'm through as a singer. I'm extinct.

Gracie: You do not!

The act quickly became a success, and the newly divorced Burns declared his love. Stunned, Gracie reacted by insisting that she still loved Benny Ryan. She met Burns's proposals with bouts of laughter, disbelief, or downright refusal.

Burns and Allen were in San Francisco, Gracie's hometown, when she got appendicitis. George swore he sent a telegram to Benny Ryan, but Benny never contacted her. She grew angry with him. Still, she would not marry Burns.

At a Christmas party in 1925, she handed Burns a present with a note on it that included the words "with all my love." Burns, dressed improbably for an emotional showdown as Santa Claus, confronted her about it, saying she shouldn't use the words if she didn't mean them. He gave her an ultimatum, to marry him or end the act. Santa then stormed out of the room.

Later that night, Benny Ryan called. Gracie spoke with him and decided on the phone to break up. She immediately called Burns and told him she was ready to get married, which they did on January 7, 1926.

Their rise after that was the stuff of dime novels and daydreams: Just six weeks after the wedding, they were at the Palace.

Burns and Allen stood in the wings as the stage card changed. Burns reached over and held Gracie's hand as their song, "The Love Nest," started, and the spotlight swung to pick them out in the wing. They smiled and casually walked out on stage.

Gracie pulled to a stop, turned around, and waved. She let go of George's hand and walked back toward the wing, still waving. Then she stopped and beckoned for someone to enter from offstage. A man came out, put his arms around Gracie and kissed her. She kissed him back. They waved to each other, and the man quickly exited. Gracie came back to George in the center of the stage.

Gracie: Who *was* that?
George: You don't know?
Gracie: No. My mother told me never to

talk to strangers.

George: That makes sense.

Gracie: This always happens to me. On my way in, a man stopped me at the stage door and said, "Hiya, cutie, how about a bite tonight after the show?"

George: And you said?

Gracie: I said, "I'll be busy after the show, but I'm not doing anything now," so I bit him.

George: Gracie, let me ask you something. Did the nurse ever happen to drop you on your head when you were a baby?

Gracie: Oh, no, we couldn't afford a nurse. My mother had to do it.

George: You had a smart mother.

Gracie: Smartness runs in my family. When I went to school I was so smart my teacher was in my class for five years.

George: Gracie, what school did you go to?

Gracie: I'm not allowed to tell.

George: Why not?

Gracie: The school pays me $25 a month not to tell.

George: Gracie, this family of yours, do you all live together?

Gracie: Oh, sure. My father, my brother, my uncle, my cousin, and my nephew all sleep in one bed and . . .

George: In one bed? I'm surprised your grandfather doesn't sleep with them.

Gracie: Oh he did, but he died, so they made him get up.

After the routine, the lights in the house went down, and a spotlight appeared on Gracie. She sang. Just at the end of the song, the music quickened, and Gracie broke into her Irish jig.

The lights came up. Burns stood next to her applauding with the audience while Gracie bowed. They did a few more minutes of patter, and for the final part of the act, they did what no team had done before. They danced together, but George stopped the music four times during the dance, did a few lines, and then resumed dancing. Then they danced off the stage.

Once backstage, Burns and Allen were exuberant. They could still hear the waves of roaring applause. Their friends rushed to greet them. Everyone offered congratulations, including Archie Leach, who would eventually change his name to Cary Grant. It wouldn't be long before the Palace would have them back as headliners.

Burns would never cherish a show business moment as much as this one. It was his first heady realization that after all the longing, all the despair, all the hope, he and Gracie had finally joked their way through the gates of show business heaven.

Gracie was not consumed by show business and never talked about the act offstage, but George lived for the straw hats, musty theaters, and asbestos curtains of vaudeville. Show business was his oxygen. He never lost faith in it, never stopped learning how to navigate its currents, and never surrendered a chance to discuss its future.

Burns and Allen went on to become the greatest comedy act in vaudeville. With considerable justification, Burns always credited Gracie for their success.

Gracie's laugh, her thin, high-pitched voice (which was not at all like her real one), her compact prettiness embodied in her curly black hair and attractive red lips, her sweetness, and her loopy but sincere way of looking at the world endeared her to the audience. She dressed well. She looked like a cute young woman with a child's attractive qualities. She had no aura of a clown, as so many other women performers such as Fanny Brice did. She did not make faces. She did not engage in sexually suggestive banter.

Gracie didn't threaten or scare the audience. They didn't want to be like her, but they wanted her to fulfill her heart's desires. They also wanted to protect her. Burns had to go out before shows to check air currents in the theater. He didn't want his cigar smoke blowing in Gracie's face. He knew audiences would never forgive him.

Gracie was as big a draw to women in the audience as she was to men. Men liked her because she was pretty and seemed to conform to the stereotypical view then current of women as hopelessly lost in the search for logic. Women might therefore easily have resented her performances. Instead, they admired her. She thought it was because they were not jealous of her, but the attraction lay also in her dignity, in the way that the much-mocked feminine logic actually made sense. Her character could even be understood and appreciated as a sly parody of men's views of women's minds.

Gracie was also a perfect symbol for women caught between Victorian morality and modern mores. It was an era of incredible restrictions on women's freedoms. Women were not, for example, allowed to smoke in public. Vaudeville's attractive women performers provided playful alternatives to the rigid gender roles in which women found themselves. The corseted American moral code was unlaced by vaudeville's brazen performers with their subtle but clear endorsement of a morality that accepted impulsive attraction and championed acting on the impulse. But many women were confused by the changes. Though they were thrilled by the new possibilities, they wanted to be respected. It is no wonder that an attractive, confused character who got respect and proved triumphant would be so interesting to women in the audience.

Burns and Allen also had perfect timing — in two senses of the word. First, their arrival on stage caught the spirit of the age. Somehow Burns, as he listened to audiences, absorbed their deepest needs and desires and knew how to shape his and Gracie's characters to reflect those feelings.

But their timing was not just deft historically; comic timing was a crucial part of their professional craft. In comedy, the straight man's "timing" refers to his ability to wait to speak until the laughter has peaked, receded, and finally stopped so that audiences can hear the next line, but not wait for so long after it has stopped that audiences might get confused or bored. The comic's timing refers to the response after the straight man has finished a line. The term "beat" is used to measure the pause between lines, and it and the "pace," or speed of the delivery, had to be perfect. The comic in the team needed an appropriate appearance and funny lines. Both the straight man and the comic needed rhythm.

Burns and Allen were experts at all of this. They knew which words to emphasize. They learned to control their voices. The staccato rhythm of their delivery was perfect. Other performers would have spoken too slowly or too fast or fallen out of the rhythm, which had to be maintained with each line and each silence. They even used pauses well. Gracie would giggle, an infectious sound and a prompt for even further audience laughter. George's repetition of much of the material was also crucial to the pacing, allowing the audience to grasp the premise precisely and be set up by George for the line to follow. It was impossible for Burns to be a comedian in such a structure. Any joke he interjected would break the patented Burns and Allen patter.

Gracie's humor would not have worked had the character not seemed to believe the illogical logic absolutely. Burns's straight man could, on behalf of the audience, show bemusement, but Gracie could not break out of character without ruining the act. It is unsurprising that many in the audience confused the real Gracie Allen with her carefully constructed character. They never saw her let the mask slip. The strain of always being "Gracie Allen" gave her devastating migraine headaches and created an early and unrelenting desire to retire from show business.

Despite these tensions, she never faltered. Through the pain, she created one of the most enduring characters in entertainment history, one whose personality and voice come through even on the printed page:

Gracie: . . . I'm a mind reader . . . All right, think of something.
George: Well, all right, I'm thinking.

Gracie: Is it green?

George: Is what green?

Gracie: Does it hang from the ceiling and whistle?

George: Does what hang from the ceiling and whistle?

Gracie: Does it run along the floor and sing?

George: Listen . . .

Gracie: Does it climb up buildings and swim?

George: Just a minute. I thought you said that you could read my mind.

Gracie: Well, George, how can I read your mind if you keep on asking all those silly questions?

Or:

Gracie: George, I've got some wonderful news for you. My brother got married, but it's the carpenter's fault . . .

George: . . . What do you mean it was the carpenter's fault?

Gracie: Well, you see, my brother was crazy about a girl who lived on the third floor . . .

George: Yes . . .

Gracie: But the carpenter made the

ladder too short, and he eloped with the girl on the second floor.

George: But what about the girl on the third floor? Bet that made her pretty mad.

Gracie: Oh, well, she didn't seem to mind it. But her husband was so disappointed he could hardly hold the ladder.

George always held the ladder tightly as Gracie scaled up the heights of comedy and eloped with fame. Even as that fame grew, neither of them ever forgot that Burns and Allen was a comedy team that came from a great American tradition.

TWO

WILD GAGS AND
MURDERED ENGLISH

The Birth of Comedy Teams

The distinguished man in formal dress with white makeup on his face dashed onto the stage. The other actors, who sat in a semicircle, had blackened their faces with burnt cork or greasepaint. They wore outlandish swallow-tailed coats with striped trousers. As a chorus concluded its song, the elegant master of ceremonies, called the interlocutor, jauntily commanded, "Gentlemen, be seated." Then, between songs and instrumental pieces, the interlocutor joked and posed riddles.

This was the format of a minstrel show in the 1840s. The interlocutor playfully ridiculed two wisecracking people at either end of the group. These endmen were known as Mr. Bones and Mr. Tambo, names taken from bone clackers and tambourines, which were noisily played right after the jokes were told — the forerunner of the rim shot. The bones hitting together produced an abrupt, sharp sound like a drum, while the tambourine sounded like a cymbal crashing. While the interlocutor spoke what was supposed to be dignified upper-class English, the two endmen, topped by exaggerated wigs, laced their dialect with puns and malapropisms. Much of the humor was primitive, the puns groan-inducing. A typical exchange went like this:

Interlocutor: He must have been a
    doctor of some standing.
Mr. Bones: No, he wasn't standing. He
    was sitting on a three-legged stool.

The back and forth among the interlocutor and the endmen led to the creation of minstrel comedy teams, white men in blackface who offered supposedly humorous parodies of African Americans as carefree folks who lived to entertain white audiences.

The next crucial step in the evolution of teams was taken when one member of the minstrel comedy team took off the blackface and served as what would later be called the straight man. These minstrel teams were popular with those who saw them, but they were not known by large numbers of Americans. While the various entertainment forms — the circuses, independent repertory theaters, showboats, road shows, and traveling menageries — often attracted large crowds, there were simply not enough shows to meet audience demands because it was so hard for the entertainers to travel.

The opportunity for entertainers to play in many places over their careers only came about with the spread of the railroad. Suddenly, traveling troupes were able to go from town to town all over the country.

It didn't take long for entrepreneurs to figure out the best way to organize. Theaters or saloons were built near a city's shopping and transportation area. Both city residents and those who came into the city to shop became potential customers. The troupes would get off the trains and be right near the places to perform.

Many of the shows were oriented specifically toward men. Saloon owners, for example, looking to fill and refill the glasses of their thirsty customers, wanted to prevent customers from returning home or to work. Entertainers were hired to perform alluring acts to keep patrons from leaving. It worked. Inhibitions were loosened, drink was bought, money spent, and an industry was created.

Despite the success of the variety shows in saloons and theaters, not everyone was pleased by the performers' rough, saucy language and the suggestive outfits worn by the women, outfits that seemed to reveal as much as they concealed. After all, families often attended the performances, and many felt that the shows were shameful and inappropriate for that kind of audience.

Outraged at the vulgarity of variety shows, a man named Tony Pastor vowed to develop a wholesome alternative and make money doing it. He labored to create a new entertainment form, one more orderly and less raucous, one that wouldn't be embarrassing to refined women and impressionable children. In doing so, he transformed American entertainment.

Born in Brooklyn to a devout Italian Catholic family, Pastor began his professional life at age six, singing at a temperance meeting. He worked at P. T. Barnum's Museum, in a minstrel show, and as a circus clown and ringmaster.

In 1881, Pastor opened the 14th Street Theater in New York. Entertaining singers and comics were on the bill, but they operated under new rules. Pastor didn't allow any liquor to be sold. Performers knew if they used words like liar, slob, devil, damn, sucker, or son of a gun they would be fired instantly. To attract family audiences, Pastor invented the tradition of giving away door prizes. Silk dresses and sacks of potatoes were especially popular.

Pastor's phenomenal success quickly enticed competitors. In 1883, Benjamin Keith and Edward F. Albee, flush with cash from staging unauthorized Gilbert and Sullivan operettas, built a theater chain in the Northeast. They staged clean shows and, sensing the willingness of people to return again and again, instituted the tradition of continuous performances.

They also used the term "vaudeville" for the shows. The word itself came from the valley of the Vive River in Normandy where drinking songs were popular.

The vaudeville theaters were temples where the masses came to revive their sagging spirits. Some of the theaters were sumptuous. The Paramount Theatre in Seattle, opened in 1928, was among the most ornate. Patrons paid their hard-earned 50 cents, and for a few hours the workers and families of Seattle became royalty as they relaxed in their lavishly decorated entertainment palace. Uniformed ushers, the palace guards, guided gawking audience members past the figurative adornments and iron handrails, past the floral gold wall patterns and the chandeliers glistening with 3 million glass beads, to one of the 3,000 seats. For many audience members, entering such a theater was the closest experience they would have to luxury. Unbeknownst to the audience, the backstage was cramped and the performers were not well paid. However, the audience members had got their money's worth before the first act even began. It's no wonder they kept coming back.

The Paramount and other theaters offered an exciting vaudeville show that usually opened with a "dumb act," one that didn't require speaking. This was done for two reasons. Vaudeville was meant to appeal to everyone, and many audience members in its early days were not yet fluent in English. Also, audience members often rushed in late, dashing from work or home. The audience could enjoy the opening silent act — such as acrobats, a cyclist, or a trick dog — while latecomers found their seats. The second act, comedy or singing, was always performed in front of a closed curtain to allow scenery to be set up behind it. These acts relaxed the audience and got them settled in their seats. The third act was typically a comedy sketch or magic act designed to get an audience excited. The acts would continue, with the next to last act (the "corker") of the first half usually featuring a major star and the closing act of the first half being a headliner.

The intermission was vital for theaters because of the huge profits they made from the concession stands — exactly as movie theaters do now. Indeed, if an act ran too long, the manager would demand that the performers cut it back. The manager's complaints made actors become precise in their timing. They learned exactly how much time to leave for laughs, how to space silences, how quickly to speak, and so on. It was the equivalent of a degree in comic timing.

After the intermission, an act was needed to calm the audience down and get them ready for the entertainment to come. The next to last spot in the second half was the major act of the show. Managers deliberately delayed it so that audience members wouldn't leave. The last spot, the "chaser," by contrast was reserved for an act that encouraged audiences to leave. It was often deliberately loud so that those who were leaving wouldn't disturb those who stayed. Surprisingly, in the early days of vaudeville, showing a motion picture was the most effective chaser. Audiences were not patient enough to watch the hazy, static shots of the earliest movies. They wanted a quick succession of acts with fast, witty repartee. The speed of such performances mimicked the helter-skelter city life they knew and the hectic nature of their own lives.

Vaudeville acts had an enormous influence on American audiences. To understand vaudeville's impact, one must consider its availability. At vaudeville's height in the 1920s, there were 4,000 vaudeville theaters and 20,000 different acts with more than 25,000 performers. More than 2 million people a day paid the average admission price of 25 cents to see a vaudeville performance somewhere in the United States. Vaudeville was a mass art form, and vaudevillians were the first stars admired by a mass audience. People sang like their favorite crooner. They bought joke books and tried to imitate the comedians they loved.

Vaudeville was a participatory rather than a private entertainment, the way radio and television would become. Audience members thought of the entertainers as familiar people. A comedian would receive an instantaneous audience judgment. There was either laughter and the stamping of feet, or there wasn't. If there weren't enough laughs, the audience would effectively stop the show, forcing the next act to appear.

But audience members didn't just mimic or applaud the entertainment. They wanted to absorb the vaudevillian's sensibilities.

The vaudeville performers, having generally come from families that were very poor, wanted to make money, seek fame, attract good-looking partners, and lead an exciting life. They wanted to escape the impoverished lives of their parents. This attitude had two profound effects on Americans. First, the vaudevillians were imbued with a deep strain of anti-authoritarianism. They rebelled against their families and against society's morals. This, in turn, set the pattern for entertainers throughout the twentieth century in this respect and ultimately for the audiences that identified with this rebelliousness. The vaudevillians taught the new immigrants that in the glorious land that was America, everyone was free to mock everyone else, including religious and political leaders and the ideas they espoused, and to speak openly about sexual desires.

Second, vaudeville stressed the enjoyment of the present, particularly the material goods provided by America. This undermined both the religious emphasis on the hereafter and the moral emphasis on delayed gratification. The vaudeville ethic was nakedly consumerist. It encouraged the idea that experience should lead to enjoyment and that work should pay for it.

The popular culture of American small towns and cities was also influenced by the vaudevillians. In a world before radio, residents of these communities relied on the vaudeville stars to let them know what was fashionable in the outside world. They learned the latest fads and jokes and the new social rules. So while the humor had to appeal to any audience, it also, in a subtle way, shaped the audience taste and slowly made the nation's cultural tastes more homogeneous.

In cities, the immigrants and working people especially found a unique institution in vaudeville. In many respects, they lived outside the major institutions of society; they fought bosses, landlords, and the legal system. But these marginalized segments of American society were the heart of vaudeville audiences. Vaudeville houses were open to them when higher education was not. The surprising and delightful shows validated the sense that they were genuinely American, that they, too, belonged in this brawny and boisterous land, that their fantasies had a basis in tangible reality. Indeed, it was only because vaudeville attracted this working-class and immigrant audience, in addition to its larger middle-class audience, that it could claim to be the first mass entertainment.

Vaudeville did have a cousin with a much less savory reputation. Burlesque had begun in the 1840s, making fun of (that is, burlesquing) the cultural habits of the upper classes. British burlesque soon added young women to the show. Unsurprisingly, it was P. T. Barnum who imported this new British entertainment by bringing Lydia Thompson's underdressed female troupe to the United States. Soon burlesque managers noted that the working-class audiences not only liked the voluptuous women but also enjoyed the interspersed comedy acts. In keeping with the ribald tone of the show, the setting was often suggestive, such as a physician's waiting room. There were jokes about men's sexual desires and the consequences of such desires. There was frequent use of slang. One standard bit, for example, mentioned "the life of Riley" referring to a pleasant, happy existence. In the skit, a man in a cast and bandages crosses the stage:

Comic: What happened to you?

Injured Man: I was living the life of Riley.

Comic: And?

Injured Man: Riley came home.

There were many suggestive jokes:

First Comic: I've been working at a ladies' bloomer factory.

Second Comic: How much do you make?

First Comic: I pull down fifty a week.

There were also jokes about a man and a woman flirting with each other:

Comic: Gentlemen prefer blondes.

Woman: But I'm not a blonde.

Comic: Well, I'm not a gentleman.

As in vaudeville, there were jokes about living conditions and, inevitably, mothers-in-law:

One comic is running along and a second comic stops him.

Second Comic: Hey, where are you going?

First Comic: My poor mother-in-law ate

some cucumbers, and now she's really sick.

Second Comic: Are you going to get a doctor?

First Comic: No. To buy some more cucumbers.

Or there were lines reflecting economic hard times, as in the skit in which a straight man goes into a cheap restaurant with a young woman he's trying to impress:

Straight Man: Isn't this a great restaurant? I'll bet you those chairs go back to Louis the Fourteenth.

Waiter: No. They go back to Macy's the fifteenth.

Mayor Fiorello La Guardia eventually banned burlesque in New York City in 1942, but it forever left a libidinal imprint on the memories of the devastated audience members who were deprived of its pleasures.

The success of vaudeville and burlesque had depended on a spectacular demographic shift. Ragged immigrants, millions of them, driven by poverty, desperation, and persecution, streamed into the ports of the United States, seduced by the glittering shores with their heart-quickening promise of a new chance in life. The newcomers had fled Europe and elsewhere yearning for a job, or excitement, or the alluring riches awaiting them in the sprawling, untamed cities of the golden dreamland that was America. The immigrants surged into the great urban centers daring to believe they were headed for a noisy paradise where plentiful and untouched treasure and romance surely awaited them.

In New York, at least, all that these newcomers found were crowded tenements and filthy factories, menial jobs and maddening noise. In vaudeville and burlesque, they found the perfect means of escape.

The vaudeville houses, recognizing the passions of this new audience, began to feature a series of ethnic comedy teams.

Although these teams were intimately familiar with the minstrel shows, a particularly American tradition, they may or may not have been aware that their comedy routines also had European roots going back at least as far as the Roman comedies of Plautus and Terence. In a typical classical comedy, a playboy son was comically teamed with a clever, funny slave to outwit a strict father. The "funny slave" tradition can also be seen in such Shakespearean comedies as *Two Gentlemen of Verona*, in which there are, in fact, two funny slaves: Speed, the witty servant of Valentine, and Launce, Proteus's humorous servant. (The "slave" character can still be seen in such modern comic characters as Jeeves, Mr. Belvedere, Benson, and the Nanny.)

American comedy teams, consciously or not, embellished these traditions with material from their own experiences, especially that of immigration. The first popular teams were Irish and then German (called "Dutch" acts, a term taken from the corruption of "deutsch"). Soon there were Jewish and Italian acts as well. That is, the chronological emergence of these teams exactly followed the order of immigration to the New World.

In each team, both members had thick accents and even thicker makeup. Their acts were filled with exaggerated ethnic stereotypes. Audience members could laugh at their own linguistic mistakes and simultaneously feel superior to the "greenhorns" who were even more baffled by the English language of their new homeland. They could laugh at the stereotypes of themselves and at the men and women who shared their workbench, ate in their restaurants, breathed the same sooty air, struggled with the same fears, and eventually, married into their families.

What the new immigrant audiences didn't quite understand was that in race-conscious America, their Irishness or Jewishness was secondary to the fact that they were white. As James Baldwin put it, "Jews came here from countries where they were not white, and they came here in part *because* they were not white." That is, the whiteness that America bestowed both homogenized the poverty-stricken immigrants and gave them a power in the new country that they hadn't had in their native lands.

Later audiences would react harshly to ethnic humor, but to audiences of the day, the humor was a reminder of their common fate, even as it, in true democratic spirit, gleefully mocked all comers. Because of the commonality of experience, the audience could feel sympathy for the comic fool. All of this was emotionally useful: The feelings removed a sense of isolation and exclusion and in so doing allowed the immigrants to develop a sharpened self-confidence accompanied by a very pleasing dose of laughter.

Not all of the stereotypes were so benign, however.

There were plenty of acts that mocked the powerless black community, one that, unlike the immigrant community, was barred from access and acceptance. Accordingly, the mocking of African Americans was qualitatively different from the mocking of the new immigrants. White audiences preferred cork-faced white actors to portray blacks as shiftless, dumb, and focused on finding a loose woman, an available card game, or a juicy watermelon.

Such racial stereotyping was facilitated by the segregated society in which vaudeville flourished. Almost all the Southern states legally prevented blacks and whites from attending the same theaters, and a separate vaudeville circuit in the South provided all-black performers for all-black audiences. Many Northern cities enforced segregation within the theaters, with the best seats reserved for whites. With blacks absent or relegated to the back of the theater, there was no check on white performers to curb their racially divisive comedy. Many acts mocking blacks therefore reinforced segregation by exaggerating, often loathsomely, black stereotypes.

The most famous of the early white acts

to use black dialect was McIntyre and Heath, starting in 1874. In one odd act, Vivian Duncan played a white character, and Rosetta Duncan, her sister, put on blackface and played a rough-and-tumble black friend. Later, D. W. Griffith made an unsuccessful film of the pair. Much later, Moran and Mack, known as the Two Black Crows, continued the tradition in films as well as onstage. Mack liked to explain to Moran, "I would go to work, if I could find any pleasure in it."

It should be noted that there were black comedy teams, too. (Blacks and whites did not ever go onstage together then.) Williams and Walker were the first successful team. Walker played a city slicker, while Williams was much slower:

Walker: . . . After you get into the bank you fill the satchel with money.
Williams: Whose money?
Walker: That ain't the point. We don't know who put the money there, and we don't know why they got it. And they won't know how we got it. All you have to do is fill the satchel . . .
Williams: And what do I do with the satchel?

Walker: All you got to do is bring it to me at a place where I tell you.

Williams: When they come to count up the cash and find it short, then what?

Walker: By that time we'll be far, far away . . .

In the act, Williams is convinced they'll end up in jail. The character types, a clear prelude to Amos 'n' Andy, were meant to combat stereotypes. George Walker explicitly set out to make "a radical departure from the old 'darky' style of singing and dancing." His penchant for high living and diamonds, and his early death did not allow him to fulfill his self-declared mission. His partner, Bert Williams, became extraordinarily famous as a great singer, but he continued to suffer the effects of prejudice. And, astoundingly, Bert Williams, a black man, always performed in blackface because that is what the white audiences wanted.

Miller and Lyles (Flournoy Miller and Aubrey Lyles), another black team, also tried to avoid racial stereotypes. This led to polar reactions: Some liked the fact that they stayed away from the standard routines about blacks, such as shooting craps, and others accused them of running away from their heritage. Miller and Lyles approached WGN in Chicago, the radio station that later produced *Amos 'n' Andy*, but were turned down. Miller later tried unsuccessfully to prove the radio series was based on their act and that Charles Correll and Freeman Gosden (the creators of *Amos 'n' Andy*) stole some standard Miller and Lyles lines, including "I'se regusted," which became a national catchphrase.

Miller and Lyles certainly did originate the comedy team classic "The Interruption Routine," borrowed and modified by later generations. In the routine, the two would interrupt each other, knowing exactly what the other was going to say and not waiting for the line to be finished. Here is one such standard routine:

Partner A: What's wrong with your car is . . .

Partner B: It ain't that. But you think maybe . . .

A: Oh, I know it couldn't be that. What you need is . . .

B: I just got one of them last week . . .

A: No, I mean the one that costs about . . .

B: Is you crazy? I can't afford that
   much . . .

   The routine worked so long for so many because it is emblematic of what teams meant: a sense of knowing a friend so well that you didn't even have to finish your thoughts.

   Not all teams consisted of friends. Teams constantly split up, regrouped, and split again. The team members argued over many matters. It only took one partner to begin dating for the second partner to suspect that the romantic pair would team up. Liquor (or "nose paint," in vaudeville parlance) sometimes threatened a team, especially when one member thought the other's drinking hurt the act. Just being together so much was stifling for some. More than a few successful team members spoke to each other only onstage or only about the act. Naturally, some teams had frequent fights over what was funny, how much money they should get, and other matters directly related to the act. It is amazing that so many comedy pairs stuck together, some for decades.

   Part of this resulted from friendship, and part of it was from fear. Performing onstage could be terrifying. The spotlight ruthlessly exposed every pore and every glistening drop of flop sweat. Comics could hope that if they weren't funny, their partner would be. It was also emotionally convenient to blame a partner for failing to get laughs or paychecks, for fumbling around looking for the skeleton key to success but never finding it.

During the early days of comedy, the straight man was considered the more important member of the pair. Indeed, both in vaudeville and early films the straight man got 60 percent of the team's pay, the comedian only 40 percent. This allocation supposedly reflected the straight man's skills: He controlled the tempo of the act with perfect timing and had to pull back and steady the sometimes manic comic from going too far for the audience. It was the straight man's reaction that helped the audience believe the absurdity of the comic. The straight man was like a tugboat, pulling and guiding the showier vessel, the one everybody watched.

The straight man's act had to seem effortless, which is why the act required so much preparation. The teams had to rehearse a lot to make the performance seem spontaneous. Additionally, the straight man had to be handsome, to attract a large number of women to the audience. He had to have a decent singing voice, dress well, speak well, and, naturally, have perfect comic timing and project a sense of confidence and control.

Finally, the straight man typically handled business affairs for the team, and so had to have a sense of the worth of the act and the art of negotiation. He had to know when to feign illness and when to threaten to walk out, how to nurse a grudge and how to be cordial, when to accept a low payment and when to move on in the team's career.

The role of straight man first emerged in the Jewish acts, and those comedy teams developed the repartee that all ethnic teams would eventually adopt.

In a typical Jewish comedy team act, the straight man would come out and sing a song. Then shots would be heard offstage, and the Jewish comic — complete with an ill-fitting suit, a beard, and a hat over his ears — would come running out.

Straight Man: Mr. Cohen, what are you running for?
Cohen: I'm trying to keep two fellows from fighting.
Straight Man: Who are the fellows?

Cohen: An Irishman and me.

The teams all played the sophistication of the straight man against the naïveté of the comic. For immigrant audiences, it was easy to understand that relationship as a metaphor for the immigrants' relationship with their new American home. They didn't resent the straight man, even if in his sophistication he became a con man, with the comic as his mark. The audience members were getting survival lessons from the straight man in their struggle to adapt to the society, to learn how to talk, dress, or act properly. The comic's ultimate triumph — because he was funnier than the straight man — let them celebrate themselves.

This straight man–comic tension allowed for all sorts of opposites to emerge: the honest against the dishonest, the thrifty against the generous, and the sober against the not so sober, for example. Because comedy was an outsider's weapon, these opposites let vaudeville (and later) audiences laugh at their everyday struggles against landlords, bosses, spouses, families, and strangers from very different cultures whose oddities became comprehensible when reduced to a series of simple stereotypes.

Audiences loved this stew of ethnic comedy teams. Indeed, they loved all of vaudeville, and they longed to know the performers, especially the talented and attractive ones.

Managers eventually recognized that audiences had favorites, and so they set out to find and nurture such performers. Vaudeville's star system began in 1893. A vaudeville manager at the Union Square Theatre in New York, miffed that a rival theater had hired well-known opera stars to attract audiences, decided to compete by using the universal language of business. He offered large sums of money to attract famous actors to make brief appearances onstage during a show. As audiences boomed, drawn, then as now, to talented, famous people, an intense competition developed. Popular performers could earn enormous salaries. Suddenly, the vaudeville stage offered a way to make a name and a fortune.

THREE

AN EXPLOSION OF STARS

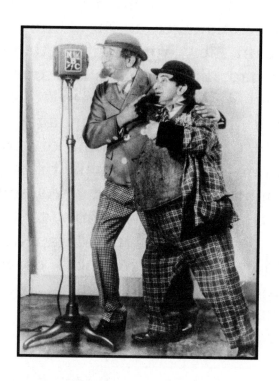

The First Classic Comedy Teams

Weber and Fields have the honor of being the first genuine team stars. Joseph Weber and Lew Fields defined "classic comedy team" because they were the first to embody what became accepted as the essential qualities of a team.

They attained national prominence. They used techniques that would become associated with team comedy such as linguistic mistakes (malapropisms, twisted or difficult-to-pronounce sentences), perfect timing (false starts, frequent interruptions), a comic sensibility (confusion, exasperation), and arguments. They contributed catchwords or some form of language to the culture. They pledged to each other that they would work together to forge a single career and create a special relationship. The joining together is crucial because in doing so the team had the opportunity to practice their act over and over, making it as perfect as possible. Team members often develop a sixth sense, an ability to know exactly what the other is thinking. This sense enables the team to put on a seamless performance — one that they couldn't do solo or with other partners. Finally, a mutual career distinguishes classic teams from simply two performers who work together irregularly or for a series of performances.

Joseph Weber came from a family with a dramatic immigrant story. His family — eleven people in all — left Poland for America but missed a ship from Liverpool. That ship was lost at sea with no survivors. When the Weber family finally embarked, the youngest child, an infant, died. Unwilling to follow the custom of surrendering the dead child to the shark-infested waters, Mrs. Weber held the baby for the rest of the voyage pretending to feed it. The family's first act upon arrival was to arrange for the burial. Joseph was born in New York in 1867.

The Promised Land was only a bit kinder to the family than the world they had left behind. Weber's father, like Nat Birnbaum's, struggled to make a living as a kosher butcher. Young Joe sought a more exciting path, and fate helped him along.

One day he found himself surrounded by a gang of boys trying to force him to surrender his money. A stranger bravely ran up to take his side. The stranger's name was Lew Schanfield, later known as Lew Fields, and he was not going to let the mere fact that they were outnumbered stop him from protecting someone in need.

Fields also came from a poor immigrant family. His father ran a sweatshop in the Bowery. Fields was toughened by the life, filled with a flinty determination to escape poverty's grasp and a desperate desire to avoid the traditional way of such escape — school.

By age ten, the two new friends were appearing together as performers, slowly perfecting their act. Incredibly, they gave birth to many vaudeville conventions when they were still teenagers. They wandered through the beer dives listening to what made people laugh. They hung out at the Bowery's famous dime museums soaking in what amused people. They went to shows and decided to "borrow" the material they liked.

They noticed that audiences loved knockabout humor with its boisterous, violent behavior. They took the crossfire dialogue from minstrel shows and earlier teams and combined that with the brutal physical humor then popular in Irish acts.

They further modified their hybrid style by developing characters with personalities. This was a crucial step, and it is the essential distinction between a comic and a comedian. Comics are performers who simply rattle off jokes. That is what the ethnic teams did. Comedians, in contrast, develop a character whose actions and words might be funny independent of the lines they deliver. (Of course, it was George Burns who offered his own definitions of a comedian: "If I get a laugh, I'm a comedian. If I get a small laugh, I'm a humorist. If I get no laughs, I'm a singer. If my singing gets big laughs, then I'm a comedian again.") The distinction between "comic" and "comedian" can be found throughout entertainment history. In early television, for example, Milton Berle was a comic and Sid Caesar was a comedian. Weber and Fields were the first to offer the alternative to the strictly comic.

They had goatees that came to a sharp point, thick accents, derby hats, and mismatched, awkwardly fitting clothing. Their characters — the con man and the dupe — had roots in comedic history, but the pair seemed so American that they became prototypes for two-acts of the future.

Weber and Fields developed or swiped many of the routines and lines that their comedic descendants would draw upon for decades. Unfortunately for them, their ethnic humor, thick accents, and roughhouse antics lost favor with later audiences, and so their names were lost to mainstream America.

They invented, or at least are given credit for, the eye poke that audiences associate with the Three Stooges. They smashed goods over each other's heads. They strangled each other. They originated the comedic convention of throwing custard pies into the face of an enemy. Indeed, in a published article, they literally listed the techniques that they had found the most effective in evoking laughter. These included: stick one or two fingers in the eye, choke and shake the head from side to side, kick, knock the other man off his feet, and slip on the other man's foot. The eye gouging came about by accident when, during a performance, Weber got some object in his eye. Fields tried to take it out, and the audience laughed. In one of their famous physical stunts, Fields attacked Weber with a hatchet and struck him over the head with it. The hatchet stuck — Weber was wearing a steel-plated wig with a cork cushion.

They uttered vaudeville's most famous lines — in about 1887. Weber said to Fields, "Who is that lady I saw you with last night?" and Fields came back with his classic response: "She ain't no lady. She's my wife."

Their "Dutch" knockabout act, making fun of German immigrants, consisted of two characters, Mike (Weber) and Myer (Fields). Weber was short, plump (he wore a lot of padding around his midsection), and generally the greenhorn, while Fields was the tall con man.

Mike and Myer did not hate each other. They did not seethe or seek revenge. Their violence emerged precisely from their friendship, from their deep knowledge of the other. They may have competed, but they needed and loved each other. The characters would never think of parting. They provided a crucial model for numerous later teams of fighting friends.

In full ethnic tradition, Weber and Fields murdered English, using language as just one more weapon in a campaign of comedic assault and battery. The clever wordplay is revealing and shows Weber and Fields anticipating the future of comedy. Their knockabout stuff emerged only after a verbal exchange. The language was as important as the seeming brutality.

Here is one routine, illustrative of the accents, the mock German-English, and the interplay. It also illustrates why the humor didn't last. The language comes from a specific and relatively brief period of immigrant history. It makes fun of people with accents in a way that now seems only mocking rather than funny.

Weber: I am delightfulness to meet you.
Fields: Der disgust is all mine.
Weber: I receividdid a letter for mein goil, but I don't know how to writteninin her back.
Fields: Writteninin her back! Such an edumucation you got it? Writteninin her back! You mean rotteninin her back. How can you answer her ven you don't know how to write?
Weber: Dot makes no nefer mind. She don't know how to read.

Vaudeville audiences noted this "Dutch" act had a strong dose of Yiddish inflection. It is no accident that Weber and Fields and so many later comedians came from immigrant Jewish families. The very notion of wordplay, the Yiddish rhythms in English, the psychological insight into character types, the distrust of authority, all these joined together to give Weber and Fields and their heirs an extra advantage. While Fields, in his career and in the way he raised his own family, tried to separate himself from a Jewish identity, his Dutch act worked in part because of the Yiddish-inflected sound and cadence.

Weber and Fields developed clever wordplays and routines that were an obvious forerunner of teams like Abbott and Costello. Here is part of one:

Fields: Vot are you doing?
Weber: Voiking in a nut factory.
Fields: Doing vot?
Weber: Nutting.
Fields: Sure. But vot are you doing?
Weber: Nutting.
Fields: I know, but vot voik are you doing?
Weber: Nutting, I tole you.

These word routines proved so popular that they became standard Weber and Fields offerings. Here (with the dialect removed) are other examples:

Weber: So tell me the street you work on. I'll come and pick you up.
Fields: Watt Street.
Weber: The street you work on. So I come pick you up, we go to lunch.
Fields: Watt Street.

Weber: The street you're working on.
Fields: Watt Street.

And:

Weber: You got a good job?
Fields: Pretty good.
Weber: What are you doing?
Fields: I'm dyeing.
Weber: You look good. . . .

Both Laurel and Hardy and Abbott and Costello adapted one of their bits. Performing it (again without the dialect) as Mike and Myer on a 1912 phonograph record, Weber and Fields created a classic:

Mike: Do you have any money?
Myer: No.
Mike: Well, all I have is a nickel, just enough for one beer.
Myer: Why don't you have one? I don't want a drink just now.
Mike: Oh, good. But it wouldn't look good if we both went in and I ordered a beer without offering one to you. Tell you what we'll do. We'll go into this bar. I'll ask if you want a beer, and you say, "I don't care for any."

Myer: Okay, I'll do that.

[A door opens. There is a pause, and then the door opens again.]

Mike: Oh, you idiot. Now see what you've done.

Myer: Why, I just done what you told me. When you asked me if I wanted a beer.

Mike: You said, "I don't care if I do," and the bartender gave you the beer, and I had to pay my last nickel.

"The Pool Room" was the sketch that most audiences associated with Weber and Fields. The use of a pool table (later made famous in vaudeville by W. C. Fields) was widely loved, in part because the table was rigged to allow for trick shots. But the typical knockabout humor, the linguistic mistakes, and the attempted bamboozling were fully present as well. Fields tried to teach Weber how to play pool while simultaneously separating him from his money. Weber didn't like such attempts, and Fields reacted by physical attack. Part of the reason for the success of "The Pool Room" was that Weber and Fields were pushing the limits of comedy from the knockabout and verbal to the level of story. The sketch was an extended morality tale, the origins of which lay in a thousand wasted afternoons that immigrants and working-class Americans alike had spent in pool halls.

Knockabout comedy allowed a release of energy and anger for immigrants. It provided a way to deal with the incredible burdens of work, family, a strange language, and economic struggles. Audiences enjoyed seeing pain and cruelty. The pain echoed the harsh reality of their lives, and it was a catharsis from the anxiety of living in the midst of such cruelty to see it on stage. The enactment of cruelty, the sheer enjoyment in its display, surely also facilitated the release of anger at people audience members wished to attack.

There is one completely different way of understanding that appeal. The immigrants wanted above all to succeed in the New Land. It was more than a matter of survival; their whole identity was at stake. They had abandoned the lands of their birth out of the conviction that America would be a land of plenty, often leaving behind skeptical families and friends. Pride demanded that they make a success of their new lives. Failure might be understandable in the Old Country but not here. The knockabout humor was, in this sense, a mirror of the assertiveness immigrants felt, an urge to push competitors aside in their hunger to succeed.

Ethnic and knockabout humor became dated and embarrassing when immigrants entered the mainstream, and audiences began to abandon ethnic stereotypes. By the 1920s, they had become unwelcome reminders of the tough early days of struggle, days the immigrants were not yet ready to romanticize as their grandchildren would. Humor grounded in the infliction of pain by one partner on another became less funny. The immigrants wanted to forget their accents and their raucous beginnings. They aspired to adopt the refined behavior of the upper classes.

By then, Weber and Fields had already opened the gateway for many other vaudeville acts. Some of them, such as Clark and McCullough, Wheeler and Woolsey, the Ritz Brothers, and Olsen and Johnson, became famous in films as well and are recognized more for work in that medium.

There were others who tried vaudeville and then went on to other fields. Walt Disney, for example, began his career not as a cartoonist but by doing imitations of Charlie Chaplin. He was in Kansas City when he won a $2 prize. He then teamed up with Walter Pfeiffer, a friend of his. Together, they developed a comedy act and performed in schools and local theaters until Disney realized his real talents lay elsewhere.

Although most of the teams consisted of two men, it didn't take long for vaudevillians to realize that if a good-looking straight man would attract women in the audience, a beautiful woman would attract men. By the late 1890s, women comedians were picked to join up with straight men. The women were selected on the basis of their appearance — their physical attractiveness, how well they wore their clothes, and how lustrous their hair was. The women rarely had any say in the act itself. Most of these teams were made up of married couples. The team got a double salary but only had to pay for one hotel room. Their romantic needs were taken care of, at least in theory. They could afford to work for less than other teams and were therefore able to work more steadily.

But the comedy team consisting of two men remained predominant. There were an extraordinary number of such teams popular in vaudeville, such as Smith and Dale, made famous by Neil Simon as the models for his play *The Sunshine Boys.* Joe

Smith and Charlie Dale met as kids when, riding bikes, they bumped into each other. They started to argue and the growing crowd pushed them toward each other. When the boys took the bicycles back to the man they had rented them from, their argument continued, and the man said they reminded him of Weber and Fields. Then the owner of the bicycle shop offered the boys a tandem bike free for a half hour so they could ride around and get to know each other. They were soon visiting vaudeville houses and working on an act. Originally named Joseph Sultzer and Charlie Marks, the two acquired their stage names when a printer who had an extra 100 cards with the name "Smith and Dale" on them offered the pair a bargain. The deal determined the act's new name.

Smith and Dale became very famous for a skit titled "Dr. Kronkhite" (*kronkhite* is Yiddish for "sickness"). The act, less clever than other bits of wordplay, evidently located a deep uneasy feeling about the medical profession on the part of the audience. Most immigrants visited doctors irregularly and were unhappy about it when they did have to go. The opportunity to laugh both at the doctor and the experience was therefore satisfying. The act included these lines, which were famous in their era:

> Smith: Are you a doctor?
> Dale: I'm a doctor.
> Smith: I'm dubious.
> Dale: I'm glad to know you Mr. Dubious.
> Smith: I'm still dubious.
> Dale: Mr. Dubious, are you a married man?
> Smith: Yes and no.
> Dale: What do you mean yes and no?
> Smith: I am but I wish I wasn't.

There were many other early teams as well. Montgomery and Stone (David Montgomery and Fred A. Stone) were comedy dancers who worked both in and out of blackface. They gained fame as the Tin Man and the Scarecrow in a 1902 production of *The Wizard of Oz*.

Savoy and Brennan (Bert Savoy, the stage name of Everett McKenzie, and Jay Brennan) began to perform together in 1913. Savoy was very popular as a brassy female impersonator. His signature line of "You *must* come over," slightly altered, may have later led to Mae West's famous "Come up and see me sometime." Savoy altered the female impersonator tradition by acquiring a male partner and developing a coquettish "boy-girl" sketch, allowing him to exaggerate the impersonation by playing off a partner. Savoy came to an unhappy ending. Lightning killed him and another vaudevillian while they were walking toward a beach.

Zeb and Zarrow (Zeb Ferguson and Walter Zarrow) were comic bicyclists who met a sad end in 1906. Zarrow was riding his bicycle across a table at an outdoor restaurant in Houston, probably to promote an appearance there. A police officer didn't much like such antics and ordered Zarrow to stop. Zarrow, a performer to what would be the end, refused. They argued and then fought. The officer drew his weapon. Zarrow turned to run away, but the officer shot him in the back. The officer was later arrested for the murder. Zeb died of pneumonia two years later.

Duffy and Sweeney (Jimmy Duffy and Fred Sweeney) were among the most physical of the comedy teams. The team, which broke up after the 1920s, introduced exaggerating the violence by including a veneer of politeness. They took to calling each other "Mister," a convention made famous by other teams, especially Laurel and Hardy.

Duffy and Sweeney sometimes got angry at audiences that didn't respond to their knockabout style, in their case most famously illustrated by slaps. They often got into trouble. Upset with one audience for their silence, Duffy interrupted the act, walked toward the edge of the stage, and threatened to "go through the aisles with a baseball bat and beat the bejesus out of you." Edward F. Albee quickly banished them from appearing in his vaudeville houses. A seemingly contrite Duffy then went to Albee's office accompanied by a boy and, noting the boy, asked Albee, "Are you going to let him starve?" Albee did not ever learn that the boy was not Duffy's son. Duffy died of alcoholism, slumped over on the corner of 8th Avenue and 47th Street.

Gallagher and Shean contributed the title of a hit song to the national discourse, "Absolutely, Mr. Gallagher? Positively, Mr. Shean." The two had worked together as teenagers but soon split up and stopped speaking to each other for six years. Anxious to revive the act, Al Shean went to the most formidable person he knew — his sister, Minnie Marx. Minnie did get the act back together, and in 1921, the two introduced what would become the most famous song in vaudeville. The song began with this introduction:

> There are two funny men
> The best I've ever seen.
> One is Mister Gallagher,
>   the other's Mister Shean.
> When these two cronies meet,
> It surely is a treat.
> For the things they say and
>   the things they do,
> And the funny way they greet.

Then the song would go into verses, which varied to reflect different settings and times.

A typical verse went like this:

> Gallagher: Oh Mister Shean, Oh Mister
>   Shean.
>   I've been away to school, that's
>   why I've not been seen.
>   The school taught Memory
>   And I took the first degree.
> Shean: Name the school please, Mister
>   Gallagher.
> Gallagher: I forget it, Mister Shean.

Gallagher and Shean were so popular that crowds gathered in the streets as they left a theater. They often wore hats from their act to acknowledge their appreciation to the crowd. Audiences also loved Gallagher's flashy gold tooth. Soon, though, the act split up again. Gallagher later had a nervous breakdown; he and his fourth wife were fighting, and he drank.

Although Al Shean continued to struggle without his famous partner, his nephews were about to create a sensation. Minnie Marx, having seen her brother's great success, was convinced that her sons could also be a smash in vaudeville. It is uncertain whether she thought her sons had talent or decided that if her brother, with his talent, could make it, then so could her boys.

Whatever her assessment of her brother, Minnie Marx was a singularly determined woman. She started her campaign by getting fourteen-year-old Groucho to try out for a dance act. (I refer here to the Marx Brothers by their nicknames, although they didn't yet have them.) Groucho complained to his mother that he had no dancing ability whatsoever; he had not yet acquired the ethic of the vaudevillian — the conviction that, of course, he had exactly the talents needed for any of the widest possible variety of job openings.

Minnie convinced him that such a minor deficiency should not stand in the way of his career, and indeed he got a job for $4 a week with the LeRoy Trio. In Denver, the naïve young performer was cheated out of his money and abandoned. Saved by a generous landlady who got him a job driving a grocery wagon, Groucho eventually made it back home to New York.

Many vaudevillians were not so lucky. There was only so much money to spend on performers. If the big stars got most of it, the less successful acts were paid very little. It became a point of honor for a vaudevillian unable to afford a hotel room to "carry the banner" — to spend the night sleeping on a park bench with a paper covering his chest and his head resting on his coat. (A "banner" is a headline spanning the width of a newspaper page.)

Groucho was forever haunted by his early poverty. Later in his life, he kept a locked room in his house. Inside the room was a shoeshine box. As Groucho explained to comedy writer Goodman Ace, "It's a holdover from my vaudeville days. I never had a dime for a shoeshine."

Once the young Groucho had made his way back home after the disastrous launch into show business, Minnie figured she'd better step in and exert more influence over her boys. They were all skipping school except for Groucho — when he was home. She knew these boys needed a mother's watchful eye. She created a singing act, The Three Nightingales, with Groucho, Gummo, and Mabel O'Donnell, who was cockeyed and sang off-key. Lou Levy soon replaced Mabel. Harpo joined the act on June 1, 1908, at Coney Island. Harpo had been playing the piano to accompany silent movies, but since he knew so few tunes, he kept playing the same ones over and over, blissfully unconcerned about how well the sound coordinated with the pictures above him.

Despite the addition, the group was a consistent failure. Once when a fire broke out, Harpo reacted by uttering the first lines that came to his panicked mind: his bar mitzvah speech. Minnie and her sister sometimes joined the act, but unsurprisingly, given Minnie's sparse singing talent, that didn't help either.

Then came Texas.

Nacogdoches, Texas, in the eastern part of the state, was not a major spot on the vaudeville circuit. The Marx Brothers were in the middle of their performance at the town opera house. The audience, like most of their audiences, was bored and unimpressed. Suddenly, there was thrilling news from outside the theater. A runaway mule was kicking a cart into small pieces. Much of the audience left to look at this more enticing alternative.

Eventually the audience returned, but the Marx Brothers were furious at this treatment. Groucho began to insult the crowd: "Nacogdoches is full of roaches" and "The jackass is the finest flower of Tex-ass." It was only a rough early version of what would soon be the great Marx Brothers repartee, but the audience — to the shock of the performers — began to laugh. Harpo then began to crawl across the stage under a rug. The laughter continued. Minnie, surrendering her dreams of producing a great singing act, accepted the verdict of the audience and the clear desires of her sons. A comedy team was born.

Also in Texas, a town sheriff had seized all of the act's stage properties. Forced to improvise, the Marx Brothers began to use whatever was around them, developing what was eventually called "spontaneous idiocy."

They had sung their last off-key song, at least without comic intentions.

Al Shean helped the Marx Brothers develop a variation of a school sketch, a type then popular. Titled "Fun in Hi Skule," the sketch wasn't very good, but the brothers had a brilliant idea. Because ethnic groups still made up the vast proportion of their audience at that time, they began to develop an act to appeal to all groups. Groucho played a German. Gummo was a Jewish character. Later, when Chico joined the act, they would broaden their array even more by having an Italian. Harpo was meant to appeal to Irish immigrants with his imitation of what was then known as a Patsy Brannigan character, a dumb but funny type. It was in this sketch that Harpo first used his famous "Gookie" face when he puffed out his cheeks and crossed his eyes. As a child Harpo had seen a cigar roller named Gehrke making the face as he did his work, which is considered the most likely origin of the face.

The sketch was also important for another reason. Groucho, very insecure about his ability to be funny, decided that he had to develop a strategy to prevent the audience from being bored. He decided to have his character talk quickly.

Meanwhile, Chico was working with various partners separate from his family, creating his Italian immigrant (modeled after a barber he had known) along the way. Minnie determined that Chico would join the act, and that, of course, meant that he did join the act.

Chico showed up unannounced on September 26, 1912, in either Waukegan, Illinois, or Lafayette, Indiana, depending on the source. Having bribed the piano player in the orchestra pit, Chico sat down to play. (Benny Kubelsky, a young violin player was also in the pit that night, ready to play as the Marx Brothers came on. Minnie would actually offer him a job as the Marx Brothers' music man, but his father wouldn't let him take it. Kubelsky would later change his name to Jack Benny.)

The sketch began when Harpo, wearing a hat with fruit attached to it, walked onto the stage. Groucho, playing the teacher, was already sitting behind the desk. Harpo noticed Groucho staring into the orchestra pit. Harpo turned, and he heard Chico's familiar playing style of running his fingers up and down the piano. Being a Marx Brother, Harpo tore an apple from his hat and threw it at Chico. Chico caught the apple and threw it to Groucho. Groucho got it and threw it to Gummo, who had peeked out from behind the curtain. It didn't take long before there was fruit all over the place. The crowd went wild.

The Marx Brothers were getting there.

Their characters were now in place, but not their names.

The nickname acquisition took place in Galesburg, Illinois, sometime around May 15, 1914. The brothers were playing stud poker with a man named Art Fisher, a comedian. Fisher, who loved their act, had acquired the habit of supplying nicknames to everyone based on the popular comic strip "Sherlocko the Monk." The process involved defining a characteristic of the person and adding an "o" to the end of the name. Fisher began to deal the cards and asked if "Harpo" wanted one. The choice of nickname in Harpo's case was easy because of his use of the instrument. Fisher's line drew some laughter from everyone, so he continued. "Chico," originally "Chicko" until a printer misspelled the name (the brothers continued to pronounce the name as "Chicko" in private), was named after his well-known and constantly practiced habit of chasing "chicks." Groucho's name reflected his temperament, although some of the other brothers later claimed that the name came from "grouch bag." Because vaudevillians stole so much from each other, it was common practice for the actors to carry their money and jewelry in a small chamois pouch, called a "grouch" bag, which they typically hung around their neck under their clothes even onstage. The nickname of the bag came because of the understandably upset vaudeville stars whose valuables had been stolen. This, though, sounds as implausible an explanation of Groucho's name as the later straight-faced but ludicrous claim that "Chico" came from the comedian's deep knowledge of fowl. Gummo was not present at the card game, but his nickname derived from the gumshoes he wore even when it wasn't raining to cover up the holes in his shoes. The origin for Zeppo's nickname is disputed. Perhaps it came from Zeppo, a trained chimpanzee. Harpo claimed Zeppo's acrobatics reminded the brothers of the animal's antics. Gummo claimed that it came from joke nicknames they gave themselves when they owned a farm. Zeppo had been Zeb, which evolved into Zeppo.

Still one more big change was about to take place.

Harpo talked in the act until a moment

marked by his mother's desperation, his uncle's apparent mistake, and a reviewer's cutting words. It was September 1914. The brothers were in Chicago, once again about to be fired. Minnie assured the theater manager that the team had a brand-new act and would try it out the next day. That night, Al Shean stayed up to write the new act called "Home Again," which was first performed the next evening. Either in haste or as a critical comment, he inserted only three lines for Harpo. Some words were added, but the incensed Harpo decided he would intrude his way into the act without lines. A reviewer noted how well Harpo portrayed his Irish immigrant character in pantomime but lamented that the whole effect was destroyed as soon as Harpo began to speak. His very identifiable New York accent immediately revealed that he had not come from anywhere near Ireland. From that time on, Harpo never again spoke in a Marx Brothers act on stage or screen. Harpo also used a wig his aunt had made, and Minnie suggested he play the harp. Harpo had discovered his grandmother's harp in the closet and had already begun to practice. He started wearing a big raincoat to cover the props he carried onstage and a horn to squeeze when he was supposed to speak.

The Marx Brothers were in business. Indeed, they were so good that they intimidated other vaudevillians. W. C. Fields claimed they were the only act he couldn't follow.

The act did undergo additional changes. When the *Lusitania* was sunk in 1915, Groucho decided to abandon the German immigrant character and substituted a Jewish immigrant instead. Gummo joined the army. Zeppo replaced him in the act.

The Marx Brothers traveled all over North America, learning as they went along. Almost no one traveled as much or saw so many places as did vaudevillians. The extensive traveling prevented audience boredom. The Marx Brothers, and all other vaudevillians, had only one act at a time. They would play the act in a city and move on, returning to that city perhaps a year later when people no longer recalled the act or remembered it fondly and wanted to hear it again. Vaudevillians knew how to please these local audiences. Many had routines in which they compared towns. They'd refer to the city where they were playing as a much nicer place than a nearby rival city.

Of course, playing the same act over and

over made the act as perfect as it could become. The performers could work on their timing and experiment with alternative words on different audiences if they wished to determine what line, for example, consistently got the largest laugh. Groucho frequently altered his lines in each town, experimenting with his language, knowing his brothers could field any ad-lib he threw out.

And in each of those towns the Marx Brothers looked for young women. Indeed, many male vaudevillians had richly deserved reputations as libertines. Even the dimmest male performers noticed that smiling women planted themselves outside theaters waiting for some additional entertainment. Hearts of young people in smaller cities across the country lay shattered from encounters with traveling stars. Prostitutes were frequent partners; many young vaudevillians caught sexually transmitted diseases. In Groucho's case, it was at age sixteen from a streetwalker in Montreal. There was, after all, little time for real romance, and the road was not a great place for a family. The vaudevillians were not welcome in too many places and found in houses of prostitution not only companionship but also food, drink, and musical entertainment.

The Marx Brothers also often had angry disputes with management. After one such struggle, the enterprising Chico arranged for them to star in a new show. The show *I'll Say She Is!* ran for a year in Philadelphia before going on the road and finally coming to Broadway on May 19, 1924. Alexander Woollcott, the famed Algonquin Club Roundtable member and witty reviewer, praised their acts and convinced them to use their nicknames publicly.

The show was important not only because it marked the break between the Marx Brothers' career in vaudeville and their career in the legitimate theater but also because it solidified the characters they would play throughout their professional lives. It also showcased Groucho's non sequiturs, puns, and other wordplay and his cynical approach to women and life. For example:

Groucho (as Napoleon): My Queen . . .
    when I look into your big blue eyes,
    I know that you are true to the
    Army. I only hope it remains a
    standing Army. France has no
    Navy, but then every man has
    qualms, even if they are only

steamed qualms . . . Where are my rubbers?

Lotta Miles (as the Empress Josephine): Here they are. [Harpo sticks his feet out from under the Empress's dress.]

Napoleon: Are those your feet? Maybe you better go to war and I'll stay here . . .

Josephine: Napoleon, when you go, all France is with you.

Napoleon: Yes, and the last time I came home, all France was with you, and a slice of Italy, too.

However triumphant they were, the Marx Brothers, and everyone else in vaudeville, would soon turn their attention to the new entertainment forms then emerging, forms that would doom vaudeville as a business and ruin the careers of many performers, but raise some of those performers to even greater heights.

FOUR

"IN THIS COUNTRY WE'RE ONLY PERMITTED ONE HUSBAND"

Comedy Teams on Radio

Astonished visitors entered through a vast mezzanine rotunda. Tingling with anticipation and curiosity, they rode special elevators to the second-floor lobby. Attractive, smiling hosts greeted them there and directed them past the public lounges and smoking rooms that opened out on terraces, past the audition studios and private, spectacularly appointed rooms for the sponsors and stars. The visitors swarmed into another elevator that would finally take them to one of the various studios.

The world's largest broadcasting complex was opened by NBC in Radio City Music Hall in 1933, filling an eleven-story wing of the skyscraper.

If the guests were lucky, they went to the large studio. It had a semicircular stage that could accommodate a one-hundred-piece orchestra. One thousand audience members could watch the show from floor level. The slightly less lucky 250 guests watched from seats in a balcony.

Some of the guests went to the fifth floor, which contained the main equipment room, all the maintenance shops, and the switching booths. They could gape at the four studios built around a single circular control room, the floor of which was actually a huge turntable that enabled workers to swing the equipment around to face any of the studios.

The guests were surprised that there were no windows, a part of the effort to soundproof the studios. The refreshing coolness came from the world's largest air-conditioning plant, right there on the tenth floor of the building.

When the shows came on, audience members who hadn't seen photographs of the stars were sometimes shocked that the performers didn't look at all as they had imagined, that the men were dressed in suits and ties, that the actors all read from scripts and didn't make up their own words, that either the actors or some other person made all the sound effects.

And the audience members were puzzled by those sounds. In publicity pictures, there were always lots of sound effects people manually producing the effects. But in the studio there were only a few people doing the effects, and the technicians were mostly using phonograph records for sounds, from the roar of an explosion to the hard-charging pounding of elephants' feet. Regular attendees would have seen plenty of acoustic tricks of the trade: twisted cellophane to mimic a crackling fire, a shaken two-foot-long inner tube, cut in strips, to sound like a wet dog vigorously shaking off the water, or an umbrella suddenly snapped open to imitate the sound of a burst of fire.

Whatever surprises awaited the audience, they always loved the shows, both in the studio and at home. And of all the radio shows, they loved comedies most.

Radio seemed to have been invented just for the comedians. Because radio audiences could only listen as they stared at their new piece of furniture, all the purely visual acts of vaudeville — the acrobats, the seal acts, and the dancers, for example — lost their jobs, driven from the entertainment world by this new upstart technology. Radio rewarded comedians with crisp verbal skills. The costumes, facial gestures, and handsome man or attractive woman, so crucial in vaudeville, were no longer necessary.

George Burns and Gracie Allen were among the comedians determined to make it in this technologically amazing but strange new medium. Gracie was invited to perform on Eddie Cantor's radio show — without George. But Burns, however much he was hurt, shrewdly agreed to the deal. Gracie's sparkle, her uncanny ability to stay in her trademark character and speak the pitch-perfect lines produced by Burns and his writers, and her ability to work with other partners guaranteed her triumph.

Burns and Allen soon got their own show, but both performers had burdens they had to keep from their audience. Burns's dyslexia made him worry that he wouldn't be able to read the scripts on the air accurately. He therefore (as he would in television when he was concerned about reading cue cards) memorized all his lines for the show. This actually helped his performance. It is very difficult for any straight man to act and read a cue card at the same time, and Burns avoided the problem with memorization. His delivery and timing were far better because he didn't have to read the lines.

Gracie feared a live radio audience. In vaudeville she had been physically separated from the audience by the lights and couldn't see people staring at her when she performed. Burns, ever sensitive to Gracie's unique talents, made sure that their radio show did not have any intrusive observers. Her fear was so intense that paper had to be taped over the studio door's glass to prevent people from peering inside. Eventually, Burns and Allen did the broadcast in front of an audience, but the still nervous Gracie hid behind a very large microphone standing at an angle so she didn't have to look directly at the people who had come to see her.

Radio also presented other perils for Burns and Allen. Once, for example, the studio's lights went out, and Gracie could not read the script. Another time, Gracie accidentally dropped the script pages, and they scattered all over the floor. Because the show was broadcast live to a national audience, both situations might have flustered less seasoned performers. But not these two. On both occasions, George simply said, "Gracie, how's your brother?" and they slipped effortlessly into a comfortable vaudeville routine. When the pages fell, for example, her response was that her brother had joined the navy, and every time they ordered "All hands on deck," he'd put them there and people would step on them.

Despite the occasional problems, Burns and Allen were wildly successful. Burns had earlier developed a habit of moving his tongue back and forth on the inside of his lower lip. This improved his punctuating a sentence and added to his pleasant, obviously amused tone, which pleased their listeners.

And the pair, especially Gracie, always worked well with the guest stars that radio offered to keep shows fresh. Once the actors James and Pamela Mason appeared on the program. The Masons were cat lovers, and the writers used that in the skit:

Gracie: My husband is a cat fancier too.
Pamela: Oh, really. How many do you have?
Gracie: Just one. In this country we're only permitted one husband.
Pamela: Well, what is your method of raising cats?
Gracie: Same as yours. Put both hands under their belly and lift.
James: Mrs. Burns, I appeal to you . . .
Gracie: You certainly do, but I still don't want any more cats.

Their humor was traditional radio humor. For example, they used a lot of puns, as in their famous 1938 bit on city names.

Gracie: You see, I tell the story by using the names of cities and towns . . . Now, for instance, Tony Martin is a Richmond who's been Macon a lot of money in Georgia, but he needs a few more Dallas to pay his Texas. Get it?

George: Well, that's not Hartford me to understand . . .

John Conte: Am I in this musical number, Gracie? . . .

Gracie: Well, I should say you are, Johnny. You're the little Boise that I'm in love with.

George: But, maybe Johnny doesn't love you.

John: Oh, that's all right, George. I'm glad to Yuma her . . .

Gracie: . . . The scene Ipswitch-es now to a town in Montana. But I can't mention the name of it.

George: Why not?

Gracie: Well, George, you're not allowed to say Helena radio.

George: Well, that was really a Butte.

Gracie: It's very funny Anaconda I made it up myself.

Of course, various matters having to do with the Great Depression were a source of Gracie's humor. For example, in 1933, Gracie announced her plans for curing unemployment:

Gracie: I've decided to put all the men

109

in the world on an island in the middle of the ocean. Then soon everybody will be working . . .
George: What will they be doing?
Gracie: Boat building.

Burns and Allen were not above some gimmicks to keep their show popular. For example, Gracie ran for the presidency in 1940, on the Surprise Party ticket. She actually did a whistle-stop tour, eventually visiting thirty-four cities and towns. She announced that her first official act would be to settle the simmering border dispute between Florida and California. A reporter, desperately trying to be serious, asked her opinion of the neutrality bill then before Congress, and she replied, "If we owe it, let's pay it." She decided not to have a vice-presidential candidate because she didn't want any vice on the ticket. Harvard University announced its support for her candidacy, but somehow that did not galvanize the masses. On election day, several thousand people wrote in her name.

Inevitably, Burns and Allen did run into some serious problems. Their strong scripts and acting sustained them through the 1930s, but eventually they began to lose the audience. Their characters of boy and girlfriend did not fit their actual ages. Burns worried constantly about the steady decline of ratings that began in 1939, but he ultimately, almost accidentally, hit on the solution. He came on the air in 1941 and simply announced the characters were now a married couple. The audience cheerfully accepted this. The change was crucial because a marriage provided built-in situations and tensions perfect for new material. Gracie could keep her character, but the character would have new and slightly more mature problems. For example, in one show, the couple had seen a Charles Boyer movie, and Gracie was smitten.

George: Gracie, could you walk a little faster?
Gracie: If you wish, Charles.
George: Gracie, I'm George Burns, your husband. Remember? I'm not Charles Boyer.
Gracie: Oh, well, that's life.

They go into a store and Gracie buys some magazines with stories about Boyer. Then they get home and go to bed.

Gracie: The article I'm reading now is

> fascinating: "Charles Boyer's Ten
> Rules for Being a Successful
> Lover."
> George: Turn out the light.
> Gracie: That's the first rule.

George and Gracie's conquering of radio
is crucial in understanding the appeal of
team comedy. Radio was the first medium
in which large audiences simultaneously
heard popular comedians. Additionally,
radio kept audiences at a further emotional
distance from its world than the minstrel
show, the theater, burlesque, or vaudeville.
Audiences, after all, generally weren't in the
same place as the performers and couldn't
see them or the acts. Only disembodied
voices created the reality of the radio world.
Listeners had to envision an entire world,
giving flesh to characters and shape and
content to places. Radio, in the famous
phrase, was a "theater of the mind."

Radio, more than any other medium, required that comedy teams create a world
for the audience. In addition to the humor
and the poignant characters developed by
the teams, it is this created world that explains the magnetic attraction of the
comedy teams for such a huge audience
for so long.

It was the comic's responsibility in a classic comedy team to establish a fantasy world for audiences, an alternative to the reality of everyday life. It was warm, safe, funny, and inviting, a world that provided relief and release from the troubled real one. Real life, seen through the gauzy pleasance of the comedy world, became more bearable.

The comic's fantasy world retained some degree of plausibility. Gracie is not just anarchically illogical. Her idiosyncratic logic makes sense to us in its own way. The comic world is an alternative to this one, but a recognizable alternative. It is reality modified, not replaced.

There was, however, a paradoxical danger for audiences in this imaginary world. Its very allure made it perilous. Rationality itself was in jeopardy if this alternative world took over for too long from the real world. People, after all, might not want to rush back to the dull, dreary demands of reality when the pleasant and carefree was just a few words away.

The straight man became the audience's attachment to reality, its lifeline back from the ultimately threatening enchantments of the comic world. The straight man was the desperately needed grown-up and the comic the child in all of us. The banter between the straight man and the comic, in this sense, was the struggle between the two worlds, and thus the straight man was much more important than simply a feeder of lines.

The underlying struggle between the rational and imaginary worlds, represented by the straight man and the comic, created a pattern that endured, with variations, across many of the most difficult decades of the twentieth century, from the vaudeville comedians like Burns and Allen to Laurel and Hardy, the Marx Brothers, Bud Abbott and Lou Costello, Martin and Lewis, the Smothers Brothers, and many others.

The recurring emergence of new teams through the 1960s reflected the fact that audiences at different times had very different anxieties and tensions and so needed to escape to different alternative worlds. Some comedy teams that played off specific momentary anxieties appealed to audiences during a limited cultural era. The teams that created worlds capable of relieving the existential anxieties embedded in the human condition lasted beyond the moment. The best comedy teams provided accurate sociological and psychological barometers for their ages and simultaneously met the deepest of human emotional needs.

Gracie Allen was popular in part because she connected the real world's logic with an alternate world's funnier logic. Audiences embraced her as a loveable guide to sweet madness, which they could freely enjoy, especially because they knew that in George they had a guide to take them back. And Burns and Allen were careful not to stray so far from reality that it could frighten the audience into worrying about a return. Throughout their careers, Burns and Allen built their act on real-life situations. They used their own lives and the ordinary world to build the comedy.

They also understood the allure of radio itself. In the 1920s, radios had been costly, with some priced at more than $120 — for a set that required assembly. Expensive and unreliable batteries powered radios in America's rural areas. But by the 1930s, manufacturers produced radios for an extremely affordable price, with some as low as $5. Rural electrification began to reach the folks in sparsely populated areas. About 90 percent of American homes had at least one radio by then. By 1942, Americans owned 27.5 million cars, 14.5 million telephones, and 14 million refrigerators. And they had 56 million radios. When *Fortune* magazine polled its readers on what they would choose to give up to save money, 79 percent said "movies," but only 14 percent said "radios."

It wasn't long after radio shows began to gain popularity that advertisers wanted to know for sure that all those people with radios were actually listening to their shows. At first, no one was certain how to tell if a program was popular. One crude method was to offer a free item and count how many people requested it. The Cooperative Analysis of Broadcasting (C.A.B.), popularly known as the Crossley ratings, began in 1929, and for the first time, statistical methods were used to verify audience numbers. The Hooper ratings became prominent in 1935. Whereas Crossley ratings depended on people recalling what shows they had listened to, the Hooper people called while the shows were on the air. They sought information from early in the morning until late at night in thirty-two cities (but no rural areas), getting immediate information about whether family members were listening to the radio and if so, what shows they found absorbing. It was not until 1949 that the A. C. Nielsen

Company bought out Hooper and updated the method of gathering audience information by installing an electronic audiometer on statistically chosen radio sets.

The pervasiveness of radio had inevitable, profound, and decidedly mixed effects upon its audience. Radio's entry into the American home meant that people no longer had to create their own entertainment. The dazzling invention expanded their horizons but also homogenized their tastes. The commercials sometimes made them want to buy what they didn't need or, in some sense, even want. Radio was also the crucial first step in making entertainment a private rather than a public activity. Audiences weren't complaining, however. The professionals on the radio made them laugh a lot more than their relatives ever did.

And radio certainly had its positive contributions beyond providing affordable entertainment. Americans, almost like newborns, discovered from radio the lure of simple sound. They became accomplished listeners. They adapted their thinking to this new medium and focused on the noises in their lives. The patter and repartee taught them new ways to talk as well as new ways to think and laugh.

The effect of radio's success in the entertainment business was staggering. Vaudeville died because audiences could now hear popular comedians for free. Even more than films, radio's music, drama, and laughter rang the mournful passing bells signaling vaudeville's demise.

Another crucial effect of radio was that its audience shaped the sort of humor presented, its content, and its pace. The masses that made up the radio audience hadn't attended college or, in many cases, high school. Reaching them meant radio performers had to talk the way they talked. There had to be familiar cultural references. For example, many Americans in the rural areas of the country during the 1930s had trouble getting telephone lines. Therefore there were jokes about that problem, jokes that later audiences obviously found baffling and outdated. There were plenty of jokes about women who couldn't drive — jokes that would remain prominent well into the 1950s. Audiences would laugh when actors flubbed lines. The good-natured laughter reflected the audience's enjoyment of language and their unease about their own use of it. They knew they were uneducated, and they relaxed when a professional made the same sort of mistakes they did. They similarly appreciated ad-libs.

Advertisers wanted to keep these listeners coming back. There were, therefore, clear rules for the performers. The pervading censorship made it impossible, for example, to discuss body parts, illness, God, and just about any other potentially offensive subject. There was no overt sexual banter and, of course, no obscenity. Advertisers wanted bland and funny, inoffensive and funny, wholesome and funny.

They wanted to appeal to as many people as possible and so sought stars with pleasant voices, unaccented, with acceptable voice rhythms, and who spoke at a rate people could understand. Already established stars were put on radio, but they did not always succeed. Some urban Jewish comedians who spoke in a distinctly Jewish rhythm — such as George Jessel — or who spoke too quickly to be understood — such as Milton Berle — did not generate huge ratings.

A comedian's pace was actually a complex problem. Although audiences needed to be able to understand the lines, they didn't want to wait very long between laughs. Delivery that was too slow could damage a career. According to a study done for the 1946–1947 radio season, there was an average of sixteen seconds between laughs on the Burns and Allen show. (The winner was Bob Hope, who had a laugh every ten seconds.) Therefore, the real challenge was speaking in a pleasant, unaccented voice that was fast enough to get to the jokes but not so fast that audiences couldn't understand or catch their meaning. That is why Burns and Allen, with their distinct voices, their hard-earned sense of what audiences around the country found funny, and their instinct for appealing subject matter, were so successful.

The new medium had its most profound effects because of the social backdrop of radio's heyday. It was an era of economic deprivation and war. Between 1929 and 1932, the average American family lost 40 percent of its income. The Great Depression, coming as it did just a few years after the emergence of both radio and sound films, created a profound need for solace from the new industries that technology had spawned. It is no surprise that radio's great success really began when the stock market crashed.

Americans desperately needed escape from a threatening present and a frightening future. The audience's optimism had sunk into despair. They thought they understood the world. Now, they questioned every aspect of their lives as the institutions they had trusted failed them. They needed to believe that there were people who could help them, laugh with them, and understand their miseries, fears, and sense of hopelessness.

The audience's need for escape, and for seeing entertainment as an oasis of hope, led them to focus on the stars who lifted them most. It was in such extreme circumstances, with such vital needs, that America created the celebrities of the era, people they could believe in when they couldn't believe in their own government, people to distract them from the pain of crawling through the horrors of everyday existence.

Radio provided escape and a justification for the lives people led. They had to be cheap, to deny their children goods they would have preferred to make available to them. Jack Benny came along as a model of the cheapest possible person. Suddenly, audiences didn't feel so cheap themselves, and they were even able to laugh about the deprivations they suffered.

Sacrificing for their families was an economic necessity and a moral obligation. Americans in the 1930s and early 1940s wanted these cultural values of self-sacrifice affirmed. They were values that would be overturned in the 1960s, but in radio's era, they were still central to American identity.

Audiences, having lost faith in economic and social institutions, might easily have turned against their government during the Great Depression. Comedies let them deflect and diffuse their political anger by letting them laugh at themselves and at their mutual condition rather than organize radical alternatives to the government.

Radio would also later be vital during World War II. Audiences during the war desperately clung to their radios not only for relief but also for news. It was their lifeline to Washington and to the front. Before the newspapers, before the newsreels, they heard about the war from the radio. Radio content was like contrasting parents, one tough parent filled with threats, danger, and strict rules about the war and one tender parent filled with the sweet laughter of escape through entertainment programs.

Although the radio audience eventually responded extremely positively to comedies, entertainers and advertisers initially struggled to find the right formula. Comedians first tried a traditional approach of patter and song. Audiences didn't react. It was only with the emergence of *Amos 'n' Andy* and its use of routines that told a story that radio comedy's real history began.

It is remarkable that the show most closely associated with radio comedy's success was a program about black characters written and performed by two white men. It was radio's first confirmation that listeners would tune in at a specific time for a particular program. It ushered in a national radio craze. It made whites more familiar with blacks — but it also promoted black stereotypes. *Amos 'n' Andy* has been the subject of so much heated controversy that it is difficult to sift through the program's history to reach a fair historical conclusion.

Freeman F. Gosden, who played Amos, and Charles J. Correll, who played Andy, created the show. Gosden's father had been a Confederate soldier in the Civil War, one of the seventy-five members of Mosby's Raiders who refused to surrender with Robert E. Lee. Gosden wanted to enter show business, and Correll taught him how to be a director. Correll, whose family also had deep Southern roots that included a relationship to Jefferson Davis, president of the Confederacy, grew up in Peoria, Illinois, and had a job managing rehearsals of production companies.

Gosden and Correll shared an apartment and developed an act. They tried it over a local radio station in exchange for free meals. They thought getting free food just for talking on this new medium was a great bargain. The raucous fun they had blending music and chatter resulted in their being asked to create a radio version of a comic strip serial. The stories they constructed for this broadcast were the quiet beginnings of a revolution.

The $150 salary sealed the deal, and the two rapidly developed the idea of creating a tale of two black men. The ten-minute show, starting in 1926, featured characters named Sam and Henry, but when the two creators wanted to syndicate the show, the station hedged. Gosden and Correll left; the character names Sam and Henry had to stay behind.

The two would-be actors went to another Chicago radio station, WMAQ, and sought new names for very similar, if not identical, characters. Most importantly, they didn't just have the characters talk to each other but had them face dilemmas and encounter unusual situations. In so doing, Gosden and Correll created narrative radio.

Amos 'n' Andy was born on March 19, 1928. This time, the stars were allowed to syndicate the show by making copies and selling them to other stations. Their show became so popular that by 1929, NBC, a national network, offered them a contract. Their salary was $100,000 a year, but money was not their only motivation. They truly enjoyed the work. They loved the characters. Indeed, their most difficult task was to avoid laughing during the show. They had to make sure not to look at each other in order to prevent such an outburst. Once, Gosden had to pour a glass of water over himself to stop from laughing.

Amos 'n' Andy was not primarily a comedy show in the sense that Burns and Allen and others would later use the word. The focus was on the continuing story, on the humanity and relationships among the characters. The humor added to the overall story, but the lines themselves weren't meant to be gags.

Amos 'n' Andy was a simple show about two African American arrivals from Atlanta who had landed in Chicago. After a year struggling in the urban jungle, all they owned was a topless car. They decided to turn the car into a cab. The topless part became an attraction; they named the company the Fresh-Air Taxicab Company. Amos was the cab driver, the hard worker, and the trusting soul. Andy claimed to be Amos's "supervisor," although that job description did not include any actual work. Two months after the program began, a character named Kingfish was added. By 1943, Amos was essentially written out of the show — his straight character didn't allow for enough story conflicts or comic possibilities, and George "Kingfish" Stevens took his place as the major character. The Kingfish was a slick con man, always trying to separate Andy from his modest funds, always scheming, always struggling with his wife and mother-in-law. Andy was his foil, the dupe, the innocent "fool."

Amos 'n' Andy legitimized radio as a successful entertainment medium. In 1931, according to one survey, 53.4 percent of those listening to radio were listening to *Amos 'n' Andy*. *Amos 'n' Andy* motivated a lot of people to buy radios for the first time. Sales of radios amounted to $650.5

million in 1928. A year later, when the program went national, sales grew to $842.5 million. Pepsodent advertised on the program, and sales of their toothpaste soared. President Coolidge let it be known that for fifteen minutes starting at seven in the evening, he would not entertain interruptions as he listened to the show.

He wasn't the only one. At movie theaters, the managers would put a stool under the screen and place a huge radio on it. People would then listen to *Amos 'n' Andy* for fifteen minutes before the manager could project the film. Managers believed, with considerable justification, that if they didn't offer the radio show, people wouldn't come to the theaters.

The show was even lauded by the esteemed playwright and critic George Bernard Shaw, who observed, "There are three things I shall never forget about America — the Rocky Mountains, Niagara Falls, and *Amos 'n' Andy*."

The listeners were not all as famous as Shaw, but they were mostly white. Amos and Andy were black characters created and performed by white actors and specifically aimed at white audiences. Indeed, only 8 percent of black families owned a radio in 1930.

There are many reasons for the show's attraction to white audiences. Of course, Americans were long fascinated with racial issues and racial entertainment, as the popularity of the minstrel shows and of blackface comedy illustrated. So the idea of portraying blacks was both well established and acceptable as a form of humor. Additionally, Amos and Andy were both likeable characters. In a crucial way, the two characters transcended race. They faced the very same economic problems their white listeners faced. As a serial, the show could and did follow reality closely, keeping audiences in touch with the world and current events. The one hundred characters Gosden and Correll invented strutted and fretted across the American stage, providing vivid sociological portraits of the country.

Amos and Andy had a crucial message, summed up by a quote from Mark Twain that Amos frequently used. "In my life I have had many difficulties — most of which never happened." They told a worried nation that hard times would pass, that it was crucial to remain hopeful and generous and to suppress worries about what could go wrong. Their encouraging, positive message was that America would come back.

It was a message that Americans desperately wanted to believe. As a cheerful Amos told a despairing Andy in a show broadcast on June 24, 1932, "Dis ain't de time to give up — when things look tough like dis an' we ain't makin' money, dat's de fust thing you think about, but dis ain't no time to do it — dat's when we gotta plug hardeh den we is plugged befo' — if peoples gived up when dey got down, why dey'd never git nowhere."

Audiences didn't mock the dialect. They huddled around their radios and nodded as Amos spoke. *Amos 'n' Andy* had heart.

It also had controversy. The creators always claimed they meant no harm in their portrayal of blacks. Black radio audience members themselves were divided about the show, with poorer blacks generally enjoying the show and finding no offense in it and more economically successful and better-educated blacks more offended by the stereotypes and by the telling fact that these stereotypes were basically the only portrayals of blacks on radio. Blacks were also offended that they couldn't perform even black roles. Originally, Gosden and Correll did all the voices — though they eventually did add a few black actors.

It is no surprise, then, that in 1931

Robert L. Vann, editor of the Pittsburgh *Courier*, infuriated by what he took to be the show's mocking depiction of blacks, aroused supporters into signing a petition. He wanted a million people to demand that the Radio Commission ban *Amos 'n' Andy*. Vann and his supporters were doubly disturbed. After all, stereotypes of blacks didn't just affect whites by perpetuating the belief that blacks were lazy, for example, but also affected young blacks who might, like any minority in any culture, come to accept and believe the majority's negative stereotypes. Vann did eventually gather 740,000 signatures, but the campaign fizzled.

Other organizations and leaders had endorsed Vann's protest, but there was lively debate within the black community. A rival black paper, probably the single most prestigious black paper in the nation, the *Defender*, published in Chicago, organized a picnic for 30,000 black children and defiantly and flamboyantly invited Gosden and Correll to attend. The two performers knew good publicity when they saw it and quickly agreed.

There is no denying that some of the characters were stereotypes. Lightnin' received his ironic nickname for his laziness.

Algonquin J. Calhoun was a scheming lawyer, a characterization some audience members, white and black, found redundant. It is certainly plausible to argue that because the show provided the only portrayal of black society for white audiences and displayed already accepted stereotypes, it dangerously reinforced the legal segregation and sense of racial superiority many whites felt. ✗

There are complications to such an interpretation. Audiences were used to and liked racial and religious caricatures. A lot of it had made the transition from vaudeville to radio. That is, blacks were not singled out for this insensitive humor, even though it must be added that the stereotypes did more harm to them than to other groups. Additionally, whites generally loved Amos and Andy. It may even be said some wanted to be Amos and Andy.

The controversy didn't diminish the radio show's popularity. And that raises another question. Why, if Amos and Andy were popular because they represented the deepest yearnings of the audience, weren't they created as white characters rather than black ones? (Surprisingly, not all listeners realized they were black characters. Some thought the dialect was just a white regionalism.) That is, what extra dimension did their color provide?

Part of the attraction of black characters for whites goes back to the original draw of the minstrel shows, which sought to calm racial anxieties by making blacks seem dumb and lazy but not dangerous. During the 1930s, blacks were leaving the South and heading to urban centers, especially Chicago. This influx, this transformation of racial ratios so tellingly chartered on *Amos 'n' Andy*, combined with the traditional fears white males had of blacks as economic and sexual competitors.

In this sense, the program can be interpreted as a way for whites to manage their fear of blacks, to see them as lazy, harmless, funny, and unsophisticated. Such an interpretation, though, still fails to grasp the show's generosity of spirit and warm humanity.

Amos 'n' Andy's real attraction was that it, like Gracie Allen, offered an alternative world, not a color-blind America but an America in which blacks weren't frightening, in which blacks became the emotional equivalent of whites, a mythical nation in which blacks were transformed into neighborhood whites but with a different color and a different dialect. It was a world without discrimination or fear. The popularity of the show illustrated the audience need for such a counterworld to offset the more troubling racial America in which they lived.

The combination of warmth, heartfelt story lines, soft humor, and the counterworld of racial harmony propelled *Amos 'n' Andy* into the most popular program in radio's history.

Meanwhile, a whole new group of radio comedians was developing. Vaudeville's great comedy stars, in some cases cursing and complaining, moved to radio simply to survive. However, regulations forbid the use of sexually suggestive material on the radio, and that meant many had to scrap their entire act. Some comedians turned to repeating usable material over and over or using weak puns.

It was Jack Benny who helped develop a radio comedy that was distinct from vaudeville. Benny supplemented the punning with other strategies. Although he couldn't mock political figures, he could mock himself without offending anyone. Benny allowed his radio co-stars to make fun of his vanity, his violin playing, his obsession with never aging beyond thirty-nine, and most of all, his stinginess. The humor on Benny's show came from the characters discussing him rather than from his lines. For example, here are the characters Mary and Rochester talking about him:

Mary: You say you just got into town, Rochester. How come? Were the trains late?

Rochester: What trains? I was out on Highway 99 . . .

Mary: You mean you hitchhiked? Why didn't you come by train with the rest of the cast?

Rochester: Well, instead of a train ticket, Mr. Benny gave me a road map.

Mary: No.

Rochester: And a short talk on the generosity of the average American motorist.

Like Burns and Allen, Benny employed an unusual narrative device. After *Amos 'n' Andy* had introduced the idea of telling a story, most of the shows used a cast that acted the part of different characters. Burns and Allen and Jack Benny were different, however. The actors on Benny's show used their real names and supposedly played themselves, but those characters and their lives were fictional. The device lent an air of reality and added tantalizing questions for audience members about the relationship between character and actor.

Benny also assembled a group of actors who would continue from show to show, confronting new situations. The comedy came from the unique characteristics of each member of the ensemble team, their individual ways of mocking some part of Benny's personality, and their need for each other. Crucially, the actors all stayed together, just as members of comedy teams did. Benny's program, therefore, helped give birth not only to situation comedy but to the comedy ensemble, a group of actors playing specific characters who would work together for the run of a show.

The characters formed a surrogate family. This was not an accident. Benny grasped that the radio audience basically consisted of small family groups. He offered them an escape from the normal confines of family life by effectively redefining the concept of family.

The ensemble approach pioneered by Benny had many advantages. For example, it allowed within its overall gang structure for the possibility of multiple teams. There were many interesting ones within the Benny ensemble, but the most interesting was the pairing of Jack Benny and Rochester (Eddie Anderson).

Eddie Anderson's father was a minstrel performer and his mother a tightrope walker. Young Eddie started a song-and-dance act at age fourteen with his brother Cornelius. Eddie had permanent laryngitis, the result of straining his voice while hawking newspapers to support his family as a youngster. In 1936 he played the part of Noah in the movie *Green Pastures*, and Benny, attracted by his acting abilities and distinctive raspy voice, cast him as a railway porter. The audience loved the rich voice, and Anderson eventually was cast as Benny's butler, Rochester.

Until 1943, the Rochester character simply portrayed the characteristic black stereotypes of the era: His life focused on gambling, liquor, attempts to avoid work, and chasing women. But even then, and much more later, the Rochester character was developing in an interesting way. In a segregated country, Benny was encouraging his writers to let Rochester join the others in mocking him. It was a subtle but important statement.

Not all the vaudeville teams would succeed on radio like Burns and Allen and Jack Benny, but they knew they had to try. In 1937, for example, the Marx Brothers appeared on *Flywheel, Shyster, and Flywheel.* The show lasted for only thirteen weeks, although fifteen routines developed during the show were eventually used in their film *Duck Soup.* The next year, they tried *The Marx Brothers Show.* It was sometimes clever, but clearly Harpo could not get a part in radio, and the visual humor that was the group's unique trademark worked only on a stage or on a movie screen. The lines in their radio act sometimes sounded forced:

Groucho: Where's my secretary?
Chico: Out to lunch.
Groucho: What time did she leave?
Chico: October.
Groucho: If she's not back by next March, I'll give her two weeks' notice.

Although there were a variety of comedy radio shows during the '30s and '40s, comedy teams roughly fell into one of two categories: domestic comedy or rural comedy. Of course, teams were the obvious choice to do domestic comedy. Such comedy had been a staple in vaudeville because, by definition, it required two performers. Models of couples successfully coping with economic hardships and war were vital during those challenging times. Rural comedy was a demographic bow to the emerging and potentially large Midwestern and Southern audiences, groups that were crucial if radio was to be a truly national medium. But why did comedy teams specifically target such an audience? Rural values focused on communal cooperation and on neighborliness. Rural listeners knew most of the people who lived in their towns. They were not urban loners, solitarily sipping coffee in a broken-down diner or huddled and isolated in an apartment surrounded by thousands of strangers. Teams mimicked the communal life led by rural audiences.

There were exceptions to this marriage and rural approach, of course, including two prominent teams. Bud Abbott and Lou Costello were popular, though it is more useful to consider their career alongside their films. And Bob Elliott and Ray Goulding were important radio talents, though in a later generation, and they should be considered in their own time.

Although Burns and Allen were, as in

vaudeville, the most famous of the domestic comedy teams, the first marital comedy team members on radio were Goodman Ace and his wife, Jane Ace. Goodman Ace was a critic and gag writer who had supplied Jack Benny with jokes for free for many years. He had his own show, and one evening in 1929, Jane stood near him waiting for the show to finish. The studio engineer failed to pick up the network show that was to follow Ace's, and the station manager frantically signaled him to keep talking. Ace motioned for his witty, intelligent wife to come over, and they began to talk first about crime and then bridge, an extremely popular national pastime at that time. Their quick-witted and spontaneous conversation led to a show, which — punning on their name and their devotion to bridge — they called *Easy Aces*.

The world on *Easy Aces* was far from the black world that Gosden and Correll created. Goody Ace created a white, upper-class world, and he did it with a merciless wit that unerringly identified what he observed to be the alarmingly high rate of human foibles. The show's comedy — drawn directly from the Dumb Doras of vaudeville and Gracie Allen's character —

was focused on Jane's malapropisms, which were eventually called Janeaceisms. Some of the most well known include the following:

Familiarity breeds attempt.
Time wounds all heels.
I was down on the Lower East Side today and saw those Old Testament houses.
We're all cremated equal.
We're insufferable friends.
I've been working my head to the bone.

The malapropisms, a clever and intelligent variation of the usually much weaker puns on most shows, nevertheless undercut Jane's character. The wit was too barbed to seem plausibly accidental. Additionally, Jane Ace was not a professional actress; indeed, fear compelled her to perform using a hidden microphone. She didn't have anywhere near the comic timing brilliance of Gracie Allen, and her voice was neither as funny nor as charming. She was Gracie for the intellectuals, not for the masses. Still, the material was fun to listen to, and audiences that loved language certainly found Jane's words both playful and illuminating.

Like Gracie, Jane Ace may have seemed scatterbrained, but she always came out as the winner, as smarter, in her own way, than her husband. Both women used the powerful weapon of language against the male-dominated world, ostensibly controlled by their spouses. In that sense, despite the obvious charge that they demeaned women, both Jane Ace and Gracie Allen actually did just the opposite, especially when one takes into consideration the prevailing culture. They developed a way to overcome a power greater than themselves. They used language to create a world in which they ruled, one that was much more inviting than the more sterile, logical world of their husbands.

Both of these marital comedy teams were aided by the fact that they were married in real life, and audiences liked to compare their radio relationships to their actual ones. Of course, Burns always idealized his marriage to Gracie, and audiences were fooled by the performance. Gracie, after all, never broke character, and George successfully hid his marital indiscretions from the public, though not from close associates or from Gracie.

A third important marital comedy on radio was *The Bickersons*, but it didn't come on the air until 1946, after the war had ended. The show, unrestrained by the emotional requirements of keeping families together during hard times, showed a darker side of the marital union. John and Blanche Bickerson (played by Don Ameche and Frances Langford) were a working-class Brooklyn family, without children, but one filled with rancor. Philip Rapp, creator of the show, based it on his own arguments with his wife, Mary. Although the show lasted for only two seasons, it did acquire a following, and Ameche used the character in one way or another for many years.

The Bickersons sought humor from domestic conflict, the depths of which can be found in an episode called "The Honeymoon Is Over," in which Blanche awakens John, who has been sleeping:

John: [groggily excited] What is it, Blanche? What's the matter? What's the matter, Blanche?

Blanche: There isn't another woman in the world who'd sacrifice her youth and her looks to live with a man who rattles himself to sleep like a lot of old bones in a bag. What do you think I'm made of, John?

John: Old bones.

Blanche: You've got to stop it.

John: Stop what?

Blanche: That snoring.

John: Oh, it's just your imagination, Blanche. I never snore.

Blanche: John Bickerson, how can you say that?

John: Very easy, listen, "I never snore." I never snore. I ne . . . ver . . . [begins snoring again].

Blanche: [waking him] John!

John: What's the matter? Why don't you let me sleep, Blanche?

Blanche: What about me? What am I to do when you grind away like a buzz saw? I never sleep at all.

John: You were fast asleep when I came home from my lodge meeting.

Blanche: What time did you come in?

John: I don't know. Put out the lights.

Blanche: You said you'd have one drink and get home at ten.

John: Well, I had ten drinks and got home at one. You knew where I was all the time; now don't start beefing about it.

The most lasting influence of *The Bickersons* was its serving as an inspiration for Jackie Gleason's creation of Ralph and Alice Kramden in *The Honeymooners*, although Gleason carefully modified the constant fighting, gave himself a male counterpart in the character Ed Norton, and always eventually reconciled with Alice.

Lum and Abner was the first of the shows to appeal specifically to small-town Southern and Midwestern audiences. The creators of the show — Chester Lauck and Norris Goff — did a hillbilly variation of *Amos 'n' Andy*. And like the creators of that show, Lauck and Goff used story lines. They combined those stories with continuing characters and in so doing expanded the notion of situation comedy into rural white settings.

Lauck and Goff had initially set out to do a blackface show, but when they got to the audition, they discovered that all the other comedy teams there were dressed as Amos and Andy. Having to improvise on the spot, they hit on the variation. Since they both had come from Arkansas, they were familiar with the hillbilly type, and so Lum and Abner were born.

The two characters owned the Jot 'Em Down Store in Pine Ridge, Arkansas. (Goff's father had actually owned a general store.) By 1931, they had gone national. The characters slowly developed. Abner liked to take chances and then complain, while Lum was always the more cautious one. Soon new characters joined the cast, including a con man, a village idiot, and other easily identifiable types.

Beginning in 1932, *Vic and Sade* (pronounced "Sayd") was set in the fictional town of Crooper, Illinois, forty miles from Peoria, that is, in the American heartland. Indeed, the setting was described as "the small house halfway up in the next block" to bring home the point that the show could be in any town. The stable small-town life was depicted through the characters of Vic Gook, a bookkeeper, his wife, Sade, a homemaker, and Rush, their son. Out of this unpromising mix, however, the show's creator, Paul Rhymer, concocted an offbeat and warm, character-centered humor. The show explored a uniquely absurd world.

Using a minimalist approach, the three characters were the only ones who performed, though "Rush" eventually left and was replaced by a new child, "Russell," and later, after Art Van Harvey, who played Vic, had a heart attack, Clarence Hartzell was brought in to play Uncle

Fletcher, an absentminded ornery old man who would go on and on about his friend, an armed guard at the Ohio State Home for the Tall. Other characters only entered through one-sided telephone talks or letters read aloud. There might be a letter from Rooster Davis, who had decided to open a restaurant that served only bacon sandwiches.

There were almost no sound effects, or music, or props. At the beginning, a lack of money forced the show to work this way, but eventually their spare approach worked because it put full emphasis on the dialogue and the characterizations. Also, the show's fifteen-minute time slot wasn't long enough to wear out the audience's welcome.

The odd characters, the highly recognizable and funny voices, and the bizarre situations created an unusual alternate world, different from the world on *Lum and Abner* and later rural comedies, both on radio and television. It was a world midway between Gracie and the Marx Brothers, filled with ridiculous situations that somehow made sense. Limited by its rural setting from deeply affecting urban audiences and lacking famous vaudeville stars, *Vic and Sade* unfortunately faded from collective memory. Nonetheless, its unique voice and diction and minimalist style rendered it a significant advance in radio comedy.

Here is part of a 1938 broadcast in which Sade accuses Vic of being mad, after seeing him fighting with a Mr. Drummond.

Vic: I wouldn't exactly condescend to get mad at a creature so handicapped. Mr. Drummond is short the normal quota of brains. Mr. Drummond moves helplessly in a fog of stupidity. Mr. Drummond, in short, is a halfwit.

Sade: [giggles] Did you tell him that?

Vic: I intimated as much — an' more — only I couched my barbs with such subtlety they went over his head like soft summer clouds.

Rush: Baseball, huh, Gov?

Vic: How's that?

Rush: You an' him were discussin' baseball?

Vic: One could hardly refer to it as a discussion. I'd vouchsafe a thoughtful opinion an' Drummond'd come back with a splatter of meaningless words boorishly strung together.

Rush: But it was baseball you were talkin' about?

Vic: Yes.

Rush: [chuckles] See, Mom?

Sade: I was just askin' Rush, Vic, how grown-up men can work theirself into a frenzy about such stuff.

Vic: Am I worked into a frenzy?

Sade: You acted like you were worked into something out by the garbage box just now. You an' Drummond both.

Vic: What did Mr. Rush reply when you quizzed him?

Sade: [giggles] He said he didn't know.

Vic: That would be his rejoinder when quizzed on any topic, I believe.

Fibber McGee and Molly was the most popular of the rural comedies. Jim and Marian Jordan, married in real life, had worked in vaudeville and struggled in radio until their new program, which began in 1935. At first, it was an odd show, a mix of Molly's Irish brogue and swing music. It took a while for the writer, Don Quinn, and the stars to develop the characters that eventually emerged. Fibber McGee was a dreamer, a man who didn't seem to have a job and never stopped plotting to get rich without much work involved. Of course, as his nickname made clear, he also inexpertly spun tall tales about his supposedly heroic past. It was the job of his patient wife, Molly, to point out his foibles and deflate his soaring ego. They lived at 79 Wistful Vista in a home through which a lot of very funny and very odd supporting characters paraded. These characters included the "Old Timer," who often repeated a line that became a national catchphrase: "That ain't the way I hear'd it." Other wildly popular catchphrases from the show included Molly's perceptive aside, "'Tain't funny, McGee," and her reaction, "Heavenly days, dearie."

The show's plots often revolved around McGee's bumbling efforts to accomplish a seemingly simple task such as mailing a letter. His inability to accomplish these tasks would be exacerbated by comments from friends, which increased his frustration. One friend who really annoyed him was Throckmorton P. Gildersleeve.

In 1941, the Gildersleeve character left the show to appear on a new radio series. With this, the spin-off had been invented. Remarkably, *Fibber McGee and Molly* was also responsible for the second spin-off, *Beulah*, based on the McGee's black maid.

It premiered in 1944. Beulah was at first played by Marlin Hurt, a white man, who loved to shock live radio audiences by keeping his back to them until his first line. He'd then turn around and speak in the Beulah voice. Audiences howled. Clearly, segregated radio in the mid-1940s still had a very long way to go.

Like the characters Vic and Sade, McGee and Molly were both married and rural; that is, they combined domestic and country humor, unsurprising given the strong emphasis on family in small towns. But the show was aimed at a broader audience than the two other rural shows.

With constrictions enforced by the sponsors and in keeping with radio's emphasis on language, Jordan's character began to use alliterative comedy. These convoluted tongue twisters were considered to be hilarious. McGee would, for example, call another character a "soggy, sap-headed serum salesman."

Their most famous recurring bit, first used on March 5, 1940, involved the packed closet in their house. Clutter from the closet fell each time McGee opened it. Typical dialogue about the closet went like this:

Fibber: Gotta straighten out that closet

one of these days, Molly . . . Oh my gosh!

Molly: Now what?

Fibber: Look! My old mandolin. Remember?

Molly: Well, what are you getting so misty-eyed about it now for? It falls out of the closet every time you open it.

Fibber: It always falls outa the closet, but this is the first time the case has busted open . . . [plucks strings]. Needs a little tuning, I guess.

Molly: A little tuning! That's about as melodious as a slate pencil.

Fibber: . . . Remember how we used to go canoeing on the Illinois River and I used to serenade you with my old mandolin?

Molly: I never knew whether you took up the mandolin because you loved music or hated paddling.

The packed closet became one of the most famous running gags in radio. It was used in clever ways. A visitor might think it was the front door and out came the contents. In one show, two burglars entered the house and tied poor McGee up. He casually informed them that all his valuables were in the closet. The hoodwinked burglars opened the closet only to be buried by an avalanche of flotsam and jetsam.

McGee's tall tales, long an American comic tradition, also pleased audiences. In one broadcast, for example, he claimed, "I'll never forget the time I rid acrost Africa on a huntin' trip on a bicycle. Yes sir, toots, that was in 1897. Capetown to Tripoli. Made it in twenty-two days exactly. Would of made it in fifteen and a half it hadn't been for bein' captured by cannibals up in the Belgian Congo."

Sometimes, Fibber could use his language to be witty, sounding more like Jane Ace than a country bumpkin. He might say, "A committee is a small group of the unqualified appointed by the unthinking to undertake the utterly unnecessary," or "Nostalgia is a longing for something you couldn't stand anymore."

Marian Jordan's career is illustrative of the pressures performers faced. Starting in November 1937, she left the show for what would prove to be an eighteen-month sabbatical. The official explanation was that she had departed for "health reasons," although the truth is that she had been battling alcoholism, a common problem among entertainers.

Fibber McGee and Molly was one of the first programs to rally support for the war once it had been declared. Indeed, on December 9, 1941 — a mere two days after the Pearl Harbor attack — there was a joke about the war. One of the characters told Molly he was searching for a globe, and she replied, "You want a globe with Japan on it? Then you better get one quick."

The success of *Fibber McGee and Molly* reinforced the shift toward situation comedies, and their low production costs — there were no expensive orchestras, guest stars, or large writing staff — also appealed to producers. This crucial development for radio comedy teams also provided a key solution for the new medium, television, where it was difficult for one actor to play many parts, as was common on radio. Jack Benny's ensemble had provided a path-breaking model for future comedy entertainment. Eventually, in television as well as radio, the situation comedy — usually set in a family residence or a place of business and populated by well-defined personalities — would rule the world of entertainment humor.

But in the 1930s and 1940s, teams were still thriving, though it must be acknowledged that radio comedy, for all its attractions, was not always great comedy. Given the incredibly confining censorship restrictions imposed on writers and performers, it is remarkable that at least some of the material still holds up so well. Radio comedy's weaknesses should also be assessed within the context of its diluted mission. The shows could never be purely funny. All comedy is performed in a social context, but rarely in so extreme a context as the economic depression and war that dominated American life during those decades. Radio comedians were heroic in their efforts to help the nation, and they were sometimes better citizens than comedians. But in their day, for their audiences, the radio comedians were vital and funny, precisely when such vitality and humor were most needed.

FIVE

COMEDY COMES TO
THE BIG SCREEN

Mr. Laurel and Mr. Hardy

Stan Laurel couldn't wait to spend a few days in England to see his parents and to tour his homeland. For years, he and his partner, Oliver Hardy, had been so busy that they had barely traveled more than a few miles away from the movie studio.

It was July 16, 1932, and the pair was set to sail for England on the fabled *Aquitania*. But neither the ship's trellis in natural teak nor its glazed windows nor wicker chairs could blot the date's grisly reminder. It had been exactly fifty months to the day since Laurel's son, Stanley Robert Jefferson, had died. The boy had been born two months premature on May 7 and slipped away nine days later. Laurel had rushed back to work, but the devastating emotional effects of the loss could be seen in his next film, titled, unfortunately, *The Laurel-Hardy Murder Case*.

Whatever sadness he may have felt, Laurel was shocked and amazed at the crowds that greeted the pair as they arrived at the pier in New York. The jubilant fans and the cars with newsreel cameras that pursued the pair down Broadway frightened both comedians.

People continued to approach them even while they were on the ocean voyage. As their ship docked in Southampton, an enormous crowd, cheering loudly and whistling their "cuckoo song" theme music, swelled toward them. Stan had trouble finding his father and stepmother. Only after an hour did they manage to get to a car to whisk them away to the Savoy Hotel.

Later, they would recall that greeting and the tour that followed with awe. Oddly, despite how closely they worked together, they didn't really get a chance to become friends until they toured. As Stan noted about their earlier career, "Between pictures we hardly saw each other." Additionally, the crowd in Southampton delivered a message to Laurel and Hardy: They were beloved international stars. The trip made them realize they were famous, and the realization overwhelmed them.

The story of Laurel and Hardy's rise to such glory is intertwined with the origins of the motion picture industry. They showed how a supremely gifted comedy team could thrive in and define the potential of the new medium of film. They brought sight gags, charm, slapstick, and narrative together. But most of all they embodied teamwork.

Technology had transformed films. No longer were they used as audience chasers in vaudeville theaters. In 1905, the first theater used exclusively to show movies was established in Pittsburgh. The owners, John Harris and Harry Davis, showed the popular western *The Great Train Robbery* and charged a nickel for admission. The ninety-six patrons sitting on folding chairs were enthralled. Soon theaters all over the country — nickelodeons — were charging a nickel to see movies. There were even daring entrepreneurs who put cushions on the chairs. It quickly became clear that it made economic sense for theater owners to show films instead of hosting vaudeville shows. Audiences were particularly interested in stars. Very few vaudeville theaters could book such stars in person on a regular basis, but it was obviously easy to bring them to the theater if they were on film.

Nickelodeon programs were changed twice a week and consisted of about five different films — a drama, an adventure, a novelty, often a documentary, and of course, given American tastes, a comedy. Together, the films ran for about an hour. A pianist, accordionist, or violin player often accompanied the silent films.

As early as 1909, 3 million Americans went to the movies each day. By 1913, there were 20,000 American movie theaters. In 1914, the 3,300-seat Strand Theater opened in New York City, effectively marking the end of the nickelodeons and ushering in the age of movie palaces.

Audiences developed a hunger for information about the new stars. In 1910, the Kalem Company became the first movie studio to provide photographs of the people in their films. However, with an incredible lack of foresight, they didn't put the stars' names on the photos. (They defended the oversight with the rationale that with acting's unenviable reputation, the stars would not want to sully their good names.) Such an approach did not stop fans from trying to contact the actors. Studios were flooded with letters, a tradition from the theater. Still, studio heads expressed shock at the number of marriage offers eager female fans bestowed upon male actors. Somehow, they thought this was not appropriate behavior for women, although they found acceptable the male marriage proposals to women stars. Also in 1910, Vitagraph and other companies offered photographs of some of the film stars, and the term "movie fan" began to be used to describe enthusiastic patrons of the nickelodeons.

All these fans meant that the movie companies constantly needed new films. People literally were taken off the street and drafted as actors. The industry was wide open; there were incredible opportunities in the new and untested movie business for groups otherwise marginalized in the society, such as immigrants, women, and ethnic minorities.

The new moviemakers knew that to succeed they had to attract the large working-class audiences. And that meant comedy, especially slapstick. Circus clowns had once used paddles to slap each other, an assault that could reliably draw laughter, and the term "slapstick" was born.

It would be misleading, however, to identify the silent comedy era only with slapstick. Despite the lack of sound, silent film comedies also depended on situations or characters to provoke laughter. In addition, slapstick shouldn't be confused with the more general notion of sight gags. Slapstick involves some violence, whereas a sight gag does not necessarily have such an element. The sight gag is structured like a joke, with a visual setup and a visual punch line that might or might not involve violence. Slapstick is aggressive and cruel but entails an explicit audience understanding that such violence does not result in any real pain or harm. A house might collapse, a hammer might hit the actor on the head, but the audience knows that it is not real and is meant to be funny.

Filmmakers had stars fall on their backsides without injury (a pratfall), or chase other actors trying to escape, or slip on ice or any of a variety of other objects, or have tumultuous fights, or engage in other fast-paced physical antics that could get a laugh, generally by mocking an authority figure. The audiences found slapstick's gleeful destructiveness to be liberating. Generally, unlike the patrons of Broadway or the opera, for example, these moviegoers were without much money or status. They relished seeing the smug representatives of society, indeed the very institutions of middle-class life, not only ridiculed but also symbolically destroyed.

Mack Sennett popularized the French approach to slapstick, including screen illusions, leavened by the influence of burlesque. In the years 1912–1917, Sennett produced a wide variety of groundbreaking slapstick films, exemplified by the Keystone Kops, and created many of the basic ingredients that came to define American slapstick.

A favorite was the camera trick, such as a paddy wagon dispensing an incredibly large number of extraordinarily inept police — a trick done by having the Kops exit, go around the camera, and enter the wagon again from the other side. The French had used the chase, but Sennett choreographed it, increasing the tempo of the chase as it continued. He filmed automobiles on public roads, with or without permission, sometimes spreading liquid soap on the road as his cars sped along, all for the inevitable spinning and general chaos. It is no surprise that insurance companies were extremely reluctant to write policies for Sennett's actors.

Sennett refined slapstick by adding unusual situations, bizarre characters and outfits, an amazing and clever array of camera tricks, and various props, such as breakaway vases.

And then there were the pies. Although Sennett claimed that his leading lady Mabel Normand was the first person to throw a pie in a film, this may have been simply a well-publicized gesture toward a woman with whom he had been allegedly personally involved. That famous first pie was thrown into Roscoe "Fatty" Arbuckle's face in the film *A Noise from the Deep*, released in 1913. Sennett had a distinctly American intuition about comedy. Trained in burlesque (thereby knowing the attraction to audiences of the pretty women in bathing suits he used in some films) and steeped in the grand American notion of excess, he soon concluded that if one pie was funny, two pies would be much funnier.

A number of comedy teams emerged during the silent era. Ham and Bud (Lloyd V. Hamilton and Edward "Bud" Duncan) starred in a series of films for the Kalem Company and even have a legitimate claim to the title of first famous comedy team in film history. Darwin Karr and Gertrude McCoy were the first fat and thin team, but they were far less famous than the more popular pairing of a hefty John Bunny and a very thin Flora Finch. Their contrasting body types became a model for many later teams. Bunny helped condition audiences to laugh simply because a comedian was overweight.

But it was Laurel and Hardy who became the first enduring team created by the Hollywood system. They were both acting for Hal Roach, a Sennett competitor, and met on camera for the first time during the filming of *You Lucky Dog* in

1921, but they wouldn't truly work together until 1926. It was Leo McCarey, a director, who noted not only the contrast in their physiques but also their similarities, especially each one's brilliant use of gestures.✳

Stan Laurel came by his talent honestly. He knew early on that he didn't like school and that he wanted more than anything to be in entertainment like his father. He made his first trip to America in 1910 with the company organized by Fred Karno. The British music hall tradition and the pantomimic skills Laurel acquired from Karno shaped his approach to comedy. Laurel also learned from his roommate, the star of the company — Charlie Chaplin. According to one story, Chaplin used to play the violin to cover Laurel's illegal frying of food.

Laurel eventually tried his hand at vaudeville, teaming with his common-law wife, Mae, who had been unable to obtain a divorce from her husband. She was the one who came up with his stage name. Stan didn't trust his real name — Stan Jefferson — because he was superstitious: The name had thirteen letters. Mae was sitting in a dressing room, reading a history book someone had left there. She came across a picture of a Roman general who wore a wreath of laurel around his head. She spoke the name aloud: "Laurel. Laurel. Stan Laurel." Stan looked up, unsure of what she was saying.

"How about that for a name?"

He also repeated the name, quickly concluding, "Sounds very good."

The name was better than the act, and the romantic relationship eventually frayed, but Stan Laurel was born.

In 1917, Laurel bumped into his old friend Charlie Chaplin, and Chaplin urged Laurel to give movies a try. A year later, Chaplin's former roommate was in his first film. But Laurel was not an instant success. He didn't like working with partners, and because of previous bad experiences, he was reluctant to work with Oliver Hardy, a Southern gentleman with a penchant for stealing scenes.

Hardy did not have Laurel's family or entertainment background. Young Norvell Hardy, born in 1892, was eleven months old when his father, Oliver, died. His struggling mother managed a hotel, but that was not a life Hardy envisioned for himself. He ran away from home to join a theatrical group. He eventually returned, and his mother sent him to a military college. Ill suited to such a regimented life, Hardy ran away again. He was a polite, timid, sentimental young man who hated being fat, and he was struggling to find his place in life.

At eighteen, he became a projectionist and part-time manager in a theater and became smitten with the fledgling movie business. He moved to Jacksonville, Florida, took Oliver as his first name to honor his father, and began making movies with the Lubin Studios. His large size and expressive face and gestures made him a natural on-screen. It was in Florida that he acquired his nickname. A local barber had the habit of applying talcum powder to his fleshy cheeks and saying, "Nice baby." The nickname became shortened to "Babe," and he used it for the rest of his life. Eventually, Hardy moved to Hollywood and began working with Hal Roach.

Both Laurel and Hardy were accomplished comic actors, but it was only when they teamed up that their fame — and even their comic talents — exploded. It was as though their full comic personalities could not emerge while playing solo or without the right partner. Once Laurel and Hardy found each other, they could focus on their individual characters and shape them more fully, but always within the context of their special relationship.

Laurel and Hardy entered the movie business after the revolution in film length. When Sennett had been at his prime, all the theaters showed short films. Most were one-reelers, lasting about ten minutes. Soon, though, there were experiments with longer films, two-reelers and beyond. By the time D. W. Griffith's 190-minute *Birth of a Nation* was released in 1915, the short film became just an extra attraction, a brief entertainment leading up to the main feature, which was significantly longer in length. In the case of Laurel and Hardy, though, audiences frequently came specifically for their shorter two-reeler as opposed to the longer main feature. Theaters were aware of this and advertised accordingly.

Some of the successful comedy teams of the 1930s and beyond — especially Laurel and Hardy and the Three Stooges — excelled in the short. Later, in the 1950s, comedy shorts were seen as having the perfect length for television, and the broadcast of these shorts on TV created a new, very large, and later influential generation of fans. In many senses, the short is a completely different form than the feature. The shorts were generally made much more quickly and with far less money and fewer production values than the features, making it difficult to compare them. Yet in many ways, Laurel and Hardy's short films were better than their features because the shorts were concise and contained, perfect for their gag style.

It took a while for them to develop that style and those characters. They didn't have a chance to spend years together in front of live audiences developing their act. Instead, they had to develop film by film, almost gag by gag, until the characters were just right.

Laurel knew that sight gags were fine for a laugh, but true emotional resonance for the audience could come only if they found the characters appealing. For example, laughs in comedy often come from the loss of dignity. To achieve the humor, the character must first be seen as dignified. In many cases, the dignified character would be a minor one, mocked with, say, a pie in the face. Part of the genius of Laurel and Hardy is that their own characters started out with dignity and would eventually lose it, but instead of the audience mocking them, as they would a banker or society matron with a face full of pie, the audience identified with them. They were still the dignified "Mr. Laurel" and "Mr. Hardy" even while they suffered.

And the actors grew to know their characters intimately. Stan used to sit in the projection room, looking at rushes and referring to himself as "the little fellow," deciding lovingly and shrewdly, for example, that a particular gag didn't work because "the little fellow wouldn't do that."

The character names of Stan and Ollie were not immediately used. Lip readers of their early silent films could tell that Laurel called Hardy by his nickname "Babe," and when Stan called Hardy "Ollie" in *A Perfect Day* (1929), Hardy responded, "Don't call me Ollie!" He never repeated that objection because they both came to see "Ollie" as fitting the character so well. And they used their names for another reason, as Hardy told John McCabe: "In the early days of comedy, the studio frequently owned the character name . . . and the comedian could be fired but he couldn't take his character name with him. So we just kept our own names."

They developed their costumes in *Do Detectives Think?* Hardy got the idea for a derby hat from Chaplin, of course. He had already found an inspiring cartoon character named Helpful Henry, who exuded confidence as he bumbled his way through life. Hardy's gesture of waving with both hands near his tie came from playing around one day in an early movie. He took Edgar Kennedy's famous slow burn — used as a silent, extended controlled expression of anger — and tied it to his desire to look directly at the camera. Hardy always made intelligent use of such brief gestures. Hardy also brushed his hair forward and grew a small moustache, and the effect was complete.

Laurel's movements came from his work in pantomime, where the face was so important. He perfected a cry, a look of perpetual bewilderment, and an open-faced innocence accompanying a grin on his long, flexible face. Laurel used makeup to make his blue eyes appear smaller. The crying — which Laurel grew to dislike but which Hal Roach loved — was started in an earlier film where, playing a butler, he acted as though he would shed tears at any second. The effect was so funny that he knew he could use it to generate an almost automatic laugh. Laurel's odd haircut came from his getting his red hair cut close for a prison film. When he put on a hat, the hair remained in an unusual formation.

The crew loved the hair so much that Laurel added it to the character. Always looking for an added touch, he began to explore how to manipulate the funny hair and came upon the idea of pulling it.

Amazingly, Laurel and Hardy worked without the usual friction and clash of ambitions and egos. It was rare for comedians to be willing and able to share the spotlight. Laurel had long lived in Charlie Chaplin's shadow and had an urgent drive to be recognized for his own talents. Hardy's own insecurities made him desire audience recognition and love. Both men, that is, deserve enormous credit in putting aside their egos to recognize that together, by sharing, they could both succeed. Hardy let Laurel make all the creative decisions. He didn't complain when Laurel got twice as much money. He followed direction well. Laurel, a quick-witted man, fully understood and appreciated Hardy's incredible acting talent and learned how to create gags to take advantage of it.

With one ego submerged and the other clearly in charge but willing to share the laughs fairly, the two had found the elusive recipe for a comedy team's longevity. It was not a recipe many other teams would be able to follow.

Their professional and personal congeniality combined with their characters to make audiences adore them and the film world they created. That world was one in which the boys tried to adapt to a society that they couldn't ultimately comprehend. Stan never grasped the reality of the world outside his perceptions. He couldn't learn from past mistakes. Like many other comedic characters, his grasp of English was not enviable. Ollie, unlike others, could understand Stan, like a brother explaining another brother's actions to uncomprehending parents. Indeed, Ollie played a somewhat older child, a child who knew there is an outside reality but wanted it to correspond to his vision and expectations. They were, in Laurel's words, "two minds without a single thought," but two minds that refused ever to give up, to surrender to the power of that nightmare world they had to wander through without that single thought. Whatever happened to them, they always had each other. Indeed, one of the team's most endearing qualities was that in the face of never-ending frustration, their innocence never collapsed into cynicism. They remained ever hopeful. The audiences of the 1930s desperately needed that hope.

Laurel and Hardy also had a special talent. David Bullard and other members of the Berth Marks Tent (one of the branches of the Sons of the Desert, the international organization for fans of Laurel and Hardy) defined this talent: "They draw us 'into' their world, rather than relegating us to a 'fly on the wall' position." It's an important observation and goes beyond Laurel and Hardy. The great comedy teams made audiences more than spectators keeping an aesthetic distance from the comical fantasy world. We love the teams that can entice us out of our world into theirs. Like other successful teams, Laurel and Hardy accomplish this by persuading us to believe in that world and by making it so pleasant, so inviting.

Sometimes Laurel and Hardy seem less a team than a couple. Some observers have suggested that homoerotic elements are present in a few of their films. The three key films cited by those who make this assertion are *Their First Mistake*, *Putting Pants on Philip*, and *Liberty*. In the first film, Stan tells Ollie that he should have a baby because "it would keep your wife's mind occupied . . . you could go out nights with me . . . and she'd never think anything about it." The couple does adopt a baby, but Ollie's wife divorces him anyway, and the baby ends up in bed between Stan and Ollie with them functioning as the parents.

In *Putting Pants on Philip*, which Laurel later claimed to be his favorite film, Laurel and Hardy depart from their already developed screen characters. Laurel plays a character who wears a kilt, and Ollie wants to replace it with pants. As they walk along, Laurel, as Philip, links his arm to Hardy, playing his uncle. In one scene, Laurel takes some sneezing powder. It performs well, but unfortunately the ensuing sneeze has the side effect of loosening his underwear. With only a kilt to cover himself, he steps toward an air vent, and off-camera, the kilt rises to embarrassing heights. Several women characters in the film faint at the sight. Hardy stares directly into the camera, asking the audience to understand his frustration.

In *Liberty*, the two are prison escapees who have managed to get some civilian clothes, but they put on the wrong pants. Much of the film focuses on their efforts to undress and exchange pants, including doing so in one spectacular scene high up on a building construction site. In a famous scene, a woman (Jean Harlow) spots them pulling at each other's trousers in the backseat of a car.

Whatever gay undertones may or may not be in the films, ultimately the Laurel and Hardy characters are not concerned with eroticism at all. Their characters are boyish, innocent, steeped in Victorian morality, and protected by their childlike natures from all the nasty realities that come with adulthood. However anti-Freudian this notion of pre-sexuality is, it is crucial for understanding the team.

A considerable part of the enduring charm of Laurel and Hardy is precisely that they symbolize adults' sense of their own lost innocence. They offer, at the very least, a nostalgia for childishness and, by extension, childhood. For some, their asexuality offers a pleasant pause from the complications of adult sexuality. Imputing any kind of profound sexual motivation to their comedy diminishes their innocence and reduces them to ordinary film characters.

Their arguments do mimic those of a married couple. This was not accidental. The pain of economic deprivation had frayed many a marital relationship, including those of Laurel and Hardy in real life. Laurel married four times (in eight separate marriage ceremonies). Hardy was married three times. The various weddings, spats, and divorces were frequently mentioned in the Hollywood press. But Laurel and Hardy's conflicts and their infliction of mutual violence was a useful release for couples in the audience — and for the actors themselves.

One of Laurel and Hardy's various claims to being the best comedy team ever is that they created the model of two friends struggling against the world, always willing to help each other despite the frequency with which their efforts are met by failure, resulting in many a "nice mess." Their deep bond is admirable. The underlying friendship, which provoked a deep empathy in audiences, involved mutual acceptance and tolerance, a sense of not being alone in having to face a frightening reality. Neither is able to abandon the other.

Laurel and Hardy faced a painful world filled with indignities, and their characters embodied human foibles and follies. Laurel and Hardy accepted such a world with dignity, with only their friendship to sustain them. Their society, or faith, or their own skills, or even a traditional family couldn't protect them. Theirs is a case for friendship above all sustaining a person through the nonsense of life. Nonetheless, Laurel and Hardy were very realistic about friendship. They knew it included mutual aggression, and they were able to define a perfect conflict model, a way of fighting while retaining the friendship.

Their focus on friendship also partially explains Laurel and Hardy's deep attraction to young people, perhaps especially to young males. The eight- and nine-year-old males in their audience were struggling to create a little distance from their parents, but they were not yet able to succeed on their own. They needed friends. Of course, later comedy teams such as the Three Stooges and Abbott and Costello copied this approach and also attracted the young. It is no surprise, for example, that the young baby boomers were so influenced by the films of comedy teams shown on television in the 1950s.

Laurel and Hardy also brought another change to team comedy. The characters they created were not the normal straight man/comic team. They added a completely new dimension to team comedy by creating a pair of distinct comic characters who always maintained their roles. Stan was always bewildered, Ollie always frustrated. Ollie's ego would not let him accept what life seemingly had offered him. He was convinced he could do better, and he dragged his pal Stan on the path to self-improvement, a path filled with constant frustrations and dangers. When they failed, Ollie could not accept responsibility. Luckily for him, he had Stan to blame. They were childlike, but not childish, in their ignorance, and they were charming because they didn't know just how ignorant they were as they tried, with a dazzling trail of failed attempts, to become competent adults.

Most comedy teams had an authority figure to balance a rebellious spirit — a straight man to rein in the comic. But not Laurel and Hardy. Ollie thought he was in charge and acted as though he were a parent or older sibling, but, of course, he clearly wasn't.

Innovating, Laurel and Hardy deployed someone outside the team to play the straight man. Jimmy Finlayson, popularly called Fin, was the outsider they most often used. Finlayson inadvertently made a contribution to American culture. Because of censors, Finlayson was not allowed to swear in the movies. He wanted, however, to express annoyance, and where he would ordinarily have used the word "damn," he substituted a sound, "D'oooohh." One famous scene in which he does this is in *Way Out West*, when he is trying to pass off one woman for another to get a deed to a gold mine. He calls out the woman's name, expecting the imposter to appear, but the real woman shows up. He is intensely frustrated and lets out his "D'oooohh." Years later, Dan Castellaneta was hired to be the voice of the animated character Homer Simpson and was reading a script in which he was called upon to make an "annoyed grunt." He asked Matt Groening, the series' creator, what that meant and was told to make whatever sound he wished. Castellaneta imitated Finlayson. Groening told him to speed the sound up, and "D'oh" was born.

The outside straight man was used so that the team could become a single unit fighting with each other but working together against the outsider. The fantasy world the team created for itself was a cocoon against the real world.

The audience had developed a growing distrust of that real world. Their greater willingness to let go of it makes sense when set against the confusing and raucous society of the Roaring Twenties and later the devastated society of the Great Depression. Audiences didn't want a straight man to provide guidance to the outside world because that world was no longer stable. Audiences wanted not comedians who were attached to the real world by the straight man's sanity but teams who mirrored the loss of that sanity. In those teams, the members were all separated from the real world and at odds with it. The members of these new teams could only rely on each other, just as audiences perceived that, because their society was in upheaval and danger, they could only truly rely on family and friends.

Laurel and Hardy also modified the Burns and Allen model in another way. In addition to having a straight man like Fin represent the real world, Laurel and Hardy largely shifted the burden of representing that real world from any one person to a situation. In almost all their films, the team started with one foot in reality. It was this reality that functioned as the "straight man." Then, slowly, Laurel and Hardy departed from it. The struggle was between the real world in which they began and the comic world they lurched toward.

Audiences, filled with a powerful need to retaliate for what they perceived as a lack of respect or justice, deeply appreciated Laurel and Hardy's ferocious attacks on the comic stand-ins for middle-class society. Nowhere is this more clearly achieved than in the 1929 two-reeler *Big Business*, the most perfectly constructed of all of their films. Laurel and Hardy are traveling Christmas tree salesmen, and Jimmy Finlayson, with his mustache and narrowed eyes, is a customer who, incomprehensibly to them, clearly has no need for what they see as such a joyous and much-needed addition to his home. The problems start out simply enough. Fin declines the sales offer, but the tree gets stuck in the door. Stan and Ollie ring again, but again the tree is stuck. Next time Stan's coat is stuck. Then the tree. This time, fed up, Fin throws the tree. Stan and Ollie leave, but Stan has a "big business" idea. He wants to take an order for next year. This time Fin clips the tree, and mutually escalating retaliation begins in earnest. Fin concentrates on their car, while Stan and Ollie merrily destroy his house and its belongings. (The house was a real one; it belonged to an appropriately compensated employee at Roach's studio.) No tree was safe; no window remained intact. The film is a perfectly choreographed battle between the middle-class home-owner and the poor salesmen. A policeman who stands by through most of the film, carefully noting each bit of damage but only belatedly stopping it, is the law the two salesmen mock. The assault on the sanctity of a middle-class home, and a beloved symbol of that sanctity, the Christmas tree, is complete. For the poor masses in the audience, the idea of attacking the supposedly inviolable sanctuary of the middle class was a perfect scenario for slapstick comedy. The destruction was a ritual of sorts, one with stages that the audience could anticipate, a knowledge that increased their laughter because it increased their sense of superiority over the characters in the film.

Leo McCarey developed the gag Laurel termed the "reciprocal destruction" of the car and house. McCarey, famously unable to comprehend the intricacies of a bow tie, was at a party when Mabel Normand pulled his tie loose. McCarey, in response to the laughter, pulled at Hal Roach's tie. Collars were not far behind. The back of dinner jackets then became too inviting a target to bypass, especially when sharpened knives were readily available.

The incident, with the mutual loss of

both dignity and property, became an almost perfect gag. It was funny. It was visual. It released emotional desires for revenge. And it would eventually turn out to be the perfect metaphor for how audiences felt about their loss of economic well-being and their resentment. (*Big Business* came out in April 1929, a few months before the stock market crash.)

McCarey's contribution was vital, but more generally it was Laurel, by all accounts, who deserves credit for crafting the bits, pushing for the best in an industry that needed to produce a lot of films in a very short time. For example, *Big Business* had been written in mid-December 1928. The film was made between December 19 and 26 of that year. Despite the crunch, Laurel spent long hours shaping and then honing the bits and gags. In a sense, he was always working because as he went through a normal day, he saw the world through a Laurel and Hardy lens and so always was on the lookout for a setting, a situation, or a funny character. However, he remained deeply intuitive. He didn't look for hidden deep meanings. Indeed, like many comedians, Laurel was upset with those who tried to overanalyze his work. As he saw it, he was just trying to be funny.

He spent his lifetime developing his sense about what would please an audience.

Laurel, very much like Chaplin, turned Sennett's concept of rapid-fire comedy on its head. Sennett wanted a laugh every twenty feet of film. It was Chaplin, first, and later Laurel — both trained in the British tradition — who elongated the gag. Their bits could take one hundred feet to get a laugh. When Chaplin first began experimenting with this form, few comedy experts recognized the genius of this method. Similarly, Laurel knew how to milk a scene, how to generate waves of laughter, how to have a topper and then another.

There was another crucial aspect to the elongation. With a live audience, a comic actor knew when the laughter stopped and it was time to get on with the next line. Silent films were made without an audience. One immense problem was deciding how much time to leave for an audience to laugh before moving on to the next bit. Pushing a lot of laughs together could, in theory, work — it did for Sennett and later for Groucho Marx. But unless the material was of very high quality, there was a danger of annoying audiences by having laughter in the theater interfere with watching for the next gag. There had to be enough gags, but they had to be perfectly paced. By elongating the gag (and creating great gags in the first place), Laurel solved this fundamental problem, one that many other silent comedians never were able to overcome.

This elongation is important in another way as well. The immense amount of sheer violence in Laurel and Hardy movies is transformed into successful slapstick for audiences precisely by the slower pace. Once the comic movements become an incredibly exaggerated reality, they enter into the world of cartoon violence. Indeed, Laurel's triumph was to match a character people cared about to that exaggerated, updated slapstick.

The slow pace was a tricky bit of business though. Hal Roach believed that comedy had a formula. He wanted each two-reeler to have a certain number of laughs — if possible, as many as seventy-five. Films would be shown to preview audiences, and a Roach employee would sit in the audience counting the laughs, in an activity called "clocking." If the film lacked the required number of laughs, additional gags were inserted or the film was re-edited. Laurel and Hardy's initial success at meeting these requirements allowed them the freedom to develop their comedic characters and to extend the length of their gags.

One clear example of the extended gag is the team's effort to top Sennett's pie-throwing records. In *The Battle of the Century*, the pie scene starts innocently enough when a pie deliveryman walking out of a store slips on a banana peel that Ollie has thrown so that Stan can slip on it and collect insurance money. The pie man then sees Ollie holding a banana. This, it goes without saying, calls for revenge. The pie man uses his only available weapon to throw at Ollie. Ollie, honor-bound to retaliate, hurls a pie right back but misses. The wayward pie instead smacks into a woman bystander's posterior. It doesn't take long after that for everyone around to get involved and start freely tossing the pies. When the custard had cleared, more than 3,000 pies had been thrown. Laurel knew that sheer numbers were not enough. Each pie had a specific target symbolic of someone of authority in the society.

Lou Costello was among those who learned a lot from *The Battle of the Century*. Costello was then a young stunt-worker at MGM, an extra in the crowd watching a prizefight at the beginning of the film. He was, no doubt, observing a lot more than the fight.

The film marked the end of an era. Audiences had mostly outgrown simple slapstick. By the time of this mother of all pie fights, the fights themselves were considered outdated.

But Laurel and Hardy had plenty of other material. They were masters of letting audiences experience comic danger vicariously. Audiences loved such scenes because placing comedians in seemingly dangerous situations reduced their own anxiety about real danger, enabling them to laugh at the pitfalls that reality too routinely opened before them. When the critic James Agee wanted to identify a favorite comedy scene, he named the wonderful bit from *Swiss Miss*, in which Laurel and Hardy move a piano across a bridge in the Alps only to meet up with a gorilla. The gorilla has an unlikely attraction to Ollie's hat. It doesn't take long for the ape and the piano to land in the river. Charles Gemora, a smallish actor with a reputation as the guy to get when you needed an ape, played the gorilla. Indeed, he had played gorillas in many films, including the Marx Brothers' *At the Circus* and an earlier

Laurel and Hardy film, *The Chimp*. He would later don the ape costume again in Bob Hope and Bing Crosby's film *Road to Zanzibar*. Seeking to expand his mastery of the animal roles, he played a bear in the Hope-Crosby film *Road to Utopia*.

Laurel and Hardy had practiced the art of piano moving six years earlier in the 1932 comedy short *The Music Box*, the only film of theirs to win an Academy Award (for "Best Short Subject"). In that hilarious film, the two had to deliver a piano to a house at the top of an exceedingly long and narrow stairway. (The 131 steps are still there on Vendome Street in Los Angeles.) Although the movie is done in sound, it has all the characteristics of their best silent work. Of course, once they get to the top of the stairs, a mail carrier tells them they could have more easily delivered the piano by a back road. They take the piano right back down, put it on the van, and drive up to the house. The front door is locked, however, and so they decide to take the piano through a window. Their efforts lead to considerable collateral damage. As in *Big Business*, they wreck a house, but this time with the best of intentions.

Laurel and Hardy were the only silent

screen comedy team to make the successful transition to sound film. In a way, this is odd, because the technology that gave voice to movies — that, in effect, married radio to silent films, thus assuring the eventual decline of both — came precisely at a time when comedy was most needed. Because the silent film's greatness lay in pantomime, whereas vaudeville's lay in verbal skill, it was the vaudevillians that triumphed. People needed to laugh and wanted as much sound as possible and as much comedy as possible. Many vaudeville teams thrived in the new movie world, but silent film comedians rarely did. Most lacked a voice that matched their physical persona.

Of course, as widely noted, part of Laurel and Hardy's charm was the pairing of a fat man and a skinny man. But their voices, the courtly Georgian tenor from Hardy and the light Lancashire accent from Laurel with its emphasis on the first syllable of a word, were perfect for their characters.

Additionally, Laurel's brilliant stretching of a routine and his exaggerated slapstick to make the violence less real were enhanced when the visual violence was accompanied by the sounds of pain and anguish. Without the cartoonish element, audiences might have felt the pain too greatly. It took the exaggeration of a Laurel or the Three Stooges to render the violence funny for American audiences. Laurel used fake sounds to reduce the sense of reality. He also used sounds well to reduce reality. He might, for example, focus on a character about to be hit by some object. The camera would then cut away to the face of a watchful bystander. The audience would not see the character being hit but would hear the faked sound and see the grimace on the face of the observer. This technique reduced the on-screen violence without removing it completely.

While Laurel and Hardy are rightly more well known for the strength of their characters, teamwork, and gestures than for their dialogue, their repartee could also be very funny. Typical of classic teams, they uttered memorable lines, such as their most famous, "Here's another nice mess you've gotten me into." This line is often misquoted because, using a music hall sketch written by Stan's father as the basis, the team made a film titled *Another Fine Mess*, and many people confuse the film title with the actual Hardy signature line.

It is unfortunate that the Roach studios did not pay the kind of money needed for more first-rate writers for their sound films. In their silent films, besides contributions from Laurel and McCarey and other directors, they used Roach's ingenious titles writer, H. M. Walker. Had brilliant writing been added to Laurel's dazzling skills with gags and the wonderful characters created by the team, their sound films would have been significantly better.

Laurel and Hardy's success was essentially limited to the end of the silent era and the 1930s, a decade during which they made forty-seven films, including one of their best in sound, *Sons of the Desert*, produced in 1933. Their humor fit seamlessly into the Great Depression, but once war preparations started improving the American economy, audiences had quite different emotional needs, and the popularity of Laurel and Hardy slowly declined, along with movie studio interest.

Laurel and Hardy weren't the only creations of Hal Roach. Convinced that great comedians were children at heart, Roach had taken the concept literally and created the Our Gang comedies in 1922. These films follow in the Jack Benny ensemble team tradition. The name for the films is confusing. The children in the original series were officially known as Hal Roach's Rascals. The first movie these Rascals made was titled *Our Gang,* and that's what distributors asked for, so eventually the group of comedies themselves began to be called Our Gang comedies. When the films were released on television, yet another name, The Little Rascals, was used. Over the next twenty-two years, 221 Our Gang comedies were made, the largest number of films in any series in movie history.

The best of the Our Gang films were created in the 1930s, before short films faced severe distribution problems. By the late 1930s, theaters were demanding full-length features for double bills, making it especially difficult for small studios to successfully market shorts. It was during the early to mid-1930s that most of the principal youngsters, who would later become famous on television, were introduced to movie audiences.

"Stymie," for example, began in 1930. "Spanky" was introduced in 1932 and "Buckwheat" in 1934. "Alfalfa" (whose name probably came from a character created by Will Rogers for an earlier Hal Roach series) came onboard in 1935, and "Darla" in 1936. Some characters did join the ensemble later. "Froggy" (who created his own odd voice without the use of dubbing and sadly died at the age of sixteen) didn't arrive until 1940. An endless stream of children from around the country auditioned to join the Our Gang team, and some surprisingly talented child actors were inevitably turned away. Both Mickey Rooney and Shirley Temple auditioned for the Gang but failed to be selected.

Viewers living through the poverty of the 1930s found the collection of poor street kids poignantly resonant. The kids were the have-nots of the world. The incredible innocence of the Our Gang members, their desire and ability to be independent and create their own amusements, and their rivalries, romances, and troubles constituted a unique child universe. They acted as a gang, complete with their own clubhouse, free of the adult world.

In real life, the Our Gang stars had big egos. Carl "Alfalfa" Switzer, whose hair, crossed eyes, and off-key singing were so adorable on camera, was a bully. He would stick nails into the other children, step on their feet, and hit them. Some of his horrid antics on the set — such as putting a large wad of gum in a camera — were so legendary that no one wanted to work with him when the series ended. He died during a dispute over $50 with a former business partner when he pulled a knife and was shot by the man. He was thirty-one. In 1938, Roach sold the Our Gang series to MGM, and the quality of the films rapidly declined.

Hal Roach also sought to replicate Laurel and Hardy's success through other interesting pairings. He believed that if two men could work as a successful team, so could two women. He was not the only one to have the idea. During a decade, from about 1926 to 1936, there was an emergence of women comedy teams. There had, of course, been romantic comedies with women comedians, but these were almost exclusively set in the domestic, private sphere. Roach's female teams were unusual in that their films were set in public arenas, reflecting the changing status of women. After all, women had fought for and won the right to vote in 1920, and the Victorian morals of the society had been permanently undermined by the liberating events of the Jazz Age. The era of new prosperity offered freedom for both genders. Later, the Great Depression made Americans uncertain about the power structure that had gotten them into such a devastating economic mess, and subtle attacks on the all-male structure were made in radio by Jack Benny. Now the vision of a community of women, not just men and not just married couples, had great appeal. The female comedy teams were also a challenge to the depiction of women presented in the all-male comedies; Laurel and Hardy's film wives, for example, were portrayed as cold and callous.

Roach tried various pairings until he finally found one that worked. He teamed Thelma Todd, a beautiful, cultured former teacher and beauty contest winner, with ZaSu Pitts, a talented actress who had appeared in such classics as Erich von Stroheim's *Greed* and who purposely exhibited considerably less glamour than Todd. The name ZaSu (pronounced "Zayzoo") was a combination of the last two letters of one aunt named Eliza and the first two letters of another aunt named Susan.

To emphasize their physical differences, Roach had Todd dye her hair a platinum blonde and wear clothes that enhanced her attractive figure. Todd was placed in provocative scenes, like taking a bath, or in otherwise revealing situations. In the film

The Pajama Party, for example, she was undressed and dressed by pretty French maids. Roach also made her sign a "potato clause," guaranteeing that she would keep her weight within five pounds of that on the day of her signing or else her contract would be terminated. ✳

Todd and Pitts were first teamed in 1933 and together made a series of seventeen short films. Later, when Pitts left the series, Patsy Kelly replaced her. The women played by Todd, Pitts, and Kelly (they used their real names for the characters) were always independent; they lived on their own, not with a parent or husband. They were financially independent as well, cast in traditional female occupations, such as telephone operators in *Catch-as-Catch-Can.*

Strong women were allowed to emerge on film partly because of the audience's view of such women in their parents' and grandparents' generations. Immigrant women usually adapted more easily than immigrant men. This may have been due, in part, to their traditional roles. Women who could cook and clean in the old country could do the same in America, but men had to learn a new language and compete for jobs that were very different than the ones they had held overseas. George Burns's father had died when he was young. Minnie Marx had to support the family because her husband was a failed tailor (he disdained the use of any measuring devices believing, with devastating inaccuracy, that his eye was sufficient). Milton Berle's father was weak, and his mother became a powerful force in his achievements. These were common family structures, and immigrant audiences were intimately familiar with strong and independent women, so that the Todd-Pitts or Todd-Kelly pairings didn't seem as emotionally odd as they might have to American audiences grounded in more traditional family structures.

It is not well remembered that there were more women in college in the 1920s than at any time in American history until 1980. There were far more women in the movie comedy business before the late 1930s than afterward until many decades later.

The characters in the Todd films were emotionally dependent on another woman, most often a roommate. The films depicted women banding together against a male-dominated world. In *Air Fright*, one of the funnier Todd-Kelly films, Todd gets

Kelly a job on an airplane. Powerful men are on the plane, but it is Kelly who controls their fate; the lowly working woman bests the wealthy, connected men. This was a perfect metaphor for audience members — male and female — who were unhappy with those who controlled the society. Seeing the male characters literally fall through the sky after they had been ejected from their seats on the plane was emotionally satisfying.

The women were always unimpressed by men. In the film *On the Loose*, Todd and Pitts are befuddled because all the males they meet just want to take them to Coney Island, a place they eventually get sick of. In a guest appearance, Laurel and Hardy were the final pair of males to invite them to the fabled Brooklyn amusement park.

The Roach all-women comedies are historically important, but they had flimsy plots and weak comic setups. It is a shame, given the outstanding talents of all three women, that they were not able to realize their full potential.

The films ended with Thelma Todd's shocking death on the morning of December 16, 1935. She was found in a car in her garage, dead of carbon monoxide poisoning. Todd was twenty-nine. The death was officially ruled a suicide, but there were persistent rumors that either her business partner had caused her death accidentally or that the gangster Lucky Luciano had killed her to keep her from talking to the police about his plans to take over Hollywood. No charges were ever brought, and the circumstances surrounding her death remain a mystery.

The era of the all-female comedy team ended when women's roles in society reverted to a familiar pattern; the continuing effects of the economic slump led more women to live at home until they married. There were so few jobs during the Great Depression that audiences were no longer comfortable with the portrayal of independent women in the workplace. There were too many men who needed jobs to support their families. The very notion of an amusing, flippant, glamorous woman became rather threatening. Mocking men, psychologically emasculating them, did not reflect the public mood in the late 1930s.

There were transitions between the independent women comedians and their eventual decline, most notably in screwball comedies, with their focus on a glamorous funny woman. But, unlike the world of Todd, Pitts, and Kelly, the screwball world was really a man's world. For a brief time, though, the cinema had recognized the daring possibilities of women banding together.

SIX

"I SHOT AN ELEPHANT
IN MY PAJAMAS"

The Marx Brothers

Harpo, Chico, and Groucho Marx were uneasy as they sat in the dining room in the Beverly Wilshire Hotel. It was September 1934, and their careers were in jeopardy. Although their last film, *Duck Soup*, had been Paramount's fifth-largest grossing film in 1933, it was nevertheless a commercial disappointment to the studio. That, compounded by a contract dispute, led the studio to drop them. A frustrated Zeppo had been unhappy with the leftovers he had been given in the Marx Brothers movies. He may even have felt guilty that he was not contributing as much artistically as the others, despite the fact that the brothers always split their paychecks four ways. He had finally decided to leave the act. The Marx Brothers were a brother short and out of work.

At that moment Irving Thalberg entered their lives. Thalberg, widely considered to be the most brilliant producer in Hollywood, was the genius at MGM who had already made *Ben-Hur* and *Grand Hotel*. Doomed by heart problems from childhood on, conscious that his life would be brief, he desperately wanted to make a dazzling comedy to display a talent without boundaries. He approached Chico, who was one of his bridge partners. Chico, the reckless gambler, nervy charmer, and persistent optimist, agreed that since the Marx Brothers were free, they would be perfect for the boy wonder's entry into comedy. Chico then tried to sell the idea to his reluctant brothers. They agreed to have lunch with Thalberg.

The lunch started with small talk. When Thalberg noted Zeppo's absence, the brothers told him Zeppo had decided to become an agent. Thalberg asked what every producer would then ask: Did the three Marx Brothers plan to be paid as much as the four Marx Brothers? Unsurprisingly, Groucho had a ready answer: "Don't be silly. Without Zeppo we're worth twice as much."

Thalberg soon got around to the purpose of the meeting. "I would like to make some pictures with you fellows. I mean *real* pictures."

Groucho, fuming, shot back, "What's the matter with *Cocoanuts*, *Animal Crackers*, and *Duck Soup*? Are you going to sit there and tell me those weren't funny?" The Marx Brothers had heard criticism before, and it always bothered them. They were proud of their rapid-fire puns and wisecracks, mockery of any authority that dared to stand in their way, and unmatched physical comedy.

Thalberg, however, remained calm. "Of course they were funny. But they weren't movies. They weren't *about* anything."

Harpo, in his thick New York accent, was agitated. "People laughed, didn't they? *Duck Soup* had as many laughs as any comedy ever made, including Chaplin's."

"That's true, it was a very funny picture, but you don't need that many laughs in a movie. I'll make a picture with you fellows with half as many laughs, but I'll put a legitimate story in it, and I'll bet it will gross twice as much as *Duck Soup*."

Thalberg pushed further. He agreed that their humor was wonderfully illogical but argued that a film shouldn't be based on an illogical idea. The comic scenes had to fit into the overall narrative. Audiences needed to be sympathetic to the brothers. Women, who had not been attracted to their movies, could be brought into the theater with romance and song. The Marx Brothers were unsure about the romance. Their movies always included a handsome male character that, with their help, finds love. Such a plot device was a convention of stage musicals at the time, and so they had added it to their films. But invariably it seemed out of place. Thalberg understood and urged that there be a seamless connection between the romantic plot and the comedy. He wanted a love story that audiences could actually believe, unlike the artificial ones in earlier Marx Brothers films. Groucho wasn't so sure.

But Thalberg was a master of sales. He told them that he did not want to change their comedy style, only how it was presented to an audience. He explained that he especially liked the way their films toppled dignity, because that was the basis of good comedy. He said he was sure, therefore, that the film he produced would have a very dignified setting into which the Marx Brothers could bring their unsettling chaos. He told them he wanted the best writers.

He had tapped into the great fear the brothers had, that their particular brand of humor had led them prematurely but permanently into retirement. Suddenly, here was a proven genius telling them to keep making movies — and, not incidentally, money — in their own style but in a new form.

Thalberg's power, reputation, and assurances tamed the Marx Brothers and resulted in their greatest film, *A Night at the Opera*. Thalberg had been at least a little deceptive, however. He believed that the

Marx Brothers were comic geniuses, but that they didn't sufficiently grasp the notion of changing their pace. All their comedy was performed at breakneck speed. Thalberg believed in a slightly more controlled pace, somewhere between Laurel and Hardy and the Marx Brothers. He had his way and tamed the anarchic style of the early movies.

But Thalberg was smart enough not to tamper with the genius of a brilliant comedy team. The Marx Brothers took the very notion of "comedy team" to its logical conclusion. They included various comedy styles within their act. In vaudeville, they had accomplished this by having each brother represent a different ethnic group. In films, though, each brother represented a different kind of comedy. Groucho became the master of wisecracking insult comedy. Chico focused on dialect humor and malapropisms. Harpo was the expert in sight gags and pantomime. With such an extraordinary variety, they could update and apply the vaudeville technique of offering some act for everyone.

Groucho was the cynical trickster trying to separate wealthy and dignified widows from their money and virtue. His rapid-fire insults left his opponents speechless, at least in his first films. Unlike George Burns, he used more than his voice and his wisecracks. He added a visual element with his greasepaint mustache and eyebrows, his cigar, and his bent way of walking. Groucho's eyebrows, glasses, and mustache are a mask. Like the many immigrants in his audience who were partially integrated into America but still anxious about the genuineness of their American identity, his character didn't want the true self discovered, because underneath, that real self was insecure about being in this strange new country, with its power elites and challenging customs. His audience liked the way that Groucho covered up his foreignness and anxiety with a barrage of insults and disguises.

Much of the emotional appeal for the audience lay in the way that the Marx Brothers played outsiders who changed their appearance to fool others into accepting them or who found tricks to enter the exclusive society. This entrance is almost literally represented in "The Password" routine from *Horse Feathers*:

Chico: Who are you?
Groucho: I'm fine, thanks, who are you?
Chico: I'm fine, too, but you can't come

in unless you give the password.

Groucho: Well, what is the password?

Chico: Aw, no! You gotta tell *me.* Hey, I tell you what I do. I give you three guesses . . . It's the name of a fish.

Groucho: Is it Mary?

Chico: Ha! Ha! Attsa no fish.

Groucho: She isn't. Well, she drinks like one . . .

Chico: Now I give you one more chance.

Groucho: I got it. Haddock.

Chico: Attsa funny. I gotta haddock too. You can't come in here unless you say "swordfish." Now I give you one more guess.

Groucho: Swordfish . . . I think I got it. Is it swordfish?

If Groucho's technique for survival in the Promised Land involved being a fast-talking con man trying to marry money, Chico's assimilationist technique was to pretend to be an innocent foreigner, complete with accent, though he was shrewd underneath the veneer. Harpo was the most fragile of all immigrants. He was so traumatized by the new life that he couldn't talk at all. He offered the third linguistic technique: silence. He wanted lots of food, and women, and a warm home, but, like many watching the movie, he stood outside normal commercial life and was too emotionally vulnerable to succeed without the kindness of others — who usually ignored or mocked him or were embarrassed by him.

The Marx Brothers took a different approach to comedy than Laurel and Hardy, who had deliberately and successfully aimed to make their humor immediately accessible to everyone, including children. The Marx Brothers included allusions and material that not everyone in the audience would understand. This worked to attract the critics and a more adult audience, but such an approach revealed its flaws when *Duck Soup* had failed to draw a large enough audience for Paramount.

It is odd that the Marx Brothers had fewer problems with the censors than some of the other comedians and teams. This is partly because Groucho was so perfect at working subtle inferences into his humor. His words might look harmless on the page but his voice and leer would make them appear suggestive on the screen.

Still, the censors posed a constant challenge. The movie industry, fearing outside interference, had set up its own censoring office in 1922, headed by Will Hays, to monitor productions. The satiric and risqué material of many comedians and teams was defanged. The Marx Brothers, though, typically mocked the system. There is one famous story that perfectly illustrates the Marx Brothers' attitude toward censorship. Harpo hired a stripper, had her dress in a way that provided minimum legal covering, and then chased her around the office of Louis B. Mayer, the powerful head of MGM. This would have been bad enough in itself, but on top of that, Mr. Mayer was at that moment having a chat with Will Hays.

This private assault on the chief censor was emblematic of the Marx Brothers' attitude toward society. The brothers had an expansive set of targets and used lots of ammunition to attack them. And the Marx Brothers didn't just mock authority; they destroyed it. No one — not heads of states or colleges, society matrons, pompous art collectors, or anyone else with pretensions — was safe. It was not just that society wasn't sacred for the Marx Brothers. Logic, and ultimately sanity, wasn't safe either. The dizzying confusion of the audience's world was reflected in a Marx Brothers funny mirror. It is no wonder that they were the first comedy team in the sound era to be a box office success.

Rich women were one of their favorite targets. Groucho, having mastered what has frequently been called verbal slapstick, with its unceasing series of insults, used his skills to mock such women, who were frequently represented by Margaret Dumont's characters. In *Animal Crackers* he says to the character, "You're one of the most beautiful women I've ever seen, and that's not saying much for you." In *Duck Soup*, the following exchange occurs:

Dumont: I've sponsored your appointment because I feel you are the most able statesman in all Freedonia.

Groucho: Well, that covers a lot of ground. Say, you cover a lot of ground yourself. You'd better beat it. I hear they're going to tear you down and put up an office building where you're standing.

Beyond insult, Groucho seeks to attract the Dumont character with his wild tales, as in the famous lines from *Animal Crackers*: "One morning I shot an elephant in my pajamas. How he got in my pajamas

I don't know. Then we tried to remove the tusks, but they were embedded in so firmly that we couldn't budge them. Of course in Alabama the Tuscaloosa. But that's entirely irrelephant to what I was talking about."

He makes no effort to hide the source of his attraction to her. In *The Cocoanuts* she says, "I don't think you'd love me if I were poor." Groucho's character replies, "I might, but I'd keep my mouth shut." In *Animal Crackers* he says to her, "You have got money, haven't you? Because if you haven't, we can quit right now."

In *Animal Crackers* Groucho offers to marry two women. Dumont protests, "Why that's bigamy." Groucho says, "Yes and it's big o' me, too."

Lawyers were another target, as seen in this exchange from *Animal Crackers*:

Groucho: Jamison, take a letter to my lawyers: Honorable Charles H. Hungerdunger, care of Hungerdunger, Hungerdunger, Hungerdunger, Hungerdunger, and McCormick. Gentlemen question mark. In re yours of the fifth inst., yours to hand, and beg to rep, brackets . . . i.e. to wit, e.g., in lieu . . . Now read me the letter Jamison . . .

Zeppo: Honorable Charles H. Hungerdunger . . . in care of Hungerdunger, Hungerdunger, Hungerdunger and McCormick . . .

Groucho: You've left out a Hungerdunger. You left out the main one, too.

As if Groucho hadn't assaulted lawyers enough in his dialogue with Zeppo, he topped it in one of his most famous exchanges with Chico in the contract scene from *A Night at the Opera*:

Groucho: Now, pay particular attention to this first clause because it's most important. Says the, uh, the party of the first part shall be known in this contract as the party of the first part. How do you like that? That's pretty neat, eh?

Chico: No, that's no good.

Groucho: What's the matter with it?

Chico: I don't know. Let's hear it again.

Groucho: Says the, uh, the party of the first part should be known in this contract as the party of the first part.

Chico: That sounds a little better this time.

Groucho: Well, it grows on you. Would you like to hear it once more?

Chico: Uh, just the first part.

Groucho: What do you mean? The — the party of the first part?

Chico: No, the first part of the party of the first part.

Groucho: All right. It says, the, uh, the first part of the party of the first part should be known in this contract as the first part of the party of the first part should be known in this contract . . . Look. Why should we quarrel about a thing like this? We'll take it right out, eh?

Eventually, the contract's parts get systematically removed until they come to the crucial part: the sanity clause. Chico expresses his opposition to this because, after all, there is no "Sanity Clause."

Their other targets, such as monied men and upper- and middle-class professionals, amply display their obsession with money, an obsession that, of course, fit perfectly with the era.

The Marx Brothers began their film career with *The Cocoanuts*. The first time we see all of them together occurs when they are chasing one another, hands out-stretched, around various pieces of furniture. Harpo chews buttons on a bellboy's uniform, and Chico and Groucho begin a verbal joust. In a single joyous moment, the three characters are established. Groucho is the con man, a social-climbing huckster whose brash exterior hides a sentimental romantic. Harpo is the silent clown, acting outside the rules of logic and rationality. Chico is the seeming foreigner, struggling to get by, but who, underneath, is the real con man.

Immediately it is Groucho who dominates with his mouth.

Bellboy: We haven't been paid in two weeks, and we want our wages.

Groucho: Wages? Do you want to be wage slaves, answer me that.

Bellboy: No.

Groucho: No, of course not. Well, what makes wage slaves? Wages! I want you to be free.

He then receives some telegrams, including one that he reads to the bellboys, "P.S. Aunt Fanny had an 8-pound boy, can you come to the wedding? . . . You're all invited to the wedding of Aunt Fanny's 8-pound boy."

Animal Crackers, Monkey Business, Horse Feathers, and *Duck Soup,* the remaining Paramount pictures, established the Marx Brothers as the lunatic fringe of comedy. It was no accident that the films had animal names in them. Paramount used the titles to tout the Marx Brothers' wild natures. These movies form a comedy set distinct from later films, primarily because they are marked by a deliberate attempt on the part of the actors to be funny every minute they are on the screen. Indeed, when *The Cocoanuts* was first released in 1929, theater owners were in a panic, convinced that audiences simply would not be able to understand the film because Groucho talked too fast. What happened instead was that the audience members, some of whom literally fell out of their seats laughing, thought they had missed a few of the great lines and so went back to see the film again. The endless visual and verbal gags — interrupted momentarily by weak romantic stories or music — defined a particular style. The story lines in the Marx Brothers films at Paramount were secondary at best. The focus was always on the galloping lines and gags.

That was why Irving Thalberg's emphasis on story and pace was so important. His analysis proved to be correct, at least financially. He greatly increased their box office appeal, just as he had promised. Groucho, at least, came to admire him profoundly.

There were a variety of reasons for the success of *A Night at the Opera*, such as a great script, talented actors, good production values, and other typical ingredients of a superior film. But there is a more subtle reason, one that justifies Thalberg's artistic assertions. As other popular zany teams of the era unfortunately demonstrated, it was possible to cross over anarchy's borderline, to be too crazy. Audiences found the looniness appealing because it made external an internal sense that their psychological center was not holding. The audience's craziness, which they had to keep under control to survive, was let loose on the screen. But just as Gracie had George to reel her back in, the Marx Brothers needed to be brought back, and without a constraining straight man on-screen, they were in constant danger of going over. Audiences, finally, were afraid of staying in the weird world too long and knew they needed to return and function in the real world, no matter how miserable it was. Thalberg rescued the Marx Brothers from permanently crossing the line.

Thalberg also paid them to try out their jokes before live audiences for both *A Night at the Opera* and *A Day at the Races*. For the latter film, the Marxes tested a hundred gags on each audience. Audience members filled out a total of 30,000 ballots, judging the funniest lines. By the end of the road shows, 175 lines were selected and those voted in the top 75 were included in the final film.

It wasn't so easy for writers to come up with a story for *A Night at the Opera*. Matters didn't start out well when the first suggestion was for Harpo to be the world's greatest tenor. Groucho then proposed bringing in Bert Kalmar and Harry Ruby, two great comedy-writing talents. Kalmar and Ruby suggested that the story be about scoundrels overselling backers a musical that would surely fail, a plotline that would later emerge in Mel Brooks's *The Producers*. Thalberg didn't want the complexity of a comedy within a comedy. Thalberg brought in two more writers. Still no workable script was produced. Finally, Groucho suggested the surefire team of

George S. Kaufman and Morrie Ryskind. These incredibly gifted writers produced a workable script.

Still, Thalberg wanted to rewrite some of the scenes. The earlier groups of writers returned, though none of the groups knew what the others were doing.

And then came Al Boasberg. Although Boasberg's name is largely unknown to the public, within the comedy-writing community he is widely considered to be among the greatest of all the gag writers. Starting as a jeweler in Buffalo who sold both jewels and jokes at the nearby vaudeville house, Boasberg went on to an amazing career. He wrote the early routines that made Burns and Allen successful. (Burns later claimed, with his typical vaudeville shine, that he discovered Boasberg.) He wrote the first joke Jack Benny ever used and helped Benny prepare for his first appearance on radio. Benny eventually signed a contract with him to go over every script. Boasberg's eye was so prized that he was paid even if he didn't make any changes. He was the person who recommended that Bob Hope be given a screen test. He wrote for Al Jolson, Buster Keaton, Eddie Cantor, Milton Berle, and many others.

Groucho Marx, who knew a thing or two

about comedy, called Boasberg "probably the funniest man who ever lived." He certainly wrote in the oddest way. Boasberg did almost all his work while sitting in the bathtub up to his neck in hot water. He spoke into a Dictaphone a few feet from the tub. The shower stall had a shelf for the books he might need.

And now he was writing for *A Night at the Opera*. Thalberg wanted more audience sympathy for the Marx Brothers without losing their antisocial behavior. Boasberg was the one who saw how to keep the trademark Marx zaniness: He made their antics into a weapon to be used against people the audience had grown to hate. For example, Harpo was hit for the first time in a film, and his assailant therefore became a completely accepted, even anticipated, target. The enemies in the film were powerful, true rivals with Groucho. The dramatic tension that arose sharpened his stinging lines.

It is unclear if Boasberg deserves credit for the contract scene. The give and take and focus on logic bear his trademark humor, so evident in Burns and Allen. However, there is one scene that was definitely Boasberg's creation.

How Boasberg shared this scene with the

Marx Brothers is a Hollywood legend. Thalberg kept bothering Boasberg, asking for new material. Finally, Boasberg called the producer and said that if he wanted the new pages, he'd have to come over and get them. Thalberg and the Marxes duly trekked over to Boasberg's office. The gagman, however, wasn't there. Neither was the furniture nor anything else, including the script. Finally, Groucho looked up. Boasberg had cut the pages apart as a practical joke. Different pieces were tacked to the ceiling. The brothers retrieved the pages and put them into the right order. Groucho recalled that the process took five hours.✱

Boasberg had written the stateroom scene, perhaps the most famous scene of all the Marx Brothers movies. Poor Groucho is put in a tiny stateroom by a rival. Three stowaways pop out of his luggage, and the four of them are eventually joined by an engineer, a manicurist, the engineer's assistant, a woman looking for her aunt Minnie, a woman who seems determined to mop the floor, and a steward and his assistants. When Margaret Dumont opens the door, everyone inside the room falls out. The scene, with so many people — including a sleeping

Harpo — crowded into so small a place, was structured perfectly and allowed viewers to laugh at their own needs for food and space. It should be noted, however, that the scene did not get great laughs when the Marx Brothers toured before filming. Only their improvisational genius, combined with the brilliant writer's concept, produced the final result.

Boasberg would go on to write gags for *A Day at the Races* as well, but, like Thalberg, he would die young, of a heart attack in 1937 at the age of forty-five. (Thalberg had died in 1936 at the age of thirty-seven, during the pre-production of *Races*.) It is not surprising that this film was the last great Marx Brothers movie. Dispirited themselves, aging, without a guiding spirit like Thalberg, the brothers drifted. The writers for their later films simply did not produce good enough scripts.

But their greatness was never forgotten. Critics and fans kept their films alive. Groucho lived long enough to host a successful television game show, and during the late 1960s and early 1970s he saw his films being re-embraced by a large new audience. This young generation, widely hostile to the Vietnam War, found in *Duck Soup* a voice for its own mocking attitudes toward the military. The young audiences saw in the Marx Brothers' crazy world a filmic example of their own generational anxieties. And the gags were still hilarious.

SEVEN

ANARCHY LET LOOSE

Other Comedy Teams
of the 1930s

The Marx Brothers were not the only famous team of the 1930s, but many of the teams that successfully competed with them are virtually forgotten by the general public today. Those teams failed to transcend their moment on the cultural stage because they met only the particular needs of the time rather than deeper, ongoing human needs and because they simply were not as funny as the Marx Brothers.

Wheeler and Woolsey, for example, were hugely popular rivals of the Marx Brothers. Bert Wheeler had been a success in vaudeville, and Bob Woolsey had appeared with W. C. Fields and in the *Ziegfeld Follies*. Originally teamed in 1929 in *Rio Rita*, they eventually made twenty-five films for RKO.

Like Laurel and Hardy, Wheeler and Woolsey developed individual characteristics. There was no straight man–comic relationship between them on-screen. Woolsey, with horn-rimmed glasses, hair parted in the middle, a swagger, and a cigar, sometimes resembled George Burns (especially in the opening scene of a later film, *Kentucky Kernels*). His character, though, was more like Groucho's. He schemed, he boasted, and he was a con man. He was a realist and a wisecracker, with a face that hid his real intentions. He sped through life, hyperactive, not very good-looking, and destined to joke about romance rather than experience it.

Wheeler's character, in contrast, was romantic, or more precisely, a comic version of a romantic. His open face revealed his optimistic dreams. He was good-looking, and he found love. The beautiful and talented comic Dorothy Lee played the object of his affections in many films. They were likeable comedians who seemed to be having a great time and invited the audience along.

Wheeler and Woolsey were extremely popular during the cynical era of the early 1930s, when, prior to the Production Code's strict enforcement, risqué material was not yet censored and when their wild brand of humor best fit the needs of the audience newly yanked from the exuberant years of the twenties and dumped into the Great Depression. A typical line came from *Cracked Nuts*: A much-married ex-queen says to Woolsey, who has just been made the new king, "Your Royal Highness is so cute," and he responds, "Yeah, well yours is not so bad either." In *Diplomaniacs*, an attractive blonde is speaking to Wheeler:

Blonde: Sing to me.
Wheeler: How about "One Hour With You"?
Blonde: Sure. But first sing to me.

Nonetheless, Wheeler and Woolsey simply didn't have the raw talent to compete with the Marx Brothers. For example, Groucho's famous line about shooting an elephant appeared in *Animal Crackers*, released on August 25, 1930. Wheeler and Woolsey's film *Half Shot at Sunrise* was released on October 4, 1930, and some lines in *Sunrise* mimicked Groucho's and demonstrated how powerfully funny the Marx Brothers were and how flat Woolsey was in contrast:

Woolsey: I spent all last summer shooting tigers in Africa.
Young Woman: But there are no tigers in Africa.
Woolsey: I know. I killed them all.

Wheeler and Woolsey made their three best films in 1934: *Hips, Hips Hooray*; *Cockeyed Cavaliers*; and *Kentucky Kernels*. In *Cockeyed Cavaliers*, their most successful comedy, Wheeler plays a kleptomaniac. The two overhear a woman saying, "I just heard that the countess has had her face lifted," and Wheeler turns to Woolsey and says, "Don't look at me. I didn't take it."

The same film also stars Thelma Todd. In a line that got them into trouble with censors, the voluptuous Todd walks in wearing a low-cut dress that she describes as "the coming thing." Woolsey then responds, "It must be coming because there's a lot of it that hasn't arrived yet."

Wheeler and Woolsey used many of the same writers who worked for the Marx Brothers, such as Bert Kalmar and Harry Ruby, S. J. Perelman, Herman and Joseph Mankiewicz, and even Al Boasberg. Indeed, Boasberg worked on four of their films. But unlike Burns and Allen, Jack Benny, or Groucho, Boasberg didn't work on developing the characters. He simply wrote gags for their existing personas. Despite the creative input of these talented writers, and some good gags, the quality of the scripts was not as consistently high as those of the Marx Brothers, in large part because — like Todd, Pitts, and Kelly — the Wheeler and Woolsey characters were not sufficiently defined.

Boasberg's work with Wheeler and Woolsey did have unintended beneficiaries: Abbott and Costello. In *Cracked Nuts,*

Wheeler and Woolsey used Boasberg's "Map of What and Which" routine, which they had used in vaudeville. Structurally, it is an obvious precursor to Abbott and Costello's "Who's on First" routine. In the film, Woolsey plays a king and Wheeler the would-be king. They are arguing over a map and how their armies will fight each other.

Wheeler: In order for your army to attack me, you . . . proceed . . . to the town of What.

Woolsey: What?

Wheeler: That's right.

Woolsey: What's right?

Wheeler: What's right.

Woolsey: That's what I said, what's right?

Wheeler: Well, I agreed with you, didn't I?

Woolsey: On what.

Wheeler: Yes . . .

Woolsey: What town is it?

Wheeler: That's What.

Woolsey: What town is next to what?

Wheeler: Which.

Woolsey: Next to what.

Wheeler: Which.

Woolsey: Which is next to what?

Wheeler: Yes.

Boasberg's script for Wheeler and Woolsey's film *The Nitwits* would later turn out to be the basis for Abbott and Costello's film *Who Done It?*

Wheeler and Woolsey did not advance the notion of team comedy as Laurel and Hardy and the Marx Brothers had, so their historical role is limited. They also suffered because Bob Woolsey died in 1938, at age fifty. The team might or might not have made better films, but in any case, Woolsey was a promoter and would certainly have worked to revive their films. Wheeler was self-effacing and modest and seemed not to appreciate the enduring value of their films.

The most important reason for Wheeler and Woolsey's decline in popularity is that they didn't adapt to the new realities of American life the way the Marx Brothers did. The worst of the Great Depression had passed by the mid- to late 1930s. President Franklin Roosevelt's New Deal policies, begun when he took office in 1933, were producing positive results, and heavy cynicism was no longer as appropriate as it had been during the really tough years of the Depression. Audiences now wanted more optimistic films. The wisecracking cynics, who were themselves not particularly likeable, became less appealing. In contrast, Boasberg's reworking of Groucho's character, making him more sympathetic, combined with Thalberg's insistence on romance and a strong story line, transformed the Marx Brothers, so that they were more compatible with the new sentiment stirring the country. Woolsey, who was funny but much less likeable as a character, was unable to effect such a change and had no one to help him do so.

Wheeler and Woolsey were not the only comedy team that failed to make the necessary transition from the wildness of the late 1920s and early 1930s anarchic comedy style to a more restrained approach. For example, few were as wild as Bobby Clark of the team Clark and McCullough. (Unlike almost every other team with a straight man, in this team the comic's name came first. It was a revealing difference.)

Bobby Clark's trademarks were his painted-on glasses, fat cigar, porkpie hat, funny walk, and perpetual leer. He also carried a cane, which he used frequently to hit the bottom of some retreating young woman. Clark was a great success in burlesque. For example, in the show *Chuckles of 1921*, he is hired to impersonate a lion tamer and is led to believe that he'll be dealing with a fake lion, but, of course, a real lion is substituted. As the reviewer for *Dramatic Mirror* wrote, "We laughed at every expression; even the eyebrows were funny." His partner, Paul McCullough, wore a fur coat, straw hat, and thick mustache. He had a hearty and infectious laugh.

It is odd to see the pair at work because they aren't really a team. Clark dominates throughout, and McCullough lurks out of the spotlight, a second banana who observes and assists but stays out of the way of the laughs. As Bobby Clark said when the Friars Club honored him in 1926, "A great many people think it is strange that McCullough and I have been together so long. . . . We don't have fights. We don't have arguments. If a question arises as to how a certain piece of business should be done . . . we sit down quietly and talk it over pro and con. I listen to McCullough's version, and he listens to mine, and then I go out on the stage and do it my way." Clark did all the comic inventions, but he did not have the emotional generosity to allow McCullough more than the tiniest sliver of the spotlight.

Their films were wild, as completely out of touch with the real world as was possible. The best, made in 1934, was *Odor in the Court*. Typically, Bobby Clark runs around a lot and smokes his cigar. The pair play two lawyers with the motto, "No case too small — No fee too large." Clark has his share of barbs. He tells a potential client, "We'll protect your rights till your lawyer's last penny is gone." He arrives at court with a marching band. In court, he advises his client: "Shut up! Quit yelling for justice. Remember you're in a courtroom." He also has a run-in with the judge:

Clark: I object.
Judge: On what grounds?
Clark: None.
Judge: Overruled.
Clark: Content.

The relentless pace, the lack of a straight man to slow Clark down, and the generally weak writing limited Clark and McCullough's appeal.

The team came to a sad ending. On March 23, 1936, McCullough was released from a Massachusetts sanitarium where he had been recovering from nervous exhaustion. A friend was driving him home when they decided to stop at a barbershop in Medford. McCullough asked the barber for a shave. The two chatted, but just as the barber finished McCullough grabbed the razor and slashed his own wrists and throat. He died two days later.

Other zany teams also failed to adapt. The Ritz Brothers never had the commercial success of the Marx Brothers or Wheeler and Woolsey, but they had another distinction. Harry Ritz, the funniest of the three brothers, was among the most influential of comedians. Soupy Sales credits him with being a principal influence. Mel Brooks put him in *Silent Movie* and, in a clever tribute, did a Ritz Brothers–like dance routine with Dom DeLuise and Marty Feldman. Jerry Lewis cites Harry Ritz's importance to his own comedy, and Harry's influence can be seen in a Sid Caesar skit or a Danny Kaye bit.

Watching Harry Ritz work with his brothers is very different from watching the Marx Brothers. Harry is clearly the center of the act, and he sometimes seems to have two people on either side balancing him. Al and Jimmy Ritz, talented as they were, seemed like adjuncts to a single personality.

The brothers, like those from many immigrant families, thought of vaudeville as an alternative to crime or factory work. Often families worked together to share in the wages and also to keep an eye on each other, to have someone trustworthy to be around, and to have someone to confide in without fear of betrayal. This was particularly true of the Ritz Brothers. Harry had offers to do a single act, but he simply would not abandon his brothers.

The Ritz Brothers — who took their name when one of them looked out a window and spotted a truck from the Ritz Laundry — were a success in vaudeville. They performed a mix of physical and verbal comedy, doing both well. In particular, their parodies were supplemented with precision dancing. They were loud and outrageous in vaudeville. They would, for example, appear in women's clothing with their own trousers rolled up and visible just below the dress for the audience to see.

But it was Harry's physicality, his frenzied energy, his ability to almost wave his body while mugging, his agility that is most impressive, and it is easy to see how these movements influenced later comedians. He made his body part of the comedy act, the way Chaplin and Groucho did. He also had a terrific wail. The Ritz Brothers did star in some interesting movies, such as *The Three Musketeers*, but generally their antics were wasted on film. Further, they had only two appearances on Ed Sullivan's career-rebuilding program and were never offered their own television show. That is, they never had a chance to reproduce for television viewers the full brilliance of their stage act.

Olsen and Johnson's method, like many of the film comedy teams of the 1930s, was to abandon the straight man–comic approach. Ole Olsen and Chic Johnson put over their act even when the material was questionable. Their comic fame rested not on a movie but on a vaudeville revue called *Hellzapoppin*, which lasted from 1938 until December 17, 1941, when the shock of Pearl Harbor rendered silliness far less amusing than it once had been.

Early in their career, Olsen and Johnson realized they weren't funny enough to carry off an act, so they gathered a whole bunch of other funny actors as part of their group. All these actors added to the eye-popping zaniness of *Hellzapoppin*. The stage was filled with trained dogs, pigeons, midgets, and much else. Olsen and

Johnson would stand there, seemingly not aware of their presence. They'd throw rubber snakes and spiders into the audience — when the lights were off. They'd hire a shill to walk up and down the aisles hawking tickets to another show. A clown walked in the aisles during intermission. They would load a young woman up with fruit and ask where she was going. "Orange, New Jersey," she'd respond. Chic Johnson's wife would walk up and down the aisle calling out for her supposed husband, Oscar, until Olsen and Johnson "shot" her.

Their intentionally low comedy was meant for everyone. There was a small touch of sentimentality as well. They would close each show with Olsen saying, "May you live as long as you want." Johnson would then respond, "And may you laugh as long as you live." They did perform in a reasonably successful film version of the show, and as late as 1956 even tried to re-create its madness on a special Milton Berle television show, though the humor seemed tired and dated. In one bit, a man with a camera comes in and says, "Gentlemen, can I take your picture?" They agree, and he, rather predictably, takes a painting off the wall.

By the beginning of the 1940s, America itself had changed along with the entertainment business. Although the Three Stooges enjoyed their golden era from the end of the 1930s until the mid-1940s, all the other comedy teams were in decline.

World War II changed much about the world, including audience taste in film comedy teams. The war brought new emotional needs. Audiences of the era were trying to become good Americans, to shake off their foreign origins, to alter their names and their accents, to leave their immigrant past to historians and novelists, to identify fully with their adopted country. From the studio moguls, to the stars, to the people paying for the tickets, Americans wanted to move on to a new understanding of themselves. They had lost touch with the vaudeville sensibilities of zany, anarchic, surreal comedy.

Film studios wanted to make not only longer films but films more acceptable to critics. The studios wanted respect. They turned increasingly away from the lowbrow comedies that had served them so well. In a way, the enforcement of the Production Code (which certainly fit in with the new mood of the country) also contributed to a change in the notion of comedy. In comedy terms, the audiences needed a straight man again. The straight man traditionally controlled the comic, knew the limits that were acceptable, and stopped the comic before he went over the line. In a post-enforcement movie world, there was once again a clear need for the classic straight man.

EIGHT

"WHO'S ON FIRST"

Abbott and Costello
Meet the 1940s

Lou Costello feared doctors, but now he needed their help to survive. It was March 3, 1943, his thirty-seventh birthday. Suddenly, the beloved comic collapsed, suffering from rheumatic fever. Confined to a wheelchair, Costello faced the end of what had been an incredible career with his partner, Bud Abbott. For the past two years, they had been voted the top motion picture box office attraction. Their popular radio show continued with guest partners for a while, but no one could reproduce the Abbott and Costello magic, and Abbott stopped the show while he waited for his friend and colleague to recover.

It took six months before Lou could take his first steps. He wanted visitors and was deeply upset that Dean Martin never came. Lou had paid for the surgery to alter Martin's large nose and expected his friend to show concern. Many others, though, came to see Lou, and he slowly recovered.

He took his first steps on his mother's birthday, in September. Even his recovery seemed to be part of a lifelong pattern of trying to please his mother. He charted his progress by the son he adored, Lou Jr., known as Butch. Butch was learning to crawl as Lou relearned to walk.

On November 4, a Thursday, Lou

Costello was finally ready to return to his live radio show, scheduled for that night. Lou bought his baby son a teddy bear. The boy would be a year old in two days. Lou went to the nursery where he played on the carpet with his son and the toys for a half hour. Before Lou left, he asked his wife, Anne, to let Butch hear the show to see if he recognized his father's voice. Anne gave her husband a bracelet that had the baby's name engraved on it. That afternoon, Lou was in the familiar Studio D rehearsing, feeling good about the return, joking as always with the crew.

Meanwhile, Anne Costello had gone to get a new stroller for the baby's birthday. She returned and assembled it with Lou's new secretary, Marty. When the assembly was finished, Marty went to get the baby, who was supposed to be in a playpen outside in the yard.

Marty went to the playpen, but it was empty. She screamed back at Anne. It was Anne who saw her son's body in the pool. Anne screamed and jumped into the pool to save her son.

A rescue unit from the fire department arrived, but it was too late. Butch was gone.

Lou's sister called the studio and spoke

to the team's manager. It was now four in the afternoon. The manager brought Lou home, and it was there that the doctor told him that his baby son had gotten out of the playpen, crawled across the patio, and fallen into the water.

Lou retreated to his home office with his father, his manager, and Bud Abbott's brother. When he came out he had a message for his sister. He wanted her to call NBC and tell them he would continue with the radio show.

She questioned his decision, but he said, "I asked Anne to keep that baby up tonight to see if he would be able to recognize my voice, and wherever God has taken my little boy I want him to hear it."

The show did go on. Lou missed some lines. The audience saw his white face and wondered why the guest star, Lana Turner, spoke barely above a whisper. When the show ended, Bud Abbott went to the microphone and said, "Ladies and gentlemen, now that our program is over . . . I would like . . . to pay tribute to my best friend and a man who has more courage than I have ever seen displayed in the theater. . . . Just a short time before our broadcast started, Lou Costello was told that his baby son . . . had died. . . . There is nothing more I can say except I know you all join me in expressing our deepest sympathy to a great trouper. Good night."

Many who knew Lou Costello said he was never the same again, that the little boy inside him had suffered too tragic a loss. He never took off the bracelet his wife had given him.

Abbott and Costello were throwbacks. In a post–Laurel and Hardy and Wheeler and Woolsey world, they returned to the straight man–comic team approach. And as surely as the Marx Brothers had defined comedy in the 1930s, Abbott and Costello defined comedy in the war-consumed America of the 1940s. The smooth-talking, thin con man with the rapid-fire delivery style and his short, plump, eternally child-like, and uncomprehending partner were characters that reflected perfectly the needs of the audience.

The attack on Pearl Harbor, carried out while the country was still recovering from the Great Depression, stunned the nation. In 1940, there were still more than 8 million people unemployed. Twelve months later, the country had to face the unwanted and fearful challenge of warfare. Gloom, even despair, descended. The war called for unquestioned unity in confronting a dangerous common enemy. The realities of the war had to be faced. Young men were drafted, sent overseas, and in many cases, died there. Hitler's terrifying march through Europe was followed through radio, newspapers, and newsreel reports. More than ever, the country needed comedians, but certainly not the anarchic types of the earlier era.

People needed an escape from the encroaching threat, but not one that undermined national institutions. An essential one, the military, was needed to defend America itself. It was time to pull together, not mock the leaders of the country.

American life was also faster and more complex. The war generation wanted comedians to reflect the quickened pace. Abbott and Costello were young and worked at a fast clip. They had to. As burlesque comedians, they were competing with both other comedians and strippers. Their fast-talking style assured audiences waiting either to be entertained by laughter or by falling dresses that if they didn't like one joke, it wouldn't be long before another one appeared.

Audiences of the early 1940s wanted a comic character that symbolically allowed them to return to a time when they were unencumbered by adult cynicism. This new character had to be childlike to allow for the retreat but could not have the childlike vulnerability of Stan Laurel or Harpo Marx. Vulnerability in wartime helped no one. The new child needed an edge. He needed to be able to get angry and get even without ever sacrificing his fundamental childlike innocence.

Lou Costello created a comic persona that was cute and childlike but still independent. He may have been frustrated and gullible, but he saw what others could not see. Costello was what America wanted, what the nation felt itself to be. He wasn't just a boy; he was, to use one of his famous catchphrases, a "baaaaaad boy." The phrase came from Costello's own life. His fifth-grade teacher had made him stay after school one day and write "I am a bad boy" 150 times.

Abbott and Costello shaped their voices to fit the characters. Bud Abbott had a carnival huckster's slickness and a rasp in his voice. At first, Costello used his regular voice, but after an appearance with Bud on Kate Smith's radio program, audiences had difficulty differentiating their voices, a problem they had never faced in burlesque, where everyone could see them as they spoke their lines. To remedy the situation, Costello changed his vocal pitch, finding one that would eventually (though not on radio) match his childlike character.

Abbott and Costello sought to combine the seemingly simple skills of wordplay and slapstick. They drew on vaudeville and burlesque sketches, the origins of which are lost in the mist of those institutions, and they made those sketches their own. In both vaudeville and burlesque, after all, comedians and teams had made their mark with not so much the set routine but what they added to the routine, how they made it distinctively theirs, and how they delivered it.

Rightly famous for being transmitters of a comedic heritage, Abbott and Costello also refined it. They developed a third variation of the straight man's connection to reality. The Burns and Allen model of the straight man bringing the audience back from the comic's fantasy world had been modified by Laurel and Hardy's use of a straight man outside the team and substitution of a situation for the straight man's version of reality. Bud Abbott and Lou Costello found a middle ground. They put the straight man back in the team and returned to using the straight man's version of reality, but it was a more troubled reality than Burns had inhabited.

Abbott modified Burns's calm and logical reality by creating a world that was deceitful, one that tried to con the innocent. The straight man no longer reeled the comic back to a reassuring reality; now the straight man brought the comic back to a reality that tried to put one over on him. It was an imaginary world comparable to the con man's in early vaudeville teams but one with a tougher edge.

The pairing of a con man and a frustrated child worked so well partly because in real life Abbott and Costello were friends, but not close friends. They got along, and yet they argued. They had disputes over the usual matters — money and billing, drinking and gambling. It is never easy to find a Solomonic way to cut fame in half, and the more fame Abbott and Costello got, the tougher the cut became.

This conflicted relationship was extraordinarily useful, however. The characters in the act had to maintain a tension, a combativeness. Had Abbott and Costello been dear friends, it would have been much harder to pretend there was tension. Had they been really angry at each other, the team would have fallen apart. Their underlying camaraderie, in fact, was one of their greatest appeals. The tension in their real relationship perfectly suited the tension in the act. Bud Abbott had to feel some anger when he got mean. Audiences could feel this real anger, and it added to the laughter.

Of course, a principal reason for their success depended on their extraordinary skill in selecting, reworking, and delivering old routines. They did more than appropriate old material, though. Word confusion, so much a holdover from the immigrant generation and radio, was transformed by Abbott and Costello. The new word confusion was aimed not at immigrant audiences, as in the earlier era, but at ordinary Americans who were confused about what was happening to their country and their economic future, and of course, about whether their spouses, siblings, or children would return alive from the war. These confusions were too painful for comedy but found some release when translated into simple linguistic confusion.

On radio and in the earlier vaudeville era, the joke came from the language itself. Abbott and Costello now added particular characteristics and underappreciated acting skills. Like the great comedy teams, they used language to develop national catchphrases, most notably Lou's sonorous "Heyyyyyy Abboooott."

Another of the reasons for Lou Costello's appeal was that he, like Charlie Chaplin, Stan Laurel, and Harpo Marx, used comedy that arose not just from a joke and not just from cultural references but ultimately from the human predicament. Chaplin, Laurel, and Harpo aroused tender emotions in the audience, feelings of pity, sympathy, and even sorrow, and when Bud pushed or slapped Lou around, the action was a prompt. Audiences immediately rooted for Lou. The character he created was very funny, but his appearance and behavior, his very being, was one of isolated pathos. He saw what no one else did, such as the moving candle in *Hold That Ghost* or Dracula emerging from the coffin in *Abbott and Costello Meet Frankenstein*. Audiences identified with his dilemma. No other characters in his movies understood his fear. None of them could comfort him. He was alone, and audiences laughed at his dilemma, at the way he handled it, and at the emotional recognition it brought of feeling alone in dealing with their own fears. It is also crucial to note that although Lou suffered, he was not helpless. He talked back. He struggled. That was a lesson the audiences cherished.

There is, however, a revealing difference between Lou Costello's character and Chaplin's. The Tramp was self-sacrificing, but Lou's character was not. In real life, Lou Costello constantly helped others. He was beloved for his acts of kindness, and therefore Lou would have had a very easy time playing such a character. Additionally, it seems logical that during a war, audiences would want a self-sacrificing hero. This, however, is the critical point: Audiences that had to be self-sacrificing in real life needed to escape this responsibility by embracing a comic character who was more focused on his own fears, not a character eager to join the military but one who had to be tricked into entering the service as in *Buck Privates*.

Abbott — by almost everyone's definition, either the best straight man who ever lived or awfully close to it — played perfectly to Costello, tricking the childlike character, immensely enjoying the sly trickery and convinced that it illustrated his intellectual superiority. He had the difficult task of selling a ridiculous premise to both Lou's character and the audience. To do this well, he had to pretend that he fully believed it himself. As a straight man, he had an almost perfect sense of when and how to draw Lou back from the edge; that is, he had to recognize Lou's thought patterns, to see where his mind was going, and to respond, and in such a way that led Lou back to the next setup and punch line. ✗

Costello was brilliant at improvisation. Sounding over-rehearsed is one of the dangers of repeat performances. To keep from being bored, the team often changed even their most famous bits each time they did them. This could, and did, result in their being lost in a routine onstage. Of course, because their humor frequently depended on confusion, audiences thought their wanderings were part of the act. They rehearsed over and over until the rhythms were right, and while Lou loved to wander off the subject, Abbott learned to remain sharp. It takes appreciable acting skill to have what in the business is called "rehearsed spontaneity," the carefully prepared semblance of making it up as one goes along. Actually, the fact that Bud had to listen so closely to Lou kept him from focusing too much on his own next line. Many straight men neglected to listen to their partner because they knew the lines so well. But listening is a key component of timing.

In a way, Bud Abbott was almost too good a straight man. Because delivering setup lines and reacting to Lou were his obvious and deeply admired strengths, writers never fully developed Bud into a character beyond being a bit of a bully and a con man. His glowering, dismissive stare, his carnival barker voice, and his crisp delivery were so good that audiences forgave the lack of a more developed personality.

Abbott and Costello's routines were memorized and mimicked. Although others could skillfully speak the words, they could never match Bud and Lou because they could not become the characters. The most famous of their routines passed from comedy history into American folklore. As Jerry Seinfeld, among others, has noted, Abbott and Costello were a vaudeville and burlesque preservation society. Many of the numerous routines they performed so well would have been lost without them.

One of the classic number confusion routines they performed came from their film *Buck Privates*:

Abbott: You're 40 years old, and you're

in love with a little girl, say 10 years old. You're four times as old as that girl. You couldn't marry that girl, could you?

Costello: No.

Abbott: So you wait 5 years. Now the little girl is 15, and you're 45. You're only three times as old as that girl. So you wait 15 years more. Now the little girl is 30, and you're 60. You're only twice as old as that little girl.

Costello: She's catching up.

Abbott: Here's the question. How long do you have to wait before you and that little girl are the same age?

Costello: What kind of question is that? That's ridiculous. If I keep waiting for that girl, she'll pass me up. She'll wind up older than I am. Then she'll have to wait for me!

Many of their routines depended on Lou misinterpreting a word. One famous example was the "Mudder/Fodder" routine first performed in *It Ain't Hay* (1943) and then, as many routines were, redone in *The Noose Hangs High* (1948). In this one, Lou doesn't understand the difference between a mudder, a racehorse that performs well when the track is wet or muddy, and a mother, a difficulty compounded by the common Brooklyn and New Jersey pronunciation of the words:

Abbott: Didn't I see you at the racetrack yesterday?

Costello: Yeah, I was there. I like to bet on the nags.

Abbott: [grabbing him] Don't talk that way about horses. Do you realize that I have one of the greatest mudders in the country?

Costello: What has your mudder got to do with horses?

Abbott: My mudder *is* a horse.

Costello: What? I will admit there's a resemblance.

Abbott: Now stop that.

Costello: Is your mudder really a horse?

Abbott: Of course. My mudder won the first race at Hialeah yesterday.

Costello: You oughta be ashamed of yourself, putting your mudder in a horse race . . .

Abbott: My mudder used to pull a milk wagon.

Costello: What some people won't do for a living . . .

Abbott: I said I've got a fine horse and he's a mudder.

Costello: *He*'s a mudder. How can *he* be a mudder.

Abbott: . . . I can't waste my time with you. I've got to go to the track and feed my mudder.

Costello: And what do you give the old lady for breakfast — oats?

Abbott: . . . Modern mudders don't eat oats. They eat their fodder.

Costello: What did you say?

Abbott: I said I feed my mudder his fodder.

Costello: What have you got, a bunch of cannibals?

Abbott and Costello also continued the slapstick tradition that most other teams had abandoned. Costello had to learn to take a punch, and he did it well. After all, he had been both a boxer and a stunt man. At home around the dinner table, he even showed his daughters how he could be slapped without being hurt.

Both Abbott and Costello had learned their trade through sheer hard work. Abbott had left school after the fourth grade, and he earned money by being a shill at Coney Island, a job that prepared him perfectly for the character he would later create. Next, his father got him a job at a burlesque house, and Abbott met many famous performers there while watching the acts. He moved on, eventually managing a theater in Detroit. One night a straight man decided he should be a comic, so the leading act was left without a straight man. Abbott stepped in, certain from his shrewd observations and his personal contacts with the performers that he could do the job. It was his first time on-stage.

He then traveled the circuit, performing skits, with his wife and others doing the comic parts. In 1936 he was at the Eltinage Theater in New York, when he decided to approach a young performer he had grown to respect deeply, an extremely talented comedian who complemented Abbott's slim good looks and fast-talking approach.

Lou Costello's journey to the Eltinage Theater began with winning a Charlie Chaplin look-alike contest. Costello viewed Chaplin's films over and over, memorizing each of the movements. Determined to succeed, he moved to Hollywood from New Jersey when he was twenty, but beyond jobs as a stuntman and a set carpenter, he could not get work.

Eventually, with his money nearly gone, he headed back home. He got as far as St. Joseph, Missouri, when his money ran out. Seeing an ad for a "Dutch" comic, Costello, desperate for a job, tried out. His German accent may not have been perfect, but he had heard enough immigrants to do a passable imitation. After a year, he headed to New York and got on the burlesque circuit, growing ever more competent and admired.

His body shape was perfect for a comic's. In burlesque, for example, the comics always wore baggy pants (the mostly male audience was not interested in seeing male legs), and Costello's portliness filled them out amply. His tight-fitting jacket, his shortness, his childlike face, all were absolutely perfect for his act.

Costello was at the Eltinage with his partner, Joe Lyons. Lou came offstage, and Bud praised the performance. Eventually, the two had dinner and agreed to team up together.

Success came relatively quickly, once they worked together as a team. Their big break came from another comedian, Henny Youngman, "the king of the one-liners." Youngman was a regular on the popular Kate Smith radio program when he got an offer to make a movie. The radio show's producer told him he could go, provided he found a replacement. Youngman suggested Abbott and Costello.

The still nationally untested team used familiar routines rewritten for them by John Grant, whose steel-rimmed glasses, white hair, and older, distinguished face made him look more like a banker than a comedy genius. Grant had an encyclopedic knowledge of routines going back to the nineteenth century. He would "borrow" one, update it if necessary, and allow the improvisational genius of Abbott and Costello to do the rest. They eventually mastered more than two hundred routines.

Soon they had their own radio show. Oddly, Lou's character on the radio show was that of a woman chaser and insulter. He mocked people. His childlike character had yet to be explored. Such a change was crucial because, although Lou's radio character could get laughs, it could not generate a sense of audience pity and sympathy. Had they tried to transfer their radio characters to film, they might not have achieved the level of success they did.

But succeed they did. In September 1940, Congress passed the Draft Bill, as the nation became increasingly concerned about the war in Europe. It didn't take long before movie studios saw being drafted as a perfect plot device for comedy films. With the United States maintaining its neutrality while war raged in Europe, there was still some laughter to be wrung from the idea of a draft. At Universal, Abbott and Costello were in a race against Bob Hope at Paramount for the first service comedy. They won the race with *Buck Privates*, their second movie. Now they were Hollywood stars.

The "Drill" routine is the centerpiece of *Buck Privates*, with Lou being smacked by a rifle and trying to stay in formation. They had done the bit many times in their act, but as usual, Lou changed it every time it was filmed. In some ways, it was a perfect routine to illustrate their talents; while Bud barked orders and tried to force Lou to conform, Lou was literally out of step. This was his attraction, especially for the young people in the audience. He violated the rules without meaning to do so. Unlike, say, the Marx Brothers, he never challenged the legitimacy of the institution. He may have been a bad boy, but he did not have a satiric thought on his mind.

Buck Privates was a personal triumph for Lou because it prompted no less than

Charlie Chaplin to call him the best clown since the silent era. It was not a title universally accepted by critics, but to Lou, Chaplin's praise was all the vindication he needed.

Buck Privates was an enormous morale booster, but Abbott and Costello did much more during World War II than provide laughter. President Roosevelt asked for their help in selling war bonds. In February 1943, just before Lou's collapse, they embarked on an exhausting trip covering eighty-five cities in little more than several weeks. Bombers flew them from one city to another; after landing they were met by state troopers and transported to what were often makeshift stages. They raised more than $5 million, a staggering sum for the time.

Abbott and Costello went on to make thirty-six feature films. These functioned in part as showcases for burlesque routines, rewritten by John Grant and sometimes improvised upon, especially by Lou. Whatever the disputed origins of many of the routines, Abbott and Costello perfected them, presented them to a wide audience, and deservedly get credit for them. Often the routines were adapted from other stars. Their hilarious "Half a Sandwich" routine in *Keep 'Em Flying*, for example, is very similar to the Laurel and Hardy "Ice Cream Soda" routine in *Men O' War*.

The "Mustard" routine was another famous bit. In it, Bud tries to convince a reluctant Lou that his refusal to use mustard on his hot dog will result in economic catastrophe.

Of course, "Who's on First" was their most famous routine. It had many precedents. Comedy writer Jim Mulholland cites "The Baker Scene" as among the earliest wordplay routines. The routine was probably written early in the twentieth century for a straight man and a comic. Unfortunately, Abbott and Costello didn't use this routine in any of their films, although it did show up in their television show in an episode titled "Getting a Job." In this rendition of the routine, as it was originally used in vaudeville, the straight man announces that he's just taken a job in a bakery, and the comic asks about the job:

Straight Man: I'm loafing.
Comic: I thought you said you were
    working.
Straight Man: I am. They pay me to loaf.
Comic: They *pay* you to loaf? How

much do you get?

Straight Man: Seven dollars a week and double for overtime.

Comic: For loafing?

Straight Man: Yes.

Comic: Can I get a job loafing?

Straight Man: I don't know. You have to belong to the union.

Comic: You gotta belong to a union to loaf?

Straight Man: Certainly, if you want to be recognized.

Comic: I wouldn't care if they didn't recognize me. I wouldn't care if they didn't even *talk* to me. I'd like to get a job in that bakery. Who's the boss?

Straight Man: Yes.

Comic: That's what I'm asking. Who's the boss?

Straight Man: Yes.

Comic: Who's the guy you're working for?

Straight Man: That's exactly correct.

Comic: I'm asking you, what's the name of the boss?

Straight Man: No, Watt's the name of the street.

The "Who's on First" routine ran into

some initial skepticism. When Pat Costello, Lou's brother, first heard the team rehearsing it in his father's garage, he told them not to do it because it wasn't funny. And when the producer of Kate Smith's radio show first heard it, he had the same reaction and told them to use another sketch. A few weeks later, Abbott and Costello told the producer they had no skit that week, and in desperation, he let them do "Who's on First." The reaction by the radio audience was immediate and enthusiastic.

Although no one knew it at the time, "Who's on First" would prove to be not only Abbott and Costello's most famous routine but also one of the last great expressions of the classic comedy teams before forces that would render them obsolete were unleashed after World War II. With its perfect construction and its use of America's national pastime as its subject, "Who's on First" functions as an apotheosis of comedy team material and an illuminating way to experience the great comedy team tradition.

"Who's on First," like most of Abbott and Costello's routines, was rarely performed the same way twice. Also, the shortstop's name, "I don't give a damn," was censored in many presentations. Furthermore, there is no authoritative version. Here is one variation taken from various television performances and performed in their film *The Naughty Nineties*:

Abbott: All right, now whaddya want?

Costello: Now look, I'm the head of the sports department. I gotta know the baseball players' names. Do you know the guys' names?

Abbott: Oh sure.

Costello: So you go ahead and tell me some of their names.

Abbott: Well, I'll introduce you to the boys. You know sometimes nowadays they give ballplayers peculiar names.

Costello: You mean funny names.

Abbott: Nicknames, pet names, like Dizzy Dean —

Costello: His brother Daffy —

Abbott: Daffy Dean —

Costello: And their cousin!

Abbott: Who's that?

Costello: Goofy!

Abbott: Goofy, huh? Now let's see. We have on the bags — we have Who's on first, What's on second, I Don't Know's on third.

Costello: That's what I wanna find out.

Abbott: I say Who's on first, What's on second, I Don't Know's on third —

Costello: You know the fellows' names?

Abbott: Certainly!

Costello: Well then, who's on first?

Abbott: Yes!

Costello: I mean the fellow's name!

Abbott: Who!

Costello: The guy on first!

Abbott: Who!

Costello: The first baseman!

Abbott: Who!

Costello: The guy playing first!

Abbott: Who is on first!

Costello: Now whaddya askin' me for?

Abbott: I'm telling you. Who is on first.

Costello: Well, I'm asking YOU who's on first?

Abbott: That's the man's name.

Costello: That's whose name?

Abbott: Yes.

Costello: Well go ahead and tell me.

Abbott: Who.

Costello: The guy on first.

Abbott: Who!

Costello: The first baseman.

Abbott: Who is on first!

Costello: Have you got a contract with the first baseman?

Abbott: Absolutely.

Costello: Who signs the contract?

Abbott: Well, naturally!

Costello: When you pay off the first baseman every month, who gets the money?

Abbott: Every dollar. Why not? The man's entitled to it.

Costello: Who is?

Abbott: Yes. Sometimes his wife comes down and collects it.

Costello: Whose wife?

Abbott: Yes.

Costello: All I'm tryin' to find out is what's the guy's name on first base.

Abbott: Oh, no — wait a minute, don't switch 'em around. What is on second base.

Costello: I'm not askin' you who's on second.

Abbott: Who is on first.

Costello: I don't know.

Abbott: He's on third — now we're not talkin' 'bout him.

Costello: Now, how did I get on third base?

Abbott: You mentioned his name!

Costello: If I mentioned the third baseman's name, who did I say is playing third?

Abbott: No. Who's playing first.

Costello: Never mind first. I wanna know what's the guy's name on third.

Abbott: No. What's on second.

Costello: I'm not askin' you who's on second.

Abbott: Who's on first.

Costello: I don't know.

Abbott: He's on third.

Costello: Aaah! Would you please stay on third base and don't go off it?

Abbott: What was it you wanted?

Costello: Now who's playin' third base?

Abbott: Now why do you insist on putting Who on third base?

Costello: Why? Who am I putting over there?

Abbott: Yes. But we don't want him there.

Costello: What's the guy's name on third base?

Abbott: What belongs on second.

Costello: I'm not askin' you who's on second.

Abbott: Who's on first.

Costello: I don't know.

Abbott & Costello: THIRD BASE!

Costello: You got an outfield?

Abbott: Oh yes!

Costello: The left fielder's name?

Abbott: Why.

Costello: I don't know, I just thought I'd ask you.

Abbott: Well, I just thought I'd tell you.

Costello: All right, then tell me who's playin' left field.

Abbott: Who is playing fir—

Costello: STAY OUTTA THE INFIELD! I wanna know what's the left fielder's name.

Abbott: What's on second.

Costello: I'm not askin' you who's on second.

Abbott: Who's on first.

Costello: I don't know.

Abbott & Costello: THIRD BASE!

Costello: The left fielder's name?

Abbott: Why.

Costello: Because!

Abbott: Oh, he's center field.

Costello: Look, you got a pitcher on this team?

Abbott: Now wouldn't this be a fine team without a pitcher.

Costello: The pitcher's name?

Abbott: Tomorrow.

Costello: You don't wanna tell me today?

Abbott: I'm tellin' you now.

Costello: Then go ahead.

Abbott: Tomorrow.

Costello: What time?

Abbott: What time what?

Costello: What time tomorrow are you going to tell me who's pitching?

Abbott: Now listen. Who is not pitching. Who is on fir—

Costello: I'll break your arm if you say Who's on first. I wanna know what's the pitcher's name?

Abbott: What's on second.

Costello: I don't know.

Abbott & Costello: THIRD BASE!

Costello: You got a catcher?

Abbott: Oh, absolutely.

Costello: The catcher's name?

Abbott: Today.

Costello: Today. And Tomorrow's pitching.

Abbott: Now you've got it.

Costello: All we've got is a couple of days on the team.

Abbott: Well, I can't help that.

Costello: Well, I'm a catcher too.

Abbott: I know that.

Costello: Now suppose that I'm catching, Tomorrow's pitching on my team and their heavy hitter gets up.

Abbott: Yes.

Costello: Tomorrow throws the ball. The batter bunts the ball. When he bunts the ball, me being a good catcher, I wanna throw the guy out at first base. So I pick up the ball and throw it to who?

Abbott: Now that's the first thing you've said right.

Costello: I don't even know what I'm talkin' about!

Abbott: Well, that's all you have to do.

Costello: Is to throw the ball to first base?

Abbott: Yes.

Costello: Now who's got it?

Abbott: Naturally!

Costello: If I throw the ball to first base, somebody's gotta catch it. Now who caught it?

Abbott: Naturally!

Costello: Who caught it?

Abbott: Naturally.

Costello: Who?

Abbott: Naturally!

Costello: Naturally.

Abbott: Yes.

Costello: So I pick up the ball and I throw it to Naturally.

Abbott: NO, NO, NO! You throw the ball to first base and Who gets it.

Costello: Naturally.

Abbott: That's right. There we go.

Costello: So I pick up the ball and I throw it to Naturally.

Abbott: You don't!

Costello: I throw it to who?

Abbott: Naturally.

Costello: THAT'S WHAT I'M SAYING!

Abbott: You're not saying it that way.

Costello: I said I throw the ball to Naturally.

Abbott: You don't. You throw the ball to Who.

Costello: Naturally!

Abbott: Well, say that!

Costello: THAT'S WHAT I'M SAYING! I throw the ball to who?

Abbott: Naturally.

Costello: Ask me.

Abbott: You throw the ball to Who.

Costello: Naturally.

Abbott: That's it.

Costello: SAME AS YOU!! I throw the ball to first base and who gets it?

Abbott: Naturally!

Costello: Who has it?

Abbott: Naturally!

Costello: HE BETTER HAVE IT! I throw the ball to first base. Whoever it is grabs the ball, so the guy runs to second. Who picks up the ball and throws it to What. What throws it to I Don't Know. I Don't Know throws it back to Tomorrow — triple play.

Abbott: Yes.

Costello: Another guy gets up. It's a long fly ball to Because. Why? I don't know. He's on third and I don't give a damn!

Abbott: What was that?

Costello: I said I don't give a damn!

Abbott: Oh, that's our shortstop.

In the 1970s, Selchow & Righter released a board game based on the "Who's on First" routine. The game makers noted what fans always knew — no right fielder is named in the routine. The clever game manufacturers created just the right name: "Nobody."

Despite their ingenious bits and incredible popularity, Abbott and Costello had their ups and downs in films because of squabbling and Bud's illnesses, among other reasons. Abbott was an epileptic, but for obvious reasons he wanted to hide that fact from the public. Lou learned to deal with the oncoming seizure. Bud would begin to veer to the side. Quickly, Lou would hit him hard in the pit of the stomach. (Oddly enough, this functioned as a temporary cure.) Audiences, thinking the punch was part of the act, always laughed. Abbott's brother Norman kept pencils in his pocket. Feeling a seizure coming on, Bud would sometimes take one to stick in his mouth. He didn't want to bite his tongue.

The team's sagging popularity was revitalized when Universal teamed them with its resident monsters for a series of "scare comedies" that began with *Abbott and Costello Meet Frankenstein*, released in 1948. The combination of monsters and comedy proved enormously successful, in part because the team treated the horror genre and the monsters with respect. Despite complaints from exhibitors that the children in the audience were scared, the children evidently loved the feeling because they kept coming back to be scared again. With the fear of war having receded with the Allied victory, monsters (the cinematic stand-ins for the real fears of the world) could be entertaining again.

The tensions of success ultimately wrecked their partnership. Younger audiences clearly went to see Lou, not fully appreciating how much Bud's feeding lines and controlling pace contributed to the humor. Both men became increasingly frustrated. They argued over money and billing. They gambled everywhere, and Costello angered studio bosses by taking furniture and other items from the set and refusing to return them. He demanded more money than Bud. At one point he wanted to change the name of the team to Costello and Abbott. Despite all this, both were extraordinarily generous people, good husbands and fathers.

Their separation became official in 1957. Lou died in 1959 of a heart attack, and Bud lived on for fifteen more years. After trying out a new partner, he quickly discovered that there was only going to be one Lou Costello.

There were imitators, of course, the most important of whom were Wally Brown and Alan Carney. Brown, the Abbott imitator, had been in vaudeville and had a decent delivery but didn't have Bud's fierceness. Carney had been in films, but he was never able to elicit the sympathy Lou could. They did several films, trying all the time to deliver Abbott and Costello–caliber dialogue, but they never even got close.

NINE

THE ROAD TO TEMPORARY TEAMS

Hope and Crosby

Bob Hope was in New York in 1932, jauntily walking past the Friars Club, the place where entertainers could relax, joke with each other, schmooze about the business, and play some cards. Suddenly, he looked up and saw a man he admired, the singer Bing Crosby. The two men began chatting, discovering they both had a passion for golf. Soon they were swapping stories and gossip.

Hope was then appearing in a play on Broadway, but he was still a year away from wide recognition as a comedian. He had been born in England, immigrated to the United States at age four ("when I found out I couldn't be king"), and grew up in Cleveland. He tried boxing but knew he had to find another career when he "not only was being carried out of the ring, but into the ring."

Having taken lessons, Hope started a dance act with his then sweetheart Mildred Rosequist. Hope was eighteen, and the $8 a night seemed enormous. He wanted to tour with Mildred but made the mistake of inviting her mother to see the act. He then worked with several partners, including an attractive, smart woman named Louise Traxill. In keeping with the vaudeville tradition, Hope did not let the audience become aware of her intelligence; he let them concentrate on her beauty.

He was always particularly good when working with an attractive woman partner, including later when he entertained American troops all over the world. Here is one of his famous bits:

Hope: Nice day.
Attractive woman: Yes.
Hope: Some sky.
Woman: Yes.
Hope: Some trees.
Woman: Yes.
Hope: Some grass.
Woman: Yes.
Hope: Some dew.
Woman: I don't.

Hope and another partner, George Byrne, were in a Broadway show, but their agent advised them to head west. They made it as far as New Castle, Pennsylvania, where Hope announced coming attractions. He got some laughs, and the manager asked him to expand the introduction to five minutes. Hope finished the three days in New Castle and left with a revelation: He should create a solo act.

Bing Crosby — whose nickname came from his affection for a comic strip titled the *Bingville Bugle* — had started singing early with various bands and eventually achieved great success, earning his first hit record "I Surrender Dear" in 1931.

Hope and Crosby's easygoing friendship led to their becoming partners onstage. They appeared together two months after their first meeting. Hope introduced Bing, ad-libbing some remarks. To Hope's surprise, Bing ad-libbed right back. Their trademark patter, which ripened into mock rivalry and mild insults, was born. After this appearance, they remained friends, eventually appearing on each other's radio shows, continuing their "feud," which had been patterned after an extremely successful ongoing Fred Allen–Jack Benny radio argument. Neither was yet a movie star.

In 1940, Paramount executives came up with an idea for a "road" picture: Put a pair of comedy stars on a perilous journey and fill the journey with laughs. The metaphor for a country on the brink of, but not yet at, war was obvious. Evidently, the aim was to reduce the fear of a strange and unfamiliar foreign location by having an audience laugh at it. The would-be film, then known as *Road to Mandalay*, was first offered to George Burns and Gracie Allen.

Their comedy did not play well off danger, so they turned it down. Paramount then considered two actors popular at the time, Fred MacMurray and Jack Oakie, but both had other jobs. Paramount went in search of actors.

Meanwhile, Hope and Crosby had remained in contact with each other. The singer co-owned the Del Mar racetrack and invited Hope to appear with him on opening night to reprise some of their vaudeville routines. Hope did, and the crowd loved it.

Paramount's chief of production happened to be there, heard the two, and knew he had found his actors, although Hope was still a risk. He was rising, but by the early 1940s he was not yet a national name, not the first choice of a producer looking for a hit. (Hope eventually was given third billing in the picture after Crosby and Dorothy Lamour.) The writers reworked the screenplay but kept in the crucial attractiveness of escape. The locale was moved to Singapore, which supposedly sounded more exotic and dangerous than Mandalay, as it proved to be in 1941.

Hope, as he would always do, brought his own gang of writers to put gags into the script. Over his career, Hope had many writers. Some comedians were notorious for mistreating them, but not Hope. He cherished them, understood them, and was kind to them. Although he was funny and quick, he unabashedly relied on them and would call his writers at any hour. Among themselves, Hope's writers referred to these as "naft" calls — as in "need a few things" — because Hope might be in a limousine on his way to the airport. He'd tell them that he would be, say, at a benefit in a few hours and needed timely, funny, pertinent jokes. But Hope didn't overly impose on his writers; at least one of them asked that Hope never call him in the middle of the night, and Hope complied.

Hope was a brilliant editor. He also enjoyed laughing. Ironically, many comedians viewed comedy as simply work and were humorless except when onstage. But Hope, like Jack Benny and Steve Allen, for example, loved writers and loved to laugh when they came up with a good line.

Of course, audiences didn't always want to know too much about the writers. The pleasant illusion of believing that the comedians thought the jokes up on the way to the microphone or as they spoke in a movie was powerful. Hope's writers seemed not to resent the fact that they were not acknowledged. They knew the illusion was part of the deal, and they nursed any wounds around their swimming pools.

Road to Singapore was not meant to be the first in a series of movies, but its success made a sequel mandatory, and it made Bob Hope a movie star. Americans who felt trapped by troubling economic and political realities found in Hope and Crosby's films an escape to a land of song and romance, of humor and fantasy, a place where evildoers were punished, love could be cheerfully pursued, and work could be avoided.

Hope's screen character was slowly evolving. In his first movie, *The Big Broadcast of 1938*, he displayed an emotional vulnerability that would soon be sifted from the character. In contrast, his character in *Singapore* was scheming, ever ready with a funny line. Hope had perfected the machine gun–like delivery style on radio and while performing for members of the armed services, where his audiences wanted a lot of rapid-fire jokes, as though they didn't have time to wait to laugh. (Later, when he worked on television, the fast delivery didn't work as well, and he had to slow his pace.) His carefree, easy delivery made it all seem effortless.

Hope's later persona as a man willing to go to any lengths to avoid a fight, someone yearning to be the hero but unable to pull it off, was not in evidence in this first *Road* film. The "false courage" that came to be a trademark hadn't quite been developed but would emerge as the series went along. His writers, drawing on Hope's real-life reputation as a bit of a braggart and a woman chaser, would also add these traits to the screen character. He also had, especially in later films, some of Jack Benny's prissiness.

What is most surprising about Hope's character in the *Road* pictures is his physicality. Hope was well known as a "talking comedian," but he demonstrated again and again a talent for slapstick as well.

Dorothy Lamour's character, unlike Hope's and Crosby's, is truly noble. She is willing to sacrifice her true love (the Crosby character) for what she believes is his real happiness. She is often considered part of the Hope-Crosby team, but she is too honest a character, and too smart, to be a foil. She's there for the songs and for her looks, not to add jokes to the comedy team. That is too bad, because a bold woman confronting the Hope and Crosby characters with some of her own sassy wisecracks would have added a lot to the mix. It was not to be. By the second film in the series, *Road to Zanzibar*, Lamour received third billing and was much less central to the plot.

Hope and Crosby's principal asset was the genuineness of their bond, one perhaps forged more by golf than art, but nevertheless a true one. They really liked each other, and that came across on-screen. They found it easy to be spontaneous, to joke around with each other. Their mutual affection and their jubilant refusal to take themselves seriously on-screen led to the creation of wonderful characters and a more intimate experience for the audience.

Hope and Crosby loved to ad-lib, consistently angering their directors. They would yell back and forth between their dressing rooms trying out new material. The crews, which always loved working with them, turned out to be their test audience. In the films, they made fun of the studio, of adventure movies, of the Hollywood system. Hope saw their work as not so much film work as live performance. He invited friends to the set to watch as he and Crosby performed, which was completely counter to the normal policy of closed movie sets. By performing before a live audience, Hope thought — correctly — he could bring movie audiences the sense of being right there with him.

Hope and Crosby transformed the social satire of the Marx Brothers into a parody of the movies and themselves, very safe and funny targets. Their low comedy was aimed at soft and easy marks and did no real damage.

That comedy included new locales that presented opportunities for unusual gags. This kept the material fresh. As other comedy teams found out as well, it made sense to put the comics in a place where they didn't belong. The very juxtaposition of the comic and the improbable location was funny in itself. An exotic setting also gave producers permission to introduce local colorful characters that could add danger or humor.

Additionally, both Hope and Crosby appealed to women in the audience. The songs, romance, and locales were pleasing, but so were their looks. At one early point, Hope's comedic career was in question because of his sleek good looks. Crosby's seductive singing voice and debonair attitude supplemented his looks to make him especially attractive.

The Hope and Crosby characters

worked extremely well against each other. They feuded over looks, women, and money. In their third film, *Road to Morocco*, Lamour kisses Hope in an embrace that straightens out the previously curled toes on his slippers. Crosby has a suggestion: "Now kiss him on the nose and see if you can straighten that out." It is a typical line, straight out of a vaudeville or radio routine. Of course, Hope gets right back at Crosby. The villain, played by a young, slim Anthony Quinn, calls Crosby "a moonfaced son of a one-eyed donkey." Hope turns to Crosby and says, "I wouldn't let him call me that even if there is a resemblance."

Hope goes out of his way to break down the fourth wall, to let the audience know this isn't really a traditional movie. Audiences loved it because they felt in on the joke. In the beginning of *Road to Morocco*, for example, Hope notes that Lamour will have to be in the film since it's another *Road* picture. He praises Paramount. Later in the film, a camel talks to the audience, saying, "This is the screwiest picture I was ever in."

The Hope and Crosby characters were both romantically eager, vying for Dorothy Lamour's affections in all but the final

Road film, when a younger, more sultry Joan Collins replaced Lamour, who, despite her understandable anger, finally agreed to appear in the film in a small part.

Their eagerness to win Lamour was not a sign of maturity, however. Both characters panicked at the very prospect of marriage, of assuming any adult responsibilities at all for that matter. They chase after attractive women and easy money. They know how to get off a wisecrack and how to fight. One famous scene repeated in several of the films is their pretense of playing patty-cake when they are actually preparing to punch their opponents. While emotionally older than Laurel's or Costello's childlike characters, they were far from mature adults.

Hope and Crosby's films continued after the war, but with new twists because the formula needed to change with the times. Meanwhile, Crosby had become famous with his rendition of Irving Berlin's song "White Christmas," which he had performed in the 1942 film *Holiday Inn*.

Road to Utopia (1946) has an odd narrative structure. It is a period piece with Robert Benchley as a narrator and with the film told mostly in flashback. It's also different in that Hope finally gets to marry Dorothy Lamour. The film contains one of Hope's most famous lines from the series. He and Crosby are in a bar in the Yukon. The villain asks what they want to drink. Crosby says, "Couple of fingers of rotgut," but Hope innocently says, "I'll take a lemonade." Seeing the reaction this less than he-man order brings, Hope quickly amends it using his version of a tough voice: "in a dirty glass." The line illustrates how Hope's character has developed into the weakling who struggles to put on a false front in a man's world. It was a character that he would successfully transfer to many other films.

One of their best scenes in the film involved Hope, trying to sleep, mistaking a bear for Dorothy Lamour in a fur coat. He fumbles a proposal saying, "I'll do things for you — big things — after we're married." He takes the paw and suggests, "Dear, you've been working too hard." The producers decided they would use a tame real bear for the scene. Hope and Crosby tried out the real bear, but one good growl and they leaped out of the bed they were in, announcing that the real bear couldn't join the team. Horribly, the next day, the bear took off his trainer's arm.

In *Road to Rio,* they reverted to the familiar formula but, evidently realizing they needed to freshen it up, decided to use guest stars. The stars included the Andrews Sisters and another popular comedy team of the time, the Wiere Brothers.

The three European brothers were a talented comedic team who could both sing and dance. In *Road to Rio,* they played Brazilian musicians hired by Crosby and Hope to pretend to be hip musical members of their band. Their characters spoke no English, so they memorized slang phrases, such as "You're telling me," "You're in the groove, Jackson," and "This is murder." Crosby and Hope used the team well, and it is surprising, given the Wiere Brothers' popularity onstage, that they did not become bigger movie attractions.

Road to Bali, made in 1952, was the first of the series in color, but it also marked the end of an era. The humor did not resonate with the new postwar, suburban audience. Despite this, the team made yet another film, *The Road to Hong Kong,* a full decade later. The poor plot hurt the film, but the stars were still charming. There was an additional film planned in the 1980s, which was to star Hope with George Burns. It had the provisional title

The Road to the Fountain of Youth, but unfortunately it was never produced.

Hope and Crosby were critical figures in the history of comedy teams not so much because of their success as a team but because they were a transition team providing clear, if unnoticed at the time, evidence of the coming decline of classic teams. Although other major teams would follow, Hope and Crosby were illustrative of the changes to come. ✳

Abbott and Costello were representative of the old-fashioned team — coming together, joining their fates to forge a single career in tandem. But with the changing audience tastes, the increasing pressures of business, and the ever-present egos, the formation of classic comedy teams had started a slow, painful decline. Still, Americans loved teams for their intimate cooperation, their clever dialogue, and the funny characterizations.

The change had actually begun with Laurel and Hardy. As actors, they were brought together by the studio rather than by their own independent decision. Their partnership had worked wonderfully because of their complementary egos.

Bob Hope and Bing Crosby took the deliberate pairing of two talented actors a step further. They were two successful performers (Crosby, at the time, the more successful) who were friends and who were cast by Paramount into a series of pictures. Between the pictures they did not perform together, and after the film series they did not continue making other films together. Hope and Crosby were the start of a new type of comedy teams — the temporary teams.

Temporary teams, which would become much more important after the 1970s, could exploit the fame of the individual stars and showcase their talents together, but the individual members of the team did not tie together their professional careers. Although Hope and Crosby showed how vital friendship was for a temporary team to flourish, studios would later bring teams together without any personal connection.

Beyond creating an alternative to classic teams, Hope and Crosby signaled the decline of traditional comedy teams in two ways. First, they helped erase the line between the two worlds created by classic comedy teams. They developed the fourth and final model of the relationship between reality and the comic world created by teams, which negated the three previous models developed by Burns and Allen, Laurel and Hardy, and Abbott and Costello. In this new model, there was no necessity for one member of a team to have a tenuous hold on reality while another character brought the team back to the real world, or for the team to create a fantasy world in which the team members banded together to overcome a strange, hostile reality represented by an outside straight man, or a team in which a straight man represented a tricky world seeking to con us.

Hope and Crosby developed a realistic humor that mocked the illusory world their movie producers had arranged for them. Their world was one in which you laughed at personal foibles and at friends, a world that you didn't take too seriously. As Crosby once defined the *Road* films, "The plot takes two fellows, throws them into a jam or as many jams as possible, then lets them clown their way out."

And, if you didn't take the real world too seriously there was no great need to create a fantasy comic world. Such an approach required a lack of sentimentality, an ability to avoid so strong an attachment to any person or place that you couldn't face the inevitable disappointments inherent in those people and places. Hope's very unsentimental comic character perfectly displayed this approach. Unfortunately, the filtering out of emotions to leave just the laughs came at a price for Hope's character. Audience members could laugh at his character but didn't feel much tenderness or pity. This lack of pathos was the character's principal weakness.

The suggestion that there was no need for an alternate reality was one more step toward the end of teams; that is, there was no need for a classic comedy team. Instead, individual comedians, or groups of performers, could just tell jokes to remind everyone to keep loose.

Second, Hope and Crosby signaled the decline of classical comedy teams by changing the relationship between the team characters. Although Crosby played the traditional straight man in the sense of getting the woman and feeding the lines to Hope who then shot back the one-liners, each character felt superior to the other. Unlike Laurel and Hardy — in which Hardy felt himself to be in charge and Laurel clearly was not — or Abbott and Costello — in which Abbott was the parent figure to Costello's childlike character — Hope and Crosby were more like squabbling brothers, ex-vaudevillians whose sibling rivalry almost always was played out in the romantic arena.

This equality of characters was a crucial departure from the relationship in traditional comedy teams. The more both characters were alike, after all, the less need there was for complementary characters with distinct differences in appearance and motivation, the less need to find a perfect balance between the characters. Soon, the two characters could blend into one person who would stand onstage alone.

The Hope and Crosby *Road* pictures continue to be entertaining time capsules, exemplars of the sort of film that helped audiences through economic deprivation and the chaos of world war and its aftermath.

And when these temporary team members ended their career as screen partners, they did all right for themselves. Crosby, of course, remained one of the great crooners of the century, and Hope became a national institution, making many successful movies and television shows and continuing his incredible dedication to the members of the nation's armed services. His ability as a wisecracking but elegant emcee served him well as the host of seventeen

Academy Award shows. He frequently but jokingly lamented never winning an Oscar. His most famous line about being ignored — "Oscar night at my house is called Passover" — was a good one, delivered by a man whose name was as well known as the trophy that eluded him.

TEN

LOCO BOYS MAKE GOOD

The Three Stooges

Of all the comedy teams that made their debuts in the 1930s and 1940s, only the Three Stooges never broke up and never lost their audience. Although the team varied in its members (it had more different members than any other comedy team in movies), the center of the act remained the three Howard brothers — nicknamed Moe, Curly, and Shemp — and Larry Fine. Oddly enough, the three brothers never worked together as Stooges; some combination of Moe and one of the other brothers with Larry, or Moe and Larry with another actor, made up the long-running Stooge team. The act lasted for almost half a century.

Moe Horwitz had decided by age eleven that he wanted to be an actor. He made his way to the Vitagraph Studio in his native Brooklyn, offering to run errands for no pay. Soon enough the actors noticed him, and Moe landed some small roles in the pictures, mostly as a poor boy or a bully, parts that would be crucial in constructing his later Stooge character.

He and his brother, Shemp (born Samuel), having Americanized their birth name to Howard, entered vaudeville. They were not very good. Indeed, they were hired because the act, put on last, dependably caused patrons to leave the theater, emptying seats before the next show would begin.

Back home, Jerome, the beloved youngest son, with beautiful hair that he would one day have to remove for the act, was about to get the first bad break of his life. After borrowing Moe's rifle, the young man who would someday be known as Curly accidentally shot himself in the ankle. Moe saved Curly from bleeding to death, but Curly would limp painfully for the rest of his life.

In 1922, Moe met an old childhood buddy then acting under the name Ted Healy. Healy was enormously successful, but he needed an assistant. Moe got the job, accepting the pay of $100 a week. It was a lot of money for the time, but it was only a very small percentage of Healy's salary. Moe's original job was to pretend to be someone in the audience. He would jump onstage and pull Healy's pants off.

In 1925, while walking onstage at the Orpheum Theatre in Brooklyn, Healy and Moe heard Shemp laughing in the audience. Healy then asked for a volunteer, and Shemp, eating a pear, eagerly came forward. Shemp offered the pear to Healy, insisting he eat it. Healy adamantly refused. The ensuing argument led to parts of the pear getting on everyone's face. Moe and Ted Healy had a new partner.

Larry Fine was from South Philadelphia. Like Curly, he, too, had had a childhood accident. He had burned one of his arms with acid. He practiced the violin to strengthen his arm. Larry also was a successful amateur boxer, a career that would prove vital to surviving Moe's later punches. Larry entered vaudeville and was playing at the Marigold Gardens in Chicago in 1925. Healy and Moe, waiting to begin their show in Chicago at another theater, saw the act. Larry had come out wearing a silk hat and tails, played his violin, and did a Russian dance. The physical dexterity impressed Moe and Healy, who went backstage. Healy asked him to join the act. He offered to pay Larry $90 a week — $100 if there was no violin involved.

Moe, Shemp, and Larry became stooges, people who worked with actors and were there to take the punches. But Ted Healy didn't want them to get the laughs, and so he made the stooges targets rather than comics.

Healy and the Stooges did old-time vaudeville slapstick, but they did it very well, with Healy doing most of the slapping. From vaudeville, they went to Broadway and then in 1930 to their first film, *Soup to Nuts*. The film itself was not a commercial success, but Healy's stooges were already being noticed for their abilities.

The Stooges resented their small cut of the earnings; Healy earned more than a thousand a week, and the Stooges still made only a hundred each. They briefly left the act but returned. Shemp struck out on his own.

Meanwhile, the seemingly inexhaustible supply of talented Howard brothers continued. Young Jerome had also entered show business. He joined a band in 1928 as a comedy conductor. He would raise his arms and pieces of his jacket would fall off. Meeting audience expectations, his pants would soon follow.

When Shemp left the Stooges, Jerome, nicknamed "Babe" by Moe, replaced him.

The new stooge was ready to receive his fair share of slaps, but Healy soon saw a problem. As Curly later recalled it, "I had beautiful wavy hair and a waxed mustache. When I went to see Ted Healy about a job as one of the Stooges, he said, 'What can you do?' I said, 'I don't know.' He said, 'I know what you can do. You can shave off your hair to start with.' Then later on I had to shave off my poor mustache."

After removing the hair, "Babe" rubbed a hand over his shaven head, looked at Healy and said, "Call me Curly." Moe said the shaved head looked "like a dirty tennis ball."

Curly was as retiring in person as he was wild in the Stooges' films. Emil Sitka, an actor who appeared in dozens of their movies, told James Neibaur about Curly, "He would address me as 'Sir' even though he was the star and I was only a supporting player. He would sit quietly waiting for his cue and instructions, but the minute he was in front of the camera he would cut up, and boy he could really ad lib."

The team did a series of films with Healy at MGM. They excelled in shorter films in which they could perform their vaudeville routines.

Finally, they decided to try to succeed without Healy. They signed a deal with Columbia in 1934 to make film shorts. They would remain at Columbia for a quarter of a century, developing the characters that would define them and building generations of fans. They ended up making 190 films for Columbia and more than 200 all together, the largest number of films by any adult comedy team.

At the beginning, it took time and effort to develop their identities, and they did so in various ways. They used their hair as a defining characteristic. Moe had his bangs, Larry the curly tufts of hair, and Curly the shaved head. The different haircuts became an easy way to differentiate them. It was an old vaudevillian's trick, but it worked well. The hair, beyond a trademark, served to divert attention away from the rest of their appearance, making them seem less like real people and more like cartoons. This was important because if they were going to keep slapstick alive during eras when it appeared to many audiences to be unsophisticated or cruel, they would need to make it clear that the violence didn't hurt. Just like Stan Laurel and the earlier comedians, they found tricks that allowed them to do this.

They learned to supplement the standard slapstick repertoire of slaps, kicks, and eye gouges with their own bits. These included Curly's catchphrase of "n'yuk, n'yuk, n'yuk," and the "woo-woo-woo" scream, which he used when he was scared or happy. Curly had borrowed this scream from another comedian named Hugh Herbert, who used "hoo-hoo-hoo." It is a sign of Curly's influence that Herbert eventually adopted Curly's version. Curly's Brooklyn pronunciation of words, like "soitenly," also became a trademark. Another Curly bit was to run around on the floor. This started one day when he forgot his lines and dropped to the floor. While lying on the ground, he began to run around in a circle, all the while spinning on his shoulder. Shemp later adopted this bit. Curly also learned a variety of different walks.

Although the Stooges became famous — and infamous — for their physicality, slapstick was not their only form of humor. They were very adept at verbal banter as well. Other comedians might say they were staying at a hotel; the Stooges stayed at the "Hotel Costa Plente" or at a place that advertised "26 Rooms–2 Bath Tubs." They would drink "Old Homicide." They came across the Cheatham Investment Company. *What's the Matador?*, *They Stooge to Conga*, *Loco Boy Makes Good*, and *Sing a Song of Six Pants* are just a few of the wonderful titles of their films.

The characters they developed at Columbia were precisely defined. Indeed, they had hit on the crucial character traits by their second film, *Punch Drunks*.

Moe was the boss, replacing Ted Healy. He did most of the hitting and eye gouging. Though he was the supposed leader, the older brother or father figure, he was one of them, not apart. The others were stooges — but so was he. Curly, the most popular of Moe and Larry's partners, was the innocent, the child in a man's body. Curly was also prepared. In the film *In the Sweet Pie and Pie*, for example, the trio find themselves in jail, and Moe bemoans the fact that they have no tools. Curly — like Harpo Marx responding to the panhandler who asks for a dime for a cup of coffee by reaching under his coat for a steaming hot cup of coffee — reveals that under his shirt he has files, saws, and other equipment.

Larry was the explainer, the brother who kept the other two from killing each other. This is an underappreciated role; it was Larry who kept the group together by acting as the go-between.

With Moe's character too bullying to be liked, and with Larry cleverly functioning as the middleman holding the "family" together, it was left for Curly to reach for the audience's sympathy. His excellent singing voice gave him a vocal control that added to the humor.

The Stooges loved to ad-lib, and they were good at it. They had mastered their own characters so well that they knew when a scripted line sounded false or wasn't funny enough. But they still took preparation seriously. Throughout their career, the Three Stooges believed in rehearsal. Like an Abbott and Costello verbal routine, the physical movements of the Stooges required each to know exactly what the other was going to be doing at any given moment.

Eric Lamond, Larry Fine's grandson, assisted them late in their careers and recalled that they still rehearsed routines they had done many times before. They made intricate, difficult simultaneous physical movements look natural and spontaneous. That professionalism and ability set them apart from other physical comedians. Emil Sitka observed, "Moe was all business and wanted the best performance possible from everyone. He was very particular about how fans were treated and how the gags were performed."

The Stooges were in many ways a holdover from the immigrant generation in which the newcomers to America and their children, who made up large parts of the urban audience, were still adjusting to the new land, still feeling as though they didn't belong. As Moe would put it, when it came time to think of plot, they considered, "Where would we be most out of place?" The emerging tensions of being in this wrong place led to disagreements, which led to slaps or insults, again a perfect mirroring of the brutal, physical immigrant experience that often depended on being good with your hands.

They found personal and universal feelings from within the immigrant experience — the constraints of family, the sense of alienation — and married them to slapstick to create their act. These feelings resonated well with the baby boom generation as well, and so the Stooges were able to attract audiences beyond their own era.

Part of the immense appeal of the Stooges was that they were a dysfunctional family. At one level, they simply acted out the way infantile children would — unencumbered by the rules of civilized life. They could physically respond when frustrated. This made them immensely popular, especially with children and males. They could break the rules and still be themselves. They were attacked from the outside, but they also attacked themselves from within. Indeed, the pathos of their act, sometimes difficult to see through the violence, lay exactly in this internal strife. Audiences recognized their own families, their own arguments, their own usually repressed desires to punch someone close.

They were also in the Laurel and Hardy tradition of being a male society, a fraternity that stuck together despite the fights. However daunting the task, however humiliating the failure, the Stooges left each film as they came in — as a team that would stick together.

The Stooges consciously worked at reflecting contemporary society. During the early years of the Great Depression they often played homeless people, then called "forgotten men." By 1935, with the economy slightly better, the Stooges sometimes had jobs. They often parodied other films and aspects of contemporary culture. The films also grew more inventive, especially after 1936. That is when the sound effects became more creative and the sight gags funnier.

The team faced crises. Curly's retirement was the first. A blood vessel broke in his head, making him unable to remember his lines. Then, in 1946, he had a stroke and was no longer able to work at all. He was heartbroken.

Jules White, the director of numerous Three Stooges films, came to visit Curly as he was recuperating. As White told the author James Neibaur, Curly was happy to see an old friend. They talked about studio gossip. Suddenly Curly grew very quiet. White recalled, "He looked up at me with a tear in his eye." Curly stared at the director and plaintively sighed, "I'm never going to make the children laugh again, am I Jules?"

Curly died in 1952 at the age of forty-eight, never to see the revival that started later that decade, a revival that would continue to make a new generation of children laugh.

Meanwhile, Moe seriously pondered ending their run but finally realized that they had to go on. He considered various actors as a replacement for Curly, including Buddy Hackett, but in the end decided that only Shemp could follow his brother. Shemp, who had had some success in films, was smart when he first replaced Curly in 1947's *Fright Night*: He purposely created his own character. He did not want to imitate Curly or try to take Curly's place because the audience would not have accepted that. Shemp was crucial to the group's future success because the

Stooges were masters of timing, and someone from outside the family would have had to spend months rehearsing before being able to be fully integrated into the team.

Any discussion of the Three Stooges has to address their violence. In one sense, of course, they were just following the classic traditions of physical comedy. In another sense, the Stooges used what comedic tools were available to them after the Hays Office and Production Code had stripped comedy of any sexual innuendo and limited the opportunity for satire. Comedy teams had to find a substitute for risqué humor. The Stooges used slapstick.

Most of the major studios had abandoned slapstick as early as the beginning of sound films. Sound had made movies seem more real, and the violence of slapstick became more troubling for some audiences. The punches and kicks were no longer substitutes for verbal insults but seemed like serious attempts to injure. Audiences wanted new kinds of films when sound became available. The slapstick done by the silent comedians was perceived as old-fashioned. This move from slapstick to verbal humor left lots of room for the Stooges; they essentially had the field to themselves.

Precisely because the audience wanted something new, the Stooges took the traditional ideas of slapstick and extended them, pushing the limits of violent comedy. The Stooges made their best films from 1938 to 1945, not an era when slapstick was widely admired.

In the early 1930s, Shemp had indirectly given the Stooges the idea of reviving the vaudeville tradition of eye gouges. Moe, Larry, and Shemp were playing cards, and suddenly Shemp got angry, stood up, and poked Larry in the eye. Moe was hysterical with laughter. The very next day, Moe tried it in a performance. He said, "Who's the manager of this act?" Each one walked toward him from either side, responding, "I am." Moe quickly raised his arms, two fingers extended, and pretended to poke them in the eyes. The audience loved it. The Stooges began to throw pies in 1936. The first bit of hair was pulled out in 1938.

To add to the mayhem, the Stooges created sound effects. A literal slapstick or whip would do for one of Moe's facial slaps, but the producers tried to make a sound like wind when a windup came before the slap. A cloth was ripped when hair was pulled. The plucking of ukulele strings accompanied a poke in the eye. The sound of a bird chirping followed a knockout; the "bird" was really whistling done by Jules White. Some of the sight gag violence was from vaudeville, such as slapping multiple faces, a technique Ted Healy had used. Others relied on well-planned sequences. The Stooges used name-calling creatively as well. Moe's insults included "half-brother to a weasel," "snoring hyena," "spotted raccoon," and "overstuffed bologna," as well as more common ones such as "knucklehead" and "nitwit." Often the verbal routines were overtures to physically violent conclusions.

The Stooges purposely limited their film production to shorts, which restricted the amount of violence that could take place. It was over in a few minutes, and it was normally cushioned between a cartoon and a longer feature. Actually, the amount of violence in cartoons far exceeded that in the Stooges' films. The Stooges were practically pacifists compared with many of the cartoon characters. Also, the Stooges limited the targets of assaults; they hurt each other or the wealthy and powerful, the bossy and annoying. By implication, they were not attacking the audience. Animals and children were treated well in the films. A society matron, on the other hand, was almost guaranteed to receive a pie in the face.

However controversial they were, the Stooges were popular in the 1940s across a wide variety of ages — unlike later, when they were marketed simply to the young. They received an enormous amount of fan mail, and theater owners demanded that the Three Stooges films accompany any new feature film from Columbia. All the Stooges' personal appearances were hugely popular events.✳

Although Columbia made an enormous amount of money from their films, Moe lived in perpetual fear that the studio would cancel their contract, which was re-newed year to year. Facing Columbia's tough-minded boss, Harry Cohn, they ac-cepted less money than they were worth.

Perhaps because of their fears, they worked very hard and kept costs down. Their films were often shot in three or four days. They used Columbia's lots rather than shooting on location, and they used stock footage. They didn't have access to well-known writers, or even to writers truly dedicated to them. Second-rate actors were often cast for the bit parts.

Given Columbia's stingy support of the Three Stooges' productions, their ultimate success is all the more impressive. Though they lacked full studio support and worked with severely limited budgets, the Three Stooges turned out films that not only survived but thrived, building an audience across generations. They became icons.

How did they do it when so many others failed?

First of all, they simply stayed together and kept working. Shemp remained with the team until his death in 1955, and then Joe Besser replaced him. They could continue, in part, because their style of comedy and the characters they created were so basic. The personalities were simple and clear, and the comedy always slapstick.

They had other strengths as well. They reduced friction within the team by splitting their income equally. They learned how to control their egos in a business where such mastery was rare. And maybe their relatively limited popularity early on contributed to their remaining together by not boosting their egos too much when they were young.

Columbia syndicated seventy-eight of their films to television in August 1958. By that time, such fame was not likely to inflate their egos beyond control.

But there were subtler factors, internal to the films, that aided their survivability. The Stooges had consistent personalities and motivations, making their Columbia movies fit well into syndication where the films were typically shown five times a week, a saturation that required such consistency for fans to get to know and like the characters. Their pace was very fast, and this sense that lots of stuff was happening all the time suited the tastes of the young baby boomers turning on televisions in 1958. The speed had another effect. People would miss lines or not catch nuances, and this encouraged repeated viewing, another factor crucial to syndication success.

It was also an era that had rediscovered the appeal of slapstick; physical comedy was making a comeback, as seen in the work of Jerry Lewis, for example. This occurred in part because the new generation felt out of place in a way comparable to their immigrant ancestors. They were living at a time when their emerging tastes in music, dress, and thought seemed foreign to their parents' world.

The Stooges greatly influenced many

young people who would grow up to become comedians and carry on their legacy. Stooge movements can be seen in the work of a wide variety of talented comedians, including the work of Michael Richards's Shemp-like character on *Seinfeld*.

Finally, another crucial factor in the Stooges' enormous success was that the families of the Three Stooges were especially skillful in preserving the team's legacy.

The Three Stooges were important for another reason, unique to them. That reason had less to do with comedy.

Any understanding of the Three Stooges' overall contribution to the movies must include the considerable bravery exhibited by the team from the late 1930s through the mid-1940s. The Howard brothers and Larry Fine were all Jewish. They watched in horror as the Nazis rose to power in Europe and anti-Semitism became more prominent in American society and in their own industry.

Starting in the 1930s, Jewish characters began to disappear from films. By 1933, even the minor Jewish characters were completely gone, though the stereotyped characters from other ethnic groups continued. Even the Marx Brothers were forced to remove their Yiddishisms and other overtly Jewish references.

Perhaps the mostly Jewish movie moguls removed Jewish characters so as not to provide ammunition for those who charged that Jewish interests overly influenced Hollywood. Perhaps the large corporations buying studios sought a homogenized product aimed at national audiences and so removed Jewish characters. Perhaps the studios, which by the mid-1930s were getting 30–40 percent of their gross revenues from foreign distribution, were worried about losing those rights in Germany and the rest of Europe. Unsurprisingly, the Nazis examined the content of all films they imported. The Hays Office applied intense pressure on studios to avoid any anti-Nazi propaganda films, and the State Department supported such a view.

American filmmakers and stars, including comedy stars, were reluctant, then, to address Nazi anti-Semitism. American audiences, eager to avoid war, did not want to see any film that might be interpreted as encouraging military confrontation overseas. With the Hays Office actively opposed, most stars simply avoided the issue.

There were a few brave souls, however. Warner Brothers released its semidocumentary *Confessions of a Nazi Spy* in September 1939, right after World War II began. There were, of course, several ways that Hollywood could have confronted the Nazis artistically. The documentary style was one, the dramatic story another. Still a third artistic method was satire: reducing the mythic power of Hitler by mocking him, his ideas, and his followers. Charlie Chaplin, for example, began filming *The Great Dictator*, his mockery of Hitler, in mid-September 1939.

The Three Stooges began filming *You Nazty Spy!* during the first week of December 1939. The film was released on January 19, 1940, nine months before Chaplin released his, although they surely knew of Chaplin's project, which was infamous in Hollywood because so many people had tried to talk him out of making the film.

In *You Nazty Spy!*, Moe Howard became the first actor to portray Adolf Hitler. The Stooges had earlier begun to smuggle the Yiddish of their childhood into their act. They found themselves going to 418 Meshugena Avenue, using the Yiddish word for crazy. They might use an insult like "Huck mir nisht a chynick, and I don't mean efsher." ("Leave me alone. Get off my back, and I don't mean maybe.") Those were all embedded in the dialogue or throwaway lines. It didn't matter if parts of the audience missed them.

But making *You Nazty Spy!* was an act of courage because they risked alienating their audience. The pugnacious Stooges wanted to puncture Hitler's image through satire. Moe Howard's daughter Joan Maurer later reported that the film remained one of Moe and Larry's favorites. They also wanted to make their satire as Jews: "Sholem aleichem" are the first collective words out of their mouths.

The film takes place in the Kingdom of Moronica where cabinet members are looking to keep power because "there's no money in peace." They want to find someone "stupid enough to do what we tell him." They choose Moe Hailstone, a paperhanger. As the cabinet members get to work on Moe, a black feather falls down and lands on his upper lip. The Hitler appearance is clear for all to see. Moe takes the job, declaring, "We must make our country safe for hypocrisy" and "Our motto shall be Moronica for Morons." He brings along Curly as Field Marshal Herring and Larry as the Minister of Propaganda. The three brutally rule Moronica until a mob chases them into a lion cage, where the lions seem satisfied with their forthcoming meal.

I'll Never Heil Again was released in July 1941, before the American entry into the war, and was a sequel to *You Nazty Spy!* Once again, the Stooges play dictators. The satire is more savage as Curly's Field Marshal Herring says to Moe's Moe Hailstone: "We bombed 56 hospitals, 85 schools, 42 kindergartens, 4 cemeteries, and other vital military objects." Hailstone is killed in the film by an exploding billiard ball, and the heads of the Stooges end up mounted on a wall — an extremely blunt attack on Hitler.

After the war began, the Stooges made a final anti-Nazi film. In *Back from the Front* (1943), the Stooges play merchant marines blown up because they mistook an unexploded bomb for a whale and charged at it. The ensuing blast causes them to take to a lifeboat. They eventually get on a Nazi warship, the S.S. *Shickelgruber* (Hitler's real family name). Moe disguises himself as Hitler. Again, their attack on Nazism is direct. When they first offer a salute to the officers, they say "Hang Hitler." Moe eventually orders the ship's officers to shoot themselves. Unfortunately, Moe sneezes, and his moustache comes flying off. The Nazis then chase the Stooges who, used to dealing with troublemakers, put grease on the ship's deck. The Nazi sailors swiftly slide into the sea.

The critics' indifference to the Three Stooges probably prevented their groundbreaking anti-Nazi films from becoming embroiled in controversy. That disdain and the fact that their audiences went largely for the laughs, not the message, allowed them to get away with making two anti-Nazi films before America entered the war.

For a variety of reasons, then, the Three Stooges hold a unique place in film comedy history. Those who cringe at the violence should look beyond it to appreciate the clever use of language and the biting and sometimes downright courageous satire. Those who see only the laughs should look beyond the humor to recognize an enduringly loyal team that produced a wide range of films, many of which concealed pointed social satire behind their physical comedy.

Their allure and their staying power lay precisely in the seeming contradiction of using high and low art without ever acknowledging either as extraordinary or anything other than just fun.

ELEVEN

"THE PLAYBOY AND THE PUTZ"

Martin and Lewis

Jerry Lewis was desperate. He had been booked into the 500 Club in Atlantic City at $150 a week, money he desperately needed for his family. Lewis was doing the act he'd been performing since he was thirteen: comic pantomime as a record played. There was also a singer on the program, someone whose talent the club's managers loudly mocked.

What happened next is a matter of dispute. The singer left the show, either because of illness or because he was fired. Skinny D'Amato, who managed the club with Irvin Wolf, approached Lewis and told the struggling comedian he was also going to be let go. Lewis told D'Amato that Dean Martin — a singer D'Amato and Wolf wanted to book — would come as a favor to Jerry, and that they did hilarious material together.

Depending on the story, either D'Amato or Lewis then called Martin's manager, Lou Perry, pleading to have Martin appear. Feeling sorry for Lewis, Perry accepted a $500 weekly salary for Martin if the club kept Lewis. Martin was then regularly commanding up to $1,000 a week, so D'Amato and Wolf were very pleased.

Martin showed up for his first performance and sang five songs. Lewis then did his comedy. Skinny D'Amato liked the singing fine, still didn't like the comedy, but mostly he was angry because Lewis had told him that the two performers did such knee-slapping material together. He called them into his office.

D'Amato stared calmly at the two performers. He was a good-looking man who always had a cigarette in his mouth, closing one eye every time he took a drag. He had perfected the ability to spin a matchbook on its corners and liked to impress people by demonstrating this talent. But he wasn't out to impress Martin and Lewis. Instead, he gave Lewis an ultimatum: Either the next show had the funny material, or Jerry Lewis would no longer be working at the club.

It was July 25, 1946. The next show was in several hours at 12:30 a.m. Worried, Lewis retreated to the dressing room. He wrote some material on greasy paper that had been the wrapping for the pastrami sandwiches the two had eaten earlier. He and Martin rehearsed in the alleyway, though both knew there would have to be a lot of spontaneity and playing off the crowd. Lewis's idea, drawn from his performances at resort hotels in the Catskills, which he dubbed "the Playboy and the

Putz," was ingenious: While the suave, handsome Martin was singing, a gawky Lewis would pretend to be an inept busboy.

They began their show. Martin sang and then along came the "busboy." Lewis dropped dishes. Martin just kept singing, pretending to ignore the interruption. Lewis put on comic teeth. He pounded drums. He took the orchestra leader's baton and pretended to lead the musicians with a shoe. And then he burned their music. He turned out all the lights. This, of course, led to waiters involuntarily dropping dishes.

The audience kept laughing. Lewis started his record act, but now Martin interrupted by squirting seltzer in his mouth. Lewis picked up some celery and smacked Martin across his expensive, surgically re-shaped nose. Martin ad-libbed, "Be careful of my new nose. The doctor didn't guarantee it against celery." They even had a few standard jokes (Dean: "Did you take a bath this morning?" Jerry: "Why, is there one missing?"), but most of the time on-stage was spent mugging and clowning.

Quickly deciding to expand the mayhem, Lewis ran over to a patron's table, grabbed a plate filled with steak and dropped it to the floor. Martin jumped in. He took a sip from a passing martini glass, coughed as though the martini had been laced with poison, and then threw the rest of the martini into a customer's face.

The entire club suddenly grew silent. No one had ever seen such an act, such outrageous behavior. Skinny D'Amato stood fuming in the corner.

And suddenly there was a response, and not from just anyone. The great singing and comedy star Sophie Tucker let out with a full-throated laugh. She had been booked in the back room and had wandered over to see the newcomers.

Sophie Tucker's laugh of approval was all the crowd needed. Suddenly the laughs were punctuated by cries of "More, more." Lewis quickly looked at D'Amato, who, no doubt shocked that the audience tolerated this mayhem, cautiously nodded.

Martin and Lewis were off and running. They started grabbing trays. Older women had to guard the front of their blouses from soda attacks. Customers joined in a conga line. They sat on the floor and sang songs. Steaks flew across the club.

Martin and Lewis were literally an overnight sensation. Skinny D'Amato had to arrange for the new team to do six shows a night. Their success never faltered for the exactly ten years to the day that they were partners.

Martin and Lewis had found a perfect venue in the nightclub — a combination bar, restaurant, and theater. Nightclubs had begun in hotels in 1918, after the end of World War I. American soldiers had seen shows in Paris and been impressed. In 1920, with the passage of Prohibition, thousands of speakeasies sprang up to supply illicit liquor (estimates range from 30,000 to 100,000 in New York alone). The fierce competition among these businesses led some of them to offer entertainment as a way to lure customers. Music, attractive women, and comics were the big attractions. The Great Depression hit these places hard — except in Hollywood, where clubs remained very popular. This was crucial because Hollywood made the clubs famous by putting them in movies beginning in the 1930s. By the 1940s, after Prohibition's end in 1933 and the emergence from economic depression and war, nightclubs were a major venue for comedians. The wealthy and powerful loved to go to the clubs, where they could dress up and go out for the evening while mingling with other wealthy and powerful people and famous entertainers. The nightclubs remained influential venues until the emergence of television, and it was in such clubs that Martin and Lewis became stars.

Jerry Lewis was a performer almost from birth. When Lewis was only six, his father, Danny, took him onstage for a fireman's benefit performance. Lewis sang "Brother, Can You Spare a Dime?" but when he was supposed to take a bow he accidentally stepped on a light. The audience laughed. Lewis even then realized that he liked the laughter more than the applause. Often left by his parents with his grandmother, he learned to playact with her. She was infinitely supportive of his clowning, but Lewis desperately missed his parents. He once explained to comedian and writer Larry Wilde how this aspect of his life affected his career choice: "An audience is nothing more than eight or nine thousand mamas and papas clapping their hands and saying 'Good boy, baby.' You'll find that people that had enough 'Good boy, baby' from their parents rarely turn to comedy. Those are our doctors and lawyers."

Lewis started as a busboy at Brown's Hotel in the Catskills, where he learned to do whatever it took to get a laugh. He gave an impromptu performance mimicking records. An ex-comedian (working as a bellboy at the hotel) named Irving Kaye asked to manage him and was able to get Lewis several bookings. Oddly, Lewis — later to become the famous loudmouth — didn't talk in the act. Eventually, he did become a master of ceremonies, but he had difficulty finding audiences that could grasp his humor.

He often ran into Dean Martin as they both struggled for recognition. One night at the Club Havana–Madrid, Lewis spontaneously got up and stood behind the performing Martin and mimicked him. The audience loved it, but the two performers didn't yet see themselves as a team. That would occur later at the 500 Club, when the real Jerry Lewis character was born as he teamed with Martin.

That character, a schlemiel from the Catskills, was endlessly in motion, a Rube Goldberg device with a laugh track. He had a face that was not vulnerable like Harpo's but equally eager for mischief. He had a voice perched precariously on the border between childhood and adolescence. His character was a nine-year-old determined to make adults pay attention to him. As Lewis told Graham Fuller in the April 1995 issue of *Interview,* "On my ninth birthday, I never had another birthday after that."

His movements have often been called awkward, or worse. For some, his twitching body and pratfalls, his oozing need to please and be loved, were repellant. He did sometimes seem to have no self-control. But his performances were clever. He somehow found a way to translate the childlike emotions of messing up and causing chaos into elaborate pantomimes accompanied by a high-pitched voice to give them a verbal dimension. His response to pressure was precisely that of an agitated child: go crazy. Lewis freed the inner hysteria of the age, this energy that had been tied down by the restraints of necessity and which was bouncing around like a pinball. Jerry Lewis's physical movements represented the inner turmoil of the postwar world, and his sophisticated early audiences reacted because he gave them precisely the sort of emotional release they needed. Abbott and Costello and Hope and Crosby brought memories of the war when people wanted to be reassured that there was a new world, a new beginning. Jerry Lewis — fresh, young, and novel — was that promise.

Lewis had an almost complete lack of inhibition. He smothered the normal social censors inside himself. He knew precisely the inhibitions he needed to lose to surprise, shock, and ultimately make his audience laugh. That was his real talent. He was a psychologist as well as an actor. The actor was able to summon up the nine-year-old, and the psychologist knew the audience so well that he could direct the kid on how to behave.

Lewis also knew how to summon pathos. He seemed lonely, isolated, deeply in need of approval and love. This was authentic because it was rooted in Lewis's own life. Had the character simply been a nuisance, as some saw him, he would have worn less well with audiences. But he was a sad clown, a funnyman whose pathos and anguish rendered him sympathetic.

When he performed a bit of nonsense, audiences laughed not only at the act itself but also from some deep-seated sympathy for the kid inside getting even for those who had hurt him so deeply. They were laughing at themselves too, recognizing Lewis's insecurities and foibles all too well, regressing to their own childhoods. Additionally, they were symbolically getting revenge on all those who had hurt them in their childhood. Lewis satisfied the craving in every sober postwar adult to squirt a seltzer bottle at a hapless victim. Lewis understood that audiences don't often really laugh at the subject of the humor so much as the emotion it expresses.

Dean Martin's handsome lover character, the nonchalant drunk, the friendly celebrant, hid his quick mind. Martin accepted Lewis; the normal, attractive man embracing the weird behavior of a crazy younger sibling gave an emotional prompt to the audience to join in the fun and accept it as well. If he liked the kid, we should too.

Dean Martin, ten years older, was also smart about the billing. They were in a car, trying to decide whether to call themselves Martin and Lewis or Lewis and Martin.

Martin said, "Let's not have an argument. Let's just call it Martin and Lewis because it's alphabetically right."

Jerry Lewis may have had some traumatic memories from school — such as being publicly humiliated when he was retained a grade — but he knew that "M" didn't come before "L."

Martin had an answer though: "D comes before J."

Martin's age and the fact that he had been in the business much longer made

Lewis realize the arrangement was appropriate. Martin did eventually make an important concession though. Initially, he had taken a higher percentage of the weekly salary, but he now agreed to an even split.

Although Martin loved to sing, he was frustrated because while singers could evoke a wide range of emotions, they generally sought to avoid having audiences laugh at them. Martin needed an outlet for his ready wit, just as Lewis needed a solid partner, an adult figure, to play against. Martin replaced the lifeless phonograph records in Lewis's act and, in so doing, ironically gave Lewis a voice.

The contrast in characters was crucial. Martin was George Burns with a handsome face and a good voice, an easygoing Bud Abbott with a soothing personality. His was a boozy, late-night club reality. Lewis mocked that reality along with any other.

The two performers obviously loved to work together, which greatly improved their act. Dean Martin and Jerry Lewis actually made team history as the first pair to face each other rather than the audience. This encouraged the audience to perceive them as emotionally close to each other.

Of course, performers live by George Burns's famous dictum: "Sincerity is everything. If you can fake that, you've got it made." Some performers indeed did learn to fake their friendship during the act, only to sulk in lonely silence afterward. For their club years, at least, Martin and Lewis's mutual attraction was genuine. Of course they needed each other, but the need was not just based on financial considerations; it was emotional as well, especially for Lewis, who saw in Martin the older brother he never had. This bond of friendship made the audience want to join in the fun they were having together and gave Martin and Lewis an energy unavailable to the merely professional performer.

Martin and Lewis were reckless on stage. They definitely were not the stock, rehearsed characters audiences were used to, but wildly funny clowns. They dragged the band members and audience into the act, obliterating the wall between performer and audience. Their very randomness was a crucial part of their charm. People thought the pair were making it up, and in many cases, they were.

Their cleverness lay in their ability to be men behaving like boys. Martin was charismatic and seductive. Lewis often mocked his own looks, sometimes comparing himself to a monkey and contrasting himself unfavorably to Martin. When they started, Lewis was twenty, six feet tall, but only 130 pounds, with a beanpole appearance, crew cut, rubber-like face, and squeaky voice. But, in fact, both were good-looking. Women in the audience loved Dean Martin, but they also found Lewis lovable. They were slapstick with sex appeal.

Their humor included not just the zaniness of the Marx Brothers, or the smooth interplay of Abbott and Costello, but — drawing on the style crafted by Hope and Crosby — a genuine sexuality. They were, in that sense, cultural prophets, hinting at the sexual revolution fomenting in the collective, but still adolescent, libidos of the baby boomers.

Their movie career began when Hal Wallis brought them to Hollywood. After their introduction to audiences through two *My Friend Irma* films, they became headliners in *At War with the Army*. The movie is important because it defined the pattern of their relationship in many future films. Lewis was the nudnik who found himself in incredible situations — a Coke machine won't stop dispensing bottles, for example. Martin was the handsome ladies' man, using songs as his weapon of seduction. Also, he was a sergeant, a step above Lewis, as he would be in other films. He was the authority figure with a maturity that included interest — intense interest — in women. As Martin and Lewis films continually grossed great sums — incredibly, none of their films ever grossed under $5 million — Wallis wanted the scripts to focus more and more on Lewis. Whereas in nightclubs both told jokes and they swapped comic–straight man roles, in films, more and more, Martin became just a singer and Lewis became the sole funnyman. This deterioration of their act contributed considerably to their breakup. Lewis was attractive to children, whereas Martin and Lewis weren't; but Martin and Lewis were attractive to adults in a way that Lewis by himself was not.

The films were generally regarded by critics as incapable of capturing the magic of Martin and Lewis live. They did sometimes try to re-create the nightclub setting, such as in their second film *My Friend Irma Goes West*, but a film by nature is not spontaneous. They could never capture that live experience in film, though they came close on their radio shows and on their Colgate television program, especially when they ad-libbed or there was a mistake.

Another factor that contributed to their eventual breakup was Martin's remarriage. In particular, Dean's new wife told him that he didn't need the kid to be funny or accepted, that in fact his career was being stifled.

The breakup was foreshadowed at the release of the 1955 film *You're Never Too Young*. The movie was supposed to premiere at Brown's Hotel, where Lewis had started out. All was arranged, but no one had asked Martin if he would agree to be there. He decided instead to go to Hawaii. A deeply embarrassed and hurt Lewis thanked reporters for not asking about Martin's absence.

Lewis's increasing importance in the films and emerging interest in all aspects of filmmaking combined to make Martin feel more and more marginal. He couldn't understand why Lewis had to try to be another Chaplin instead of being content as a comedian. Martin also felt that his comedic talents would never be fully appreciated if he was constantly being pushed out of the spotlight, in deference to Lewis's need to be the funny one.

The breaking point came in 1956 when

Martin saw the script for their new film *The Delicate Delinquent*. Martin had been cast as a uniformed police officer, but he didn't want to play the part. Lewis coolly replied, "We'll have to get somebody else," and Martin, no stranger to coolness himself, said, "Start looking, boy."

The end came at the Copacabana ten years to the day after their first performance at the 500 Club. Jack Benny, Eddie Cantor, Milton Berle, Sammy Davis Jr., Jackie Gleason, and many other stars attended their last show. Martin and Lewis were onstage for over an hour. Their movie *Pardners* was opening the next day, and so they sang the title song. They hugged, and then they separated. Lewis went back to his dressing room, feeling numb and shaking. He began to cry and suddenly felt a deep uncertainty about whether he could perform alone. Lewis called his wife, crying. Then he called Martin, who said, "Hey, pally. How are ya holding up?"

Lewis said, "I don't know yet. I just want to say . . . we've had some good times, Paul." Paul was Martin's middle name, and Lewis sometimes used it when he felt especially close to his now ex-partner.

"There'll be more."

"Yeah . . . well . . . take care of yourself."

"You too, pardner."

Then the two wished each other luck and said their final good-bye. But the hurt and pain were deep. The success each found alone tasted sweet, so there was no push to reunite. They didn't perform together onstage until Frank Sinatra brought them together for a muscular dystrophy telethon in 1976.

Their act may have ended, but their impact lingered. Lewis trained a generation of baby boomers to give full vent to their emotions. He turned out to be a spectacular teacher. They laughed at his mugging and his bodily contortions, but they mostly absorbed his chutzpah, his insistence on letting his feelings be known without concern for social conventions.

Of course, Martin and Lewis had imitators. After all, their act had seemed so easy: Take a nut and a nice-looking singer, mix together, let them go wild, and success and money would follow. One young man named Sammy Petrillo looked a bit like Lewis, and so Petrillo hired Duke Mitchell, had Mitchell's hair cut to look like Martin's, and began an imitation act. Petrillo was far better at being Lewis than Mitchell was at being Martin. The level of their success can be judged by the fact that they were teamed with an aging actor from monster movies in the happily forgettable *Bela Lugosi Meets a Brooklyn Gorilla.*

As it turned out, Martin and Lewis had no successful imitators at all. They were the last spectacularly successful classic comedy team, the last ones to make major movies together as partners, to perform in clubs and on radio and on television. There would be other teams, other types of teams, but there would never again be a team that conquered all the audiences of film, stage, radio, and television. They were heroically successful, and though they were the end of the line, the tradition would soon branch out into different forms.

TWELVE

"HELLOOOO, BALL"

Comedy Teams of the 1950s

One reason for the disappearance of classic comedy teams was that they were simply running out of new material.

There were other teams in the 1950s, but they did not achieve the level of success of Martin and Lewis. For example, one popular team emerged from a series of "Bowery Boys" films (forty-eight in all), which featured a gang of adolescent delinquents and social outcasts searching for trouble as the "Dead End Kids." The original cast came from the Broadway play and then the Samuel Goldwyn film. Because of what he saw as their incorrigible behavior (they kept calling him "Pop" and complained about not being allowed to go swimming), Goldwyn fired them, and they went over to Warner Brothers to make seven "Dead End Kids" movies, again showing their tough side. They made other series as well, including the "East Side Kids" films, and it was in the East Side comedies that the formula began to change. Most of the films were still serious, but there were increasing elements of comic relief. Over time, the comic interplay grew between the two main characters, Slip Mahoney, played by Leo Gorcey, and Horace Dubussy Jones, more affectionately known as Sach, played by Huntz

Hall. More and more humor was added until it was the predominant element of the films. Young Gorcey had developed a great ability to mug and to speak with appropriately urban malapropisms. He was a comic caricature of a criminal, learned from working with those types in other films. James Cagney had slapped him for ad-libbing during the filming of *Angels with Dirty Faces.* Gorcey was deeply influenced by Edward G. Robinson, and even his most comic turns retain that tough-guy core.

His work with Hall, though, was always the highlight of the pictures. Sach was childlike, somewhat of a dimwit, but he could see what Gorcey, as "the Chief," overlooked. This was, of course, familiar comic territory. The Chief-Sach relationship paralleled the Laurel and Hardy relationship, in which one member of the team thought he was smarter than the other member but wasn't. Also like Laurel and Hardy, Gorcey and Hall were a comic-comic team rather than a straight man–comic team. Sach was the child constantly duped by a domineering partner. Like Bud Abbott, Slip was allergic to real work but quick with a con game. And like all the two-man teams, there was a close male bond between the two. The Bowery Boys were something like the Little Rascals grown up and still trying to entertain themselves.

The life of the Bowery Boys was attractive to its young audience. After all, they got by in life without undertaking any real responsibilities. They didn't age or marry. They hung out in a soda shop run by a character named Louie — played by Leo Gorcey's real-life father, Bernard — where they ran up an ever-growing tab from their overindulgence in banana splits. (As a clever inside joke, the writers actually made the tab get larger as the series progressed.) Louie's role in the ensemble was the straight man, trying to control the wild antics of the gang, but sputtering in exasperation, as though the straight man realized that the gang's anarchic spirit could not be put into one of his shop's seltzer bottles.

His failure as a straight man symbolized in a way what was happening to team comedy: The straight man's center could not hold, as evidenced by the separation of Martin and Lewis in 1956 and of Abbott and Costello in 1957.

There were other members in the gang comedy, but the ensemble possibilities were never as fully realized as the Gorcey-

Hall teaming. In the end, Gorcey's increasing inability to maintain self-control led to his departure, and the charm of the movies ended.

Radio comedy also remained popular for a while in the 1950s. Most of the radio comedians eventually either abandoned that medium or simultaneously appeared on television. There was, however, one significant team from the 1950s that owed its success to radio. Indeed, although they were successful elsewhere, their genius seemed built for radio.

Bob and Ray had an elusive, almost surreal comedy style that very gently mocked the smaller aspects of life. They created dozens of fascinating characters such as Tex, a drawling cowboy, and Wally Ballou, a completely inept reporter who would forget to turn on his microphone and so would begin in mid-sentence. Naturally, his wife was named Hulla Ballou, and it didn't surprise anyone that his son was named Little Boy Ballou.

They could also be serious, such as when they created the character of Commissioner Carstairs to satirize Senator Joseph McCarthy, at a time when others in the media were, mostly out of fear, treating him with respect.

Bob Elliott and Ray Goulding began work at a Boston radio station in 1946 — Bob as the host of a talk and music show and Ray as the announcer. They experimented with different voices and developed trademark elements of their partnership, such as the sign-off: "This is Ray Goulding reminding you to write if you get work . . . And Bob Elliott reminding you to hang by your thumbs." They also created bizarre "commercials," such as this one for sweaters: "We have two styles: turtle or V-neck. State what kind of neck you have."

In 1953 they landed a network radio show, which ran on Saturday nights at 8:00 and then Mondays through Fridays at 5:00 p.m. They were especially adept at mocking popular culture and their own medium. Bob, interviewing Ray, might suddenly say, "You don't have to smile all the time. This is radio."

Given their penchant for spoofing ads, with a light satirical touch, it's not surprising that Piel's beer hired them to do a funny commercial. Playing Bert and Harry Piel, the two developed commercials that became a national sensation.

But Bob and Ray were at the end of the great era of radio comedy. Now television was the realm of the new comedy successes, and the television age coincided with the immense post–World War II changes in American life.

Buoyant with victory in the war, made bold by youth and a thriving economy, the veterans returned home eager to settle down, marry, and start a family. The baby boom that started in January 1946 led to a desperate need for new housing. Concerned about urban life and armed with G.I. loans, parents headed for the lush paradise they supposed lay just over the rainbow in suburbia. Their young children, they knew, would be safer there and would be educated by gifted teachers in new schools. Between 1946 and 1962, 23 million new homes were built in America, two-thirds of them in new suburban subdivisions.

Along with new homes, Americans needed new refrigerators and stoves and furniture. They needed paved roads and gas stations for their dutifully washed and waxed cars to get to and from this Eden. Americans, drunk with hope and driven to consume, thought they had found the Promised Land.

But this Norman Rockwell America soon revealed a darker underside. The women staying home to raise their 2.1 children realized that their sparkling new homes could also be velvet prisons. Accustomed to the independence they experienced in the workplace and in the armed services during the war, women were now largely confined to their homes and neighborhoods. Seeing the attractive appliances on television or in a neighbor's house, they bought new goods on installment plans, incurring ever-growing household debt. The marketplace offered so many new goods to buy. In 1928, the average American grocery store stocked 870 different items. By 1952, the grocery stores carried approximately 4,000 different items.

Suburban women had other problems as well. Their children were not as compliant as they were supposed to be. Their husbands complained of crowded commutes, ruthless gray-flanneled and coldhearted co-workers, and uncontrollable spending. There was a fear of economic sliding and being forced to return to the urban centers they had so recently escaped. This fear drove an increasing number of women to get a job they didn't necessarily want. In 1950, 21.6 percent of wives worked outside the home. By 1960, the number had risen to 30.5 percent. Families needed the money to pay for the homes and buy the goods.

And one of the household items they treasured most, and which alleviated the new suburban anxieties, was that incredible new invention, that radio with pictures, television.

At first, when televisions were scarce, people gathered in bars or in a fortunate neighbor's house, sitting in front of the small box, gazing at the black-and-white images. Soon viewers wanted to have their own set.

In 1950, only 9 percent of American homes had a television set; by 1955, 64.5 percent had one. By 1958, more than 45 million American households had televisions. Television became the entertainment of choice. Radio listening, at least in the evening, plummeted. In 1948, radio listeners tuned in for an average of 5.20 hours a day. By 1953, radio listening (in homes with televisions) had dropped to 1.71 hours a day, while in those same homes people watched television 5.76 hours a day. By the mid-1950s, children spent more time watching television each week than they spent in school.

The reasons for the rapid switch from radio to television may seem obvious, but it should be noted that at the time there were people who were not entirely convinced television was the better choice. After all, listeners enjoying their favorite radio programs could engage in other activities; they might do homework or housework, read or talk. Television, in contrast, seemed to demand their full attention, a bit like the movies, although people spent only a few hours a week at the movies, though movie attendance was declining, too. In 1946, 4.1 billion movie tickets were sold. By 1954, that number was down to 2.3 billion, and by 1962, it had dropped to 1.1 billion. Of course, there were social and economic factors other than television purchases that might have explained the decline in movie attendance, but television was becoming the dominant medium, the one that entertained virtually all Americans. It shaped culture in the 1950s.

Television, the magic box, seemed to be the perfect medium for its era. It brought stars, and comedy, and tears, and thrills into the safe environment of the home. Exhausted fathers came home from work and stared at the screen until its soothing pictures released the tensions. Young children could stare at it for so long and so devotedly that parents used television as an electronic baby-sitter. At night, unified families gathered around the single set.

Television also unwittingly delivered messages into the home. It fed national fears by presenting chilling news about the Cold War and the atomic bomb. It made Elvis Presley's unstoppable hips, mesmerizing sneer, and rhythmic music immensely popular. Though it was much less clear in the mid-1950s than it would be a decade later, rock 'n' roll was rehearsing to shake a whole generation.

Television also changed viewers. They stayed up later to keep watching and so got less sleep. They ate precooked "TV dinners" on small tables in front of their sets. They spent more time sitting and less time exercising.

Americans loved the parade of shows. They loved to laugh, and the sponsors and producers, on the hunt for the mass audience that would generate the most profit, turned to familiar faces. There were some comedy teams that survived and thrived on television.

George Burns and Gracie Allen's television show debuted in October 1950. The writers and Burns focused on Gracie's zany character. Audiences, forever in love with Gracie's charm and taken with

Burns's gravel-voiced asides, embraced the new show.

Burns loved playing in front of a live audience, but television was more difficult for him. In radio, he had left the scripts almost entirely to the writers, but in television he found that he had to work with them more. On television, writers had to work within the limits of sets and realistic situations, whereas in radio the audience's imagination allowed much more in the way of fantastic material. It's no wonder that the great comedian Ed Wynn complained that "television is the glass furnace," burning bits and actors up in a way that all could see.

George Burns may have thrived, but Gracie, who had long wanted to retire, was much less comfortable in the new medium. The necessity of memorizing her complex lines, live television's intolerance of mistakes, and the demand that she be perfectly dressed and made up tormented her until she finally fled in 1958, no longer able to continue, despite George's pleas. Gracie died of a heart attack in 1964 at the age of sixty-nine.

Amos 'n' Andy also ventured onto television. The creators tried to avoid the radio controversy by using exclusively African

American actors. Audiences embraced the characters of Kingfish, Andy, Amos, Sapphire, Lightnin', and Algonquin J. Calhoun all over again. Ratings were good for the two years (1951–1953) that the show aired. After it left the CBS network, the show was broadcast frequently and successfully on local stations. In 1963, as the civil rights movement was gaining prominent national attention in America, CBS announced that the show had been sold to networks in two African countries. However, one of them, Kenya, decided to ban it. Suddenly, there was new life to what had been intermittent protests. By 1966, after a series of complaints, CBS decided to withdraw the program entirely.

The debate was never settled, even within the African American community. The issue remained the same as when the show had aired on radio: Although the show featured many black professionals, it also included black stereotypes. The arguments echo on.

Some classic comedy teams, such as Abbott and Costello and Martin and Lewis, were also successful on television, but generally television instigated an important shift. A new hybrid was created: the temporary team. Two performers teamed together for a specific comedy series, but they weren't necessarily close associates, and they didn't perform together outside the show. These "television teams" were not true comedy teams in the traditional sense, but they were the inheritors of the comedy team tradition nonetheless.

Although classic teams were disappearing, American audiences continued to be attracted to comedy friendships, and television created new formats to house them: the variety show and the thirty-minute situation comedy.

Sid Caesar and Imogene Coca were the first of these new television teams. Caesar started his comedy career as a child in his father's restaurant, imitating the various languages spoken by customers. After some musical work in the Catskills, Caesar tried his adept hand at comedy. He enlisted in the Coast Guard and had a comic part in a Coast Guard musical, *Tars and Spars*, which toured the country. That show had a civilian director named Max Liebman, a man who would play a crucial role in the development of Caesar's television programs.

Liebman produced the *Admiral Broadway Revue*, Caesar's first television variety show, and the first one to have a permanent cast and staff. Imogene Coca was in the cast of the show, which lasted for only nineteen weeks. It was cancelled because it was too successful; the sponsor of the show sold so many televisions that they needed to withdraw advertising money to pay for the production of the newly ordered sets.

Imogene Coca, daughter of a Spanish orchestra conductor and an Irish dancer and actress, took piano lessons at age five, singing lessons at six, and dancing lessons at seven. Her father got her small parts in various theatrical productions until she reached Broadway at age fifteen.

Her big break came when she and her partner, Leonard Sillman, were rehearsing for a 1934 production of a show called *New Faces*. During a break, the diminutive Coca, shivering in the cold theater, borrowed a large polo coat. She noticed how ridiculous she looked in the oversize coat, and in fun, she began pretending to do a fan dance. Sillman saw her joking around and decided to include the bit in the show. It made her a star.

By 1939, she had a stage hit in *Straw Hat Revue*. A director of a theater in Pennsylvania had brought the show to Broadway. He was Max Liebman.

Liebman got the idea of pairing Coca with Caesar when Coca and her husband showed Liebman a pantomime they did together. Liebman liked it, but he wanted her to do it with Caesar. She was too shy to disagree, but she thought she would have to show Caesar how to do the pantomime. Indeed, she later recalled Caesar being suspicious of her at rehearsal because it was her material. The skit, about a woman who is trying to kill herself and the man who tries to save her but almost goes over the edge of the roof himself, was so intriguing to Caesar that he asked his writers to do other skits for the two of them.

Your Show of Shows, Caesar and Coca's next program, made them television superstars. Lasting from 1950 through 1954, the ensemble variety show included brilliant satires and clever parodies written by the greatest writing team in television history, which included Woody Allen, Mel Brooks, Larry Gelbart, Carl Reiner, and brothers Danny and Neil Simon. Together, the creators and stars of the show cleverly ridiculed and mocked human vices and weaknesses, holding an all-too-accurate mirror up to the audience.

Although Caesar appeared with other actors on the show, and Coca sometimes performed without Caesar, their pairings were always a highlight. Like any great team, each one sensed what the other was going to do. They were an immediate sight gag because of the difference in their sizes. Caesar was tall and broad while Coca much shorter and wafer thin. Caesar dominated the screen. He needed someone who could seem to accept the dominance so that there would not be unintentional conflict, but someone who, in that acceptance, maintained dignity and radiated poignancy. Though later programs had other, more physically attractive and highly talented counterpoints to Caesar, none could match Coca's emotional depth or her clownlike pathos.

Additionally, Caesar was a method actor, a man who became immersed in his characters. There was no emotional distance. This approach was crucial for him. He didn't believe in a chain of one-liners. He, like all the great comedians, focused on delivery and character. This not only reflected Caesar's strongly held views about comedy but also was crucial in maintaining his comic distinctiveness. Other comics could steal gags, but no one could steal Caesar's characters or his style.

Coca, unlike Caesar, always kept a self

that was separate from the character. Her maintenance of that distance relieved some of Caesar's intensity for the audience but also magnified its brilliance by providing a contrast. With her impish grin and large eyes and her ability to seem joyous one moment and desolate the next, Coca was a perfect comedic foil for Caesar, a fact reflected in the show's soaring ratings.

The show — incredibly — was performed live for ninety minutes each week. Making mistakes and missing lines were the usual drawbacks to a live show, but all the performers were extraordinarily quick-witted and their ad-libs and cover-ups were part of the charm of the performance. Also, broadcasting live gave the show the crucial advantage of being able to talk about what was currently on people's minds. It could make fun of a recent foreign movie or the latest trend in marriage. It could not, however, engage in overtly political satire because of network fears of being branded as left-wing. It was, after all, the McCarthy era, when viewers' ears were attuned to hear whatever hinted at subversive themes. Given the brilliance of the staff and, of course, of Caesar and Coca, this was a staggering loss because the show was so on-target in other areas of American life that a political satire surely would have been both hilarious and salutary.

Their satiric voice, though, was not to be denied. Caesar was prevented from turning the show's brilliant writing minds loose on politics, so he and Coca instead focused their enormous acting talents on a study of the dark side of American marriage.

They became famous for their ongoing skits as "the Hickenloopers." So convincing was their portrayal of a sparring married couple that many viewers believed Caesar and Coca were actually married. In the skits, Coca played Doris, who wanted to improve the couple's social standing. Her desire was ferocious and relentless. Caesar, as Charlie, was content to maintain their current existence and to lead an ordinary life. Doris was combative in her assessment of Charlie:

Coca: You know what the trouble is with you? You have no spirit of adventure. Didn't you ever try something new, strange, unusual, a little off the beaten path, something a little weird, something you thought you'd never have anything to do with?

Caesar: [Looking directly at her] Once.

They have small disagreements that slowly grow into ferocious verbal warfare. Poor Charlie is made to suffer as Doris vainly makes various attempts to improve him. He goes to the theater, or a French restaurant for dinner, complaining all the while. At a symphony concert, for example, Coca, as Doris, tries her best to educate him:

Coca: Oh, look. In the second half of the program, they're playing Tchaikovsky's Pathetic Symphony. Tchaikovsky had a very pathetic life, you know. When you hear his music, you actually feel all the pain and agony and torture and misery.

Caesar: I got my own aggravation. I don't have to come here and listen to his torture.

Coca: You'll enjoy this. Look . . . the musicians are taking their places.

Caesar: [Listening] He must've had a miserable life.

Coca: They're just tuning up.

The Hickenloopers don't have a very happy marital life. Charles doesn't like her cooking ("Who boils bread?") or the fact that she had to have her own way:

> Caesar: You and your stubbornness. Stubborn, stubborn, stubborn. Why don't you apologize?
> Coca: You apologize.
> Caesar: I should apologize? For what? What?
> Coca: You know.
> Caesar: I'll never apologize for that.
> Coca: I think it's absolutely ridiculous for two grown-up people to act like children. Let's talk it over, discuss the whole thing from your point of view, look at the situation like adult people, and then we'll find out that I've been right all the time.

Charlie's summary of their marriage is telling: "You know what, Doris? I'm for you. You're for me. But we're not for each other."

There must have been a lot of nods or silent agreement among audience members. Caesar and Coca had tapped into the dark underside of American marriage. Their satire was so brilliant because it had located what the culture kept trying to hide, and that made it invaluable for the audience. As Caesar said about the sketches,

"We showed couples how they felt, that they weren't alone, and just how ridiculous they could be . . . Believability was critical. If they didn't believe us, they wouldn't care."

Caesar and Coca were both essentially loners and didn't see each other socially away from the set. Even at lunchtime, Caesar tended to go with his writers and she with the dancers.

Your Show of Shows and later Caesar programs, such as *Caesar's Hour*, were among the greatest variety shows, though the genre would soon be eclipsed by situation comedies, which were more profitable and easier to produce.

Situation comedies assembled a cast that continued week to week, and the situations, based on the characters created, formed the basis of the humor. Almost all situation comedies came from farce, with an improbable plot, exaggerated characters, and moments of slapstick.

A full history of situation comedies would be needed to trace how team comedy influenced American television since the 1950s. Alternatively, it is useful to find the models for television situation comedy and identify in them the spirit of comedy teams. Jackie Gleason and Lucille

Ball were two vital figures in the emergence of television situation comedy and the new television teams that would soon replace the classic teams.

Although Caesar and Coca had frequently focused on marital conflict as the basis of comedy, the subject was most deeply mined by Jackie Gleason in *The Honeymooners.* He found a perfect foil in Audrey Meadows, who played his character's long-suffering wife. He found a buddy with whom to have adventures, and it was the buddy teaming that came to be even more comically interesting than the marital teaming.

In September 1951, Gleason arrived to meet the production team for his show *Cavalcade of Stars.* Gleason suggested a sketch in which a husband and wife fought. Someone asked if he wanted to get a copy of *The Bickersons* to use as a model, but Gleason, while acknowledging the influence of the radio show, wanted to create his own couple. The brief sketch, under five minutes, appeared on October 5, 1951. Gleason played Ralph Kramden, a loud-mouthed Brooklyn bus driver who got into an argument with his wife about his going out to get some bread. Pert Kelton portrayed his wife.

The sketch's success, and Gleason's emotional attachment to the character, made him want to continue. A new actor, Art Carney, was brought in as Ralph's friend and neighbor for the follow-up Kramden sketches. Ed Norton, the neighbor, proudly served the citizens of New York by working in a sewer.

As with other teams, appearance was important. Gleason was rotund and filled the screen with his presence. *Time* once described him: "He looked like a big basset hound who had just eaten W. C. Fields." Carney was thin and much more retiring, happy to stay off to the side. It is no surprise that they were nicknamed "the Laurel and Hardy of Brooklyn." Indeed, the real-life Laurel and Hardy were fans of Gleason and Carney.

And so were a lot of Americans. Gleason and Carney realized this when they went on a vaudeville-like tour to promote *Cavalcade of Stars*' move to CBS from the much smaller DuMont network. At CBS, "The Honeymooners" continued to be a sketch within the larger variety show. It eventually did become a full-length series in 1955 and had various incarnations after that. Ironically, the thirty-nine "classic" episodes of 1955 were initially considered to be a failure; they found enormous acceptance only later when the show went into syndication.

Pert Kelton was a casualty of the move to CBS. Although she did have some minor heart problems, the key reason for her dismissal was her rumored past affiliation with the Communist Party.

Gleason found that it was difficult to replace her. Kelton was forty-five years old when she was released in 1952, and she looked and sounded like she came from the working class. It is not surprising, then, that when twenty-six-year-old Audrey Meadows tried out for the part, Gleason thought her far too young and attractive to play the hard-bitten Alice.

Meadows was determined to get the part, and depending on the story, she either submitted a series of still photos in which she was made up to look like Alice Kramden or went directly to Gleason in full character dress and makeup. In any case, Gleason immediately saw the obvious: She was perfect. Supposedly, he was shocked to discover that this Alice was the actress he had dismissed because of her attractiveness.

Gleason decided that Ralph and Alice would not have children; in his opinion, children were impossible to work with. Besides that, they couldn't ad-lib, and they might be so cute that they would steal his scenes.

Joyce Randolph as Trixie, Ed Norton's wife, rounded out the cast.

Because Gleason never liked to rehearse, the other cast members, especially Carney, developed a remarkable ability to ad-lib, to cover Gleason's flubs. Of course, with live television anyone could forget a line, be distracted when someone else skipped lines, or simply lose where they were in the story. The actors in *The Honeymooners* decided to go to the kitchen table when one of them was lost. This would prompt the others to help. There were also cases in which Gleason, always notoriously unhappy with his writers, would toss the entire script, and the actors would have to improvise on the air. It was not a show for the fainthearted.

The show used some standard humor, especially "fat" humor, which Gleason encouraged. In one episode, for example, Ralph tells Alice about his latest great idea, concluding, "This is probably the biggest thing I ever got into," to which she snaps, "The biggest thing you ever got into was your pants."

But the humor went beyond the fat jokes. Gleason wanted to get his humor out of relationships and situations, not just jokes. *The Bickersons* was filled with clever lines; *The Honeymooners* wasn't. Gleason's joke lines were put-downs, not witty and memorable aphorisms. Gleason, like Caesar, wanted to let the humor flow from the psychological truths the characters displayed when they were in conflict with other characters. Gleason wanted to show the comic frailties of humanity, and he was very talented at doing so.

He had learned all about human misery and weakness from his childhood. Gleason had been born poor in Brooklyn. His only brother died when Jackie was two years old. Later, Jackie's father went to work one day and simply never came home, abandoning the family when Jackie was only eight years old. Before he left, though, his father had made a major contribution to Jackie's life; he'd brought the boy to the Halsey Theater to see vaudeville, and Jackie was immediately enthralled. He'd sat on his father's lap, engulfed by the laughter, finally finding a place, so unlike his home, where there was joy. He begged his father to keep taking him, one day announcing that he wouldn't be afraid to be on the stage, and he began doing imitations that made his parents laugh.

He dropped out of school after the eighth grade and started to hang around pool halls. His mother moved to a flat at 358 Chauncey Street, where the rent was cheap and the neighbors were kind to the struggling family. It was the address Gleason would later use for the Kramdens. The show's set, with its cramped quarters, spare furnishings, and barely functioning sink and icebox, were Gleason's attempts to re-create his childhood upbringing, to show the national audience where he had come from, and to transcend that past at the same time.

Ralph was always trying to make his life better, and he could never quite grasp why life was so tough on him, so unfair. He was the classic comedic child, wanting to do well but frustrated by life. He could laugh and cry at the same time.

He could also express anger, especially at Alice. This anger erupted from him as a series of physical threats: "One of these days, Alice. Pow. Right in the kisser," or "Bang, zoom, to the moon, Alice." He never carried out these threats, but, especially given his bulk, they were believable and certainly created additional sympathy for Alice. The threat and the removal of the threat were crucial to the emotional structure of the show.

That anger was the subject of much interest at the time. Indeed, *TV Guide* published a story in which experts offered explanations for why the audience found it so compelling. Most of them saw the Kramden relationship as distinctly American, because in the current culture, males were no longer the undisputed heads of the household. Women held an equal — and sometimes superior — position. Ralph thereby represented males revolting against such a situation, with their anger being safely released through humor.

Gleason, in an interview published by the *American Weekly* in its April 8, 1962, issue, reflected on his interpretation of Ralph: "I've met a lot of Ralph Kramdens in Brooklyn. He is the guy who is trying to make [a] living and can't provide better for his wife. In order to hide his guilt he's boisterous and flamboyant and opinionated. But the good thing about Kramden is that after he tries to make a point and gets deflated, he shuffles and rubs his toe in the gravel and apologizes to Alice. He tells her he loves her, which in his simple mind makes everything all right. And in Alice's greater mind it *does* make everything all right. If a guy's trying to do the best he can for you, and he loves you, you know he's sincere. She loves him for that reason."

Gleason's insights are crucial. The character goes through a transformation in each show — but then returns to his old form for the next show, only to be transformed again. Audiences wanted to see that transformation — that change from the angry loser, the guy with a thousand get-rich ideas that all fail, that yells at his wife and his neighbor, that never seems to get ahead — to the Chaplin-like, sad and sympathetic soul who is touched by love and, in Gleason's view, by grace and somehow finds the means to express it. As an episode was about to close, he often gazed lovingly at his wife and said, "Alice, you're the greatest."

Audiences saw in Ralph's transformation hopes for redemption in their own marriages and lives. Struggling to pay for mortgages and new cars, beset by debts, peer pressure, and advertising, the viewers could feel Ralph's struggle, even as they felt superior to it because mostly they were in better circumstances than he was. He comically expressed their frustrations at having to struggle so hard, at having to come to terms with the limits reality placed on their dreams. And somehow, as he found that love gave him solace and hope, so could they.

Ralph's character also signified a considerable change in audience views of poverty-stricken protagonists. Audiences in the 1930s, who were often poor and struggling to make ends meet, resented the rich in part because they viewed that wealth as unattainable. Those audiences loved it when a penniless hero caused wealthy characters to slip and lose both their balance and their dignity. By Gleason's day, however, the audiences no longer resented the rich; they wanted to join them. And given the postwar economic boom, they believed that they actually had a chance at becoming rich if they worked hard enough. Ralph Kramden schemed to become wealthy. He exemplified the altered attitudes and renewed expectations.

Alice's character was strong, self-reliant, and unafraid of confronting her much more physically powerful husband. Alice was a woman poised for social recognition as a new type of wife. There seems to be little physical love between Ralph and Alice; there is more of a mutual emotional need.

The marital struggles on Gleason's show belie attempts to idealize family life in the 1950s or to portray the decade as the epitome of marital bliss in the twentieth century. The seemingly content couples raising happy children in suburban paradises maintained their smiles only by repressing their anger, or laughing at it, or believing that love rendered the anger meaningless. This repression would end, and the explosive results erupted in the late 1960s and 1970s when traditional marriages were ending at rates never before seen in American life.

In *The Honeymooners*, the comedy team made up of a friendly member of the same gender proved stronger than the marital comedy team. These friends provided an escape from marriage and an alternative satisfying emotional relationship. The "buddies," that is, did more than provide wry commentary about the central marital relationship; they provided, in all ways other than physical love, a complete, and more satisfying, substitute for the marriage.

The pairing of Gleason and Carney presented a significantly different kind of team comedy, though there were still the fat jokes:

> Gleason: Did you ever see a picture of
>   me when I weighed 165 pounds?
> Carney: No, Ralph, I never did see any
>   of your baby pictures.

Ed and Trixie Norton lived upstairs from the Kramdens. Like Ralph, Ed was poor, but he accepted his place. He remained cheerful, friendly, and, to put it as kindly as possible, naïvely optimistic. He was always willing to help Ralph but was not very good at it, and many times his boastful support of his friend got Ralph into trouble. He might, on Ralph's behalf, challenge a pool hall bully to a fight. Ever proud of his membership in the sewer-working fraternity, Norton served to soften, even to humanize, Ralph. Gleason's real-life ongoing rage could be overwhelming if there wasn't a counterforce, and the Norton character provided that force deftly.

Carney had used an Ed Norton–type character before in his work both on radio and television. He knew the Ed Nortons of the world. Carney had been badly wounded in World War II; he spent nine months in the hospital recovering from a shrapnel wound in his leg. When he got out, he rode the subway a lot while he was seeking an agent, and he listened carefully to all of the other passengers. He heard and grew to admire a Brooklyn-Bronx, distinctly New York accent and syntax. An accomplished mimic, Carney found himself re-creating the accents.

He then tried it out when he played a cop in a skit in which Gleason played another of his characters, Reggie Van Gleason. Gleason knew Ralph Kramden could have a neighbor who sounded just like that. Carney also worked on how Ed Norton would dress. He immediately decided that he would use a felt hat that he had bought in high school sixteen years earlier. The pin-striped vest over a tee shirt soon followed. Carney's timing and his skill at pantomime helped him shape the character's movements and speech. Carney enjoyed making Norton extroverted because in real life the actor was extremely shy.

The character was crucial in another way. If Ralph was the essence of American ambition, Ed was the one who shrewdly decided he was unwilling to suffer the agony that resulted from the seemingly inevitable defeats.

Both Ralph and Ed, though, did want the goods America had to offer. Both wanted a television set and a vacuum cleaner but had trouble affording these accoutrements of middle-class life. They were clever to inject this longing into the show. Many audience members, through hard work, loans, and struggle had acquired the very goods Ralph and Ed wanted. Seeing the two Brooklyn working families still without those goods made the viewers feel as though they had accomplished an important goal, as measured by the failures of the Kramden and Norton families.

Ed was a friend and neighbor along for the ride but not quite as brave as Ralph. He was the audience member's alter ego, watching the Great One fail without having to go through the pain himself.

Carney and Gleason created some classic scenes. Perhaps the most famous was the scene in which Ralph, bragging to his boss in an effort to get ahead, claimed an expert ability to play golf. In real life, Gleason loved the game, but Ralph had no experience at all. Ed Norton got a how-to book and began to tutor Ralph, but the two were immediately stumped when the first command was to "address the ball."

Gleason, adorned in a mismatched, loud outfit, struggled until Carney decided he understood the instructions. He grabbed a club, stared down, and in an exaggerated pronunciation of the first word, said, "Helloooo, ball."

Gleason and Carney seem to fit well in the buddies comedic tradition going all the way back to vaudeville through Abbott and Costello and Martin and Lewis, but there is a crucial distinction. Gleason always wanted full control and to be the center of the action, with Carney as the junior partner.

Carney was able to master and submerge any competitive feelings he might have had, which enabled him to keep working with Gleason when other, less talented actors would have quit in disgust. Gleason craved the spotlight; Carney didn't need it. Indeed, he didn't really want to be responsible for carrying the show.

Carney may have been a second banana, but he was not a stooge. Gleason never mistreated him on the air. If Gleason came up with an idea that resulted in Carney's getting a laugh, the joke stayed in. This was not a practice universally honored by comedians. Indeed, Carney recalled one famous star he wouldn't name who kept someone in the audience during the dress rehearsal to gauge laughs. If anyone in the cast got a bigger laugh than the star, that line was removed. Gleason lived for the laugh, wherever it came from.

Gleason and Carney were among the most important models for the many television comedy pairs that would emerge. In an important way, television teams in sitcoms would allow the virtues and values of classic comedy teams to survive their apparent extinction.

Of all those influential television teams, the most important one centered on a red-headed, attractive, bright and driven woman. Lucille Ball had starred on a popular radio program titled *My Favorite Husband*, playing Liz Cugat, a socially prominent and sophisticated wife to a bank vice-president. Just a few weeks after the show began, a CBS radio network programmer called a young comedy writer named Jess Oppenheimer and asked the writer to do a script for the show.

Oppenheimer looked at the scripts for *My Favorite Husband* and came up with a fresh idea. He didn't know Lucille Ball, but he decided the show would be funnier if he shifted her character and made her behave more like an impulsive child. Her character now would be determined to get on the stage, an impulsive quest that would keep getting her into embarrassing messes. The network loved the show made from Oppenheimer's idea and hired him as the head writer.

Lucy, meanwhile, had learned slapstick. But she had a problem: She was still nervous in front of her radio audiences. The nervousness could be incorporated into the sophisticated character because it came across as reserve, but the new childlike character needed to be free of inhibitions.

Oppenheimer considered the problem and came up with a solution. He had worked for Jack Benny, replacing Al Boasberg as the writer who heard the final draft and made suggestions. Oppenheimer arranged for the cast of *My Favorite Husband* to see Benny's cast perform. The effortlessly relaxed Benny was an eye-opener for Lucille Ball. She realized she could have fun and let go, and the audience would love her all the more. (Jack Benny later repaid the compliment by having all his writers see the *I Love Lucy* episode in which William Holden sets Lucy's putty nose on fire.)

It wasn't long before Lucy's brilliant comedic talents became noticed. The *Hollywood Reporter* observed that it was "too bad that her funny grimaces and gestures aren't visible over the radio."

Lucy was definitely ready for television. And television was ready for Lucy. CBS executives ordered a filmed version of the radio show. Lucy liked the idea, except for one crucial matter. She did not want to include Richard Denning, her radio co-star, in the new show. Instead, she wanted her real-life husband, Desi Arnaz, to play her television husband.

The executives were flabbergasted. Arnaz was a Cuban bandleader who spoke broken English. Who would believe the two were married? They didn't like the idea at all. But Lucy was determined.

She had always been determined.

Her father had died before she was four, and her grandfather then helped raise the family. She hadn't been allowed to play with the neighborhood children out of fear of contracting a disease or learning inappropriate language. For seven years, she remained apart. Perhaps that was why she later could play a childlike character so well because, as she once told a reporter from *Photoplay*, "Comedians don't laugh. I don't know why. Perhaps they were sad children." The Lucy Ricardo character gave her the opportunity to let that sad child have another chance at life, as Jerry

Lewis had done with the nine-year-old in himself.

It was her grandfather who took Lucy to a vaudeville show each Saturday. At fifteen, she went to New York City to learn to act, but she felt useless and overwhelmed by the talents of another young student named Bette Davis and returned home. She became a model and eventually achieved enough success to be brought to Hollywood, where she never quite attained the breakthrough she had hoped for. But she did find love. No one was going to tell her she couldn't marry the handsome Cuban musician.

And no one was going to tell her that Desi Arnaz was not going to be in the new television show. To prove their attractiveness to audiences, Lucy and Desi embarked on an old-fashioned vaudeville tour with a twenty-minute act featuring a trick cello, a seal routine, and some songs. The Cuban and the redhead were, she triumphantly noted to the CBS bosses, a big hit.

Nevertheless, Lucy and Desi still needed to produce an audition show, what today is called a "pilot." CBS refused to offer them a contract, and their agency took the idea to NBC. Once NBC became interested, CBS grew to like the idea much more.

Lucy, several months pregnant and struggling to hide it, filmed the audition show. There were no neighbors, just Ricky Ricardo the bandleader and his wife, Lucy, who wants to break into show business exactly as much as her husband wants her to stay home. The show business theme mirrored the ever-growing American fascination with celebrities. The audition show was a hit with the network, and a series was set to air.

Oppenheimer, now the producer, and the writers came up with new characters for the show, Fred and Ethel Mertz, who were older, slightly less well-off neighbors and landlords, and who would serve as foils for Lucy and Ricky.

Casting the neighbors was a concern. There have been more than one pair of co-stars who sounded right, who were brilliant, but who failed. The most famous case of such spectacular failure was W. C. Fields teaming up with Mae West in the 1940 film *My Little Chickadee*. The two great comedians hated each other and had no chemistry. But Lucy's producers got it just right, at least in front of the camera. William Frawley, a veteran vaudevillian, was selected for Fred, and Vivian Vance, a respected but not widely known actress, was picked for Ethel. Vance was on her third marriage and had already had a nervous breakdown. Bill Frawley was a heavy drinker. The producers knew they were taking chances.

Surprisingly, Lucille Ball never got a chance to see Vance perform before she was hired. At first, there was tension between the two performers, but that soon subsided, and they became close. Vance and Frawley, though, were bitter, hostile partners. Vance, who was only two years older than Lucy and twenty-two years younger than Frawley, didn't like the fact that the public thought she would be married to him. Her feelings were so strong that when the pair was eventually invited to do a spin-off, Vance refused, infuriating Frawley, who saw the new show as his big chance to be the well-paid star.

I Love Lucy was first broadcast on October 15, 1951, right after Arthur Godfrey's program, the top-rated show in the nation. From the beginning, then, *I Love Lucy* had a fair chance at success, but no one predicted the extent to which the show would become an entertainment tornado that swept through American television, destroying competitors in its path and remaking the landscape. *I Love Lucy* did nothing less than create the conventions that came to define the situation comedy form.

The success of the show can mostly be ascribed to Lucille Ball's remarkable skills. On the May 5, 1952, episode of *I Love Lucy*, Lucy Ricardo was seen slugging down shots of a product she was supposed to be advertising. The drink was Vitameatavegamin, a supposedly healthy potion that, unknown to Lucy, was 46-proof. She kept trying to get the commercial right, but the more she sampled the product, the more she struggled to pronounce its name. When she tried to pour a spoonful from the bottle, the potion kept missing the spoon and landing on the table. Finally, she figured it out. She put the spoon on the table, grabbed the bottle using both hands, and poured its contents into the spoon, which was now finally full. She was beaming. Then she forgot the spoon, picked up the bottle, and took a healthy belt.

Lucy was hysterical all on her own, but she was even more hysterical with a comic partner. She re-created the mirror scene from *Duck Soup* with Harpo Marx. When William Holden guest starred, Lucy, in disguise, had a fake putty nose that accidentally caught on fire. Thinking fast, she blew out the fire and then dipped the nose in a cup of coffee.

Lucy worked well with Desi, but she worked especially well with Vivian Vance. For example, in another 1952 episode, Lucy and Ethel tried to wrap chocolate bonbons on a conveyor belt that mercilessly increased its speed. Rushing feverishly to keep up, they put the chocolates everywhere, including in their mouths, under their hats, and down the front of their uniforms — a place that even escaped Charlie Chaplin in the classic conveyor belt scene in *Modern Times*. In another show, Lucy and Vivian became furious at each other because they had each worn the same dress, having believed the other was going to return her dress. In their fury, they tore each other's dresses, all the while singing Cole Porter's "Friendship." They stopped only when their husbands forcibly broke up the mutual destruction.

Ball and Vance were the first important all-woman comedy pairing in decades. Though it's a rather loose use of the concept, they, too, were a comedy team.

Although Lucy and Ricky carried on the team tradition of the world of irrationality brought back by the rational partner, there was a crucial difference. Ricky's ethnic background and his accent, which had so worried CBS executives, turned out to be charming to viewers. However, that very charm depended in part on his exoticism, and Ricky, despite being the rational partner, could never be a George Burns. He could be beloved, but he could never be an "ordinary" American. That's why Ethel became so crucial and why Lucy and Ethel were a more provocative team. It was Ethel who stood in for the audience.

Lucy and Ethel became like sisters on the show, with Ethel the older, supposedly more responsible one. Lucy was impulsive and anxious to get what she wanted. They developed a formula: Lucy would come up with an idea; Ethel would fret about it; Lucy would convince or hoodwink Ethel into going along; and together the pair would get into plenty of trouble.

Emotionally, the women in the audience were actually much more like Ethel Mertz than Lucy Ricardo. Ethel was a surrogate for those who wanted to have great adventures, to get out of the house and find some excitement, but who did not quite have the courage. They lived vicariously through Lucy, who had the guts. Like both Lucy and Ethel, the women in the audience were discovering the stifling effects of their cookie-cutter suburban existence.

Women viewers deeply identified with Lucy Ricardo when she became pregnant. Oppenheimer and the writers had decided that television's Lucy Ricardo would also become pregnant when Ball announced her pregnancy. The networks were shocked at the idea, but they had already learned all about Lucy's determination. The episode about the birth, broadcast on January 19, 1953, attracted approximately 44 million viewers. Arnaz had phoned Oppenheimer to tell him that the actual birth had virtually coincided with the television birth. Oppenheimer was pleased and joked, "Tell Lucy she can take the rest of the day off."

But Lucy, actor or character, didn't need to be told what to do. The character was pre-feminist, someone who heroically asserted her independence, who constantly defied her husband's orders, and who had a lot of fun doing it. Lucy was acting out the fantasies of the women in the audience, letting them emotionally rehearse for a time when they were ready to stand up for themselves, keeping them sane in a male-dominated world that considered their lifestyle to be privileged and idyllic. Lucy reminded them that the culture's definition of their lives as perfect was nonsense that needed to be challenged. But Lucy did it through humor, and as always, that was a potent weapon.

Her greatest trick was to do all this without losing the crucial 1950s virtue of femininity. She didn't mind getting hit with pies, falling over furniture, being locked in a freezer, or chased by a man with a knife, as long as she remained beautiful and well dressed. She wore expensive jewelry and was married to a handsome, successful celebrity. Many viewers copied Lucy's wardrobe and wrote letters requesting information about her elegant clothes. Lucy's enormous eyes and flaming red hair made her appear amusing but not funny-looking. She was, as *Time* once dubbed her, a "clown with glamour." Of course, this glamour aged. Her voice, a sweet soprano at the beginning of the series, would coarsen.

Ball's tremendous talent for physical humor came in part from her entertainment background. During the first several decades of the twentieth century, in such entertainments as the Ziegfeld Follies, beautiful "chorus girls" acted with funny comedians. The "girls" who were selected were the ones who were the best at comedy. Lucille Ball had been a "Goldwyn Girl," and she had acted with Eddie Cantor, and she had been in *Room Service* with the Marx Brothers.

Ball's combination of beauty and humor was crucial because she was still working in a male-dominated world. The public hesitated before laughing at attractive women. They were more comfortable laughing at loud women, women who made themselves unattractive and portrayed themselves as such, like ZaSu Pitts, Patsy Kelly, and Fanny Brice. That's why Lucille Ball was so revolutionary. She also had the ability to give her character a childlike poignancy as well as a certain silliness, in the same way Lou Costello did.

Even though Lucy achieved almost instant success, it was a Hollywood assumption that the public would tire of her in a few months. As an unnamed movie producer told the entertainment columnist Hal Humphrey, "She'll kill herself with the public in six months. No entertainer can come into a person's home every week and not wear out his welcome." Instead, Lucy was accepted like a winsome, hilarious, adored neighbor. Audiences were entertained, but they also cared about her. Viewers were curious to see what problems and crazy adventures Lucy would get into each week.

The audience's empathy would be vital for Lucille Ball as she faced the greatest crisis of her career.

On September 11, 1953, she admitted that she had once registered as a Communist. On March 19, 1936, Ball had registered with the Los Angeles County Registrar of Voters as intending to affiliate with the Communist Party. On June 16, 1936, Ball signed a sponsor certificate on behalf of Emil Freed, a Communist Party candidate for the State Assembly. On September 15 of that year, Freed appointed Ball as a member of the State Central Committee of the Communist Party, although Ball later said that she never authorized her name to be used and never even knew about the appointment.

In April 1952, William Wheeler, an investigator from the House Un-American Activities Committee, visited Ball. She later gave testimony before Wheeler in an executive session of the committee. During the testimony, Ball said that she, her mother, and her brother had registered as Communists to please her grandfather.

For seventeen months, she spoke to no one outside the family about the situation. That is, for almost a year and a half, during a time when Communists were deeply hated, during a time when FBI director J. Edgar Hoover kept files about the personal secrets of Hollywood celebrities in his office, during the height of Senator Joseph McCarthy's power, Lucille Ball carried on her career at the top of the entertainment business. She may not even have thought about any potential threat because she wasn't very political. Or she may have been deeply worried that the information would be made public. Whatever her private thoughts were, she maintained an iron-willed ability to carry on.

And then Walter Winchell wrote a column that included these words: "The most popular of all television stars [has been] confronted with her membership in the Communist Party." Though no names had been mentioned, five days later the story broke when Donald Jackson, a California member of the House Un-American Activities Committee in Congress, revealed the facts, although he made it clear that Ball had never played a role in the Communist Party.

Despite the official clearance, Lucy and Desi decided to face the press.

On September 13, 1953, the *Los Angeles Times* ran an extended story about Lucy and Desi's meeting with reporters. Arnaz had tried to joke that the only thing red about Lucy was her hair, and even that wasn't real. But the press wanted answers. One press agent stepped forward to note that she had voted in the primary that year but not in the general election. Defiantly, Lucy replied, "Okay, I voted. Big deal."

The night the story broke, Lucy had to appear before a live audience for the taping of her show. It was clear that all she had worked for, her entire future, the future of this groundbreaking show, was in the balance.

I Love Lucy never missed a beat. The audience that night and the much larger audience at home did indeed love Lucy. They sympathized with her and understood that her registration was simply an attempt to please an aging grandparent. They identified with her need to keep it secret to protect her family. Lucy later reported that even Lou Costello, who was politically conservative, had been supportive.

In a way, this event marked a crucial change in American life. Lucille Ball overcame the purgatory that haunted the

1950s: McCarthyism. Within a few years, McCarthy would be disgraced. Lucy was a historic figure, the clearest example that Americans were ready to move on. She was, as on her television show, the perfect embodiment of her country.

THIRTEEN

"MOM ALWAYS LIKED YOU BEST"

Comedy Teams of the 1960s

On April 3, 1969, Robert Wood, the new president of CBS television, sent a wire to Tom Smothers. The message was crisp: Tom and his brother Dick were fired. Their hit show would no longer be on the air. The reason that Wood gave for the firing was that the Smothers Brothers had failed to provide a preview tape to the network for the network's censors and affiliated stations.

Tom Smothers began a campaign to have the network reverse its decision, and a lawsuit was filed. (The Smothers Brothers won the suit four years later, but by then it was too late to matter. The cultural energy of the era that had so perfectly matched their own talents had itself dissipated.)

The end of the show was a huge moment in the life of the Smothers Brothers and, in many ways, a pivotal event in the youth culture wave that would soon engulf American life. The Smothers Brothers didn't know it, but they were going to be one of the last classic comedy teams to achieve national success.

There were other teams that emerged in the 1960s, but they were fragile, often short-lived, sometimes of an experimental nature with roots that did not go deeply into the fertile ground of team comedy. They emerged on records, or in improvisational comedy groups, or for a few last glorious moments, on television.

Comedy albums, first released in 1948, were usually reserved for obscene or suggestive material. They were known as "party albums," the marketing euphemism of the day. Redd Foxx, Belle Barth, and Rusty Warren were the most successful practitioners. Mort Sahl first recorded in 1955 and became a model for other cutting-edge comedians to do the same.

The first of the great teams to record had gone to the Sid Caesar School of Comedy. They couldn't have had a better education.

Mel Brooks and Carl Reiner had written for Caesar, but Brooks really wanted to perform. Reiner encouraged his very funny friend. The two would go to parties, and Reiner would present Brooks with a new character. They would then improvise a dialogue. Reiner noted, "I never told him what it was going to be, but I always tried for something that would force him to go into panic, because a brilliant mind in panic is a wonderful thing to see."

One day Reiner came in and told his co-workers about a television show he had seen titled *We the People Speak*. The show employed actors to portray newsmakers.

Reiner didn't much like the show but saw in it perfect material for satire on *Your Show of Shows*. No one in the office had seen the program, so Reiner began to make fun of the announcer. Suddenly, he pointed at Mel Brooks. "Here with us today, ladies and gentlemen, is a man who was actually at the scene of the Crucifixion, two thousand years ago. Isn't that true, sir?" Brooks reflexively went into character, starting with a deep sigh, and continued on for most of an hour to the delight of some of the best comedy minds in America.

Suddenly, the 2,000-Year-Old Man was born. Mel Brooks portrayed him, complete with Yiddish accent and Borscht Belt attitude, as a man who had seen all that 2,000 years of life had to offer but wasn't too impressed by any of it.

At 11:30 p.m. on June 21, 1960, the two men had just finished performing the routine at a party in Beverly Hills. George Burns walked up to Mel Brooks and asked if the material was on a comedy album. Brooks told him there was no album. Burns puffed his cigar, exhaled, and said, "If you don't put it in an album, I'll steal it. I'm serious." A few minutes later, the television and comedy star Steve Allen came over, offering to pay for studio time to record the material.

Brooks and Reiner had been reluctant to release the material to the public because they thought the Yiddish accent might be seen as mocking Jews and therefore inappropriate. But Allen, who was not Jewish, was sure that their genius would be widely appreciated.

Stanley Ralph Ross, a writer and actor, was one of about one hundred people at the two-hour recording session. "It was a big studio, a recording studio where they usually have an orchestra. Instead of an orchestra, it was just the two guys up on stage. They had chairs and coffee and juice. That was it. They just went on. Carl had some cards for asking the questions. I don't think Mel had any idea of what Carl was going to say to him."

Reiner had perfected the role of straight man/interviewer in performing with Sid Caesar's "Professor" character. As with previous straight men, his understated brilliance at directing the flow of conversation, feeding Brooks good lines, and controlling the timing was invaluable. For example, Reiner would ask, "Who was the person who discovered the female?" Brooks ad-libbed his answer: "Bernie . . . One morning he got up smiling . . . He went into such a story. It was hundreds of years, I still blush."

Going back to the original line, Reiner asked the 2,000-Year-Old Man about Jesus.

Brooks: I knew him. Nice boy. He wore sandals. He was quiet, a quiet lad. He came to the store, never bought anything . . . He made a cabinet for me.

Reiner: Did you know he was going to be the Jesus that shook the world?

Brooks: If I knew that he was going to be a hit, I would have made him a partner in the store.

Later, the 2,000-Year-Old Man expressed some concern about dying and meeting Jesus. It turns out that Jesus had been paid just "four bucks" for the cabinet. He also noted, "If Shaw and Einstein couldn't beat death, what chance have I got? Practically none."

And, naturally, the 2,000-Year-Old Man had some complaining to do about his children. "You know how they are, children. Good luck to them. Let 'em go. I don't want . . . Listen. Let 'em be happy.

As long as they're happy, I don't care. But they could send a note and write, 'Hiya, Pop. How ya doin' pop?' You know. *Something.*"

The success of the album spawned a mini-industry. Though they never performed in public, they did produce four albums from 1960 to 1973. There was a cartoon special and a book. In 1973 they made a sequel about the 2013-Year-Old Man, and in 1997 they wrote and recorded *The 2,000-Year-Old Man in the Year 2000* with a subtitle that included a promise to show listeners how to avoid death. Ironically, the success of the original album doomed any prospect of an ongoing team because both developed extraordinarily successful personal careers.

The ad-lib nature of Brooks and Reiner was perfectly in keeping with the spirit of the age. Improvisation was exciting because it shed the safety of a script. It was a psychological rebellion. Improvisation provided a model for making life up as you went along, a sense that all was possible, that a person letting go of an unhappy life didn't need a clear place to land, just a zest for the journey. Improvisation gave birth to itself, as many young people wanted to do emotionally.

Many of the other comedy teams that emerged in the 1960s had their roots in improvisational comedy, a form in which actors band together to perform in front of an audience and make up characters and dialogue as they go along or base their efforts on suggestions from audience members.

Contemporary American improvisation has a clear lineage back to the 1920s when Viola Spolin, a Chicago theater educator, determined that she could best teach theater to her young students by the use of games. When Spolin was appointed supervisor of drama for the Works Progress Administration, she organized improvisational groups for adults.

Spolin's son, Paul Sills, was a student at the University of Chicago in 1951 when he and a group of friends started performing plays and, with David Shepherd, formed the Playwrights Theatre Club. The club, after splits and reorganizations, had by December 1959 become Second City (the derogatory name given to Chicago in a *New Yorker* article by A. J. Liebling). Alumni from Second City include Jerry Stiller, Anne Meara, Jack Burns, Avery Schreiber, David Steinberg, Joan Rivers, and Robert Klein. Later, many of the people who would gain fame on *Saturday Night Live*, including Dan Aykroyd, Jim Belushi, John Belushi, Chris Farley, Bill Murray, Mike Myers, Gilda Radner, Martin Short, among others, got their start at Second City.

The success of Second City spawned many other improvisational groups such as The Committee and Firesign Theatre. Eventually, Second City's Toronto counterpart would have a major effect on comedy with the creation of *Second City TV.*

Mike Nichols and Elaine May were the first major team born from improvisation. They had begun working together in 1955 when they were members of the Compass Players. They began to improvise literally from the moment they first met. Nichols had seen May, or rather someone he didn't know but thought of as an "evil, hostile girl," glowering at him as he performed. One night at a railroad station, he saw her again. He walked up to her, effected a German accent, and said, "May I sit down?" May, never slow, responded in a vaguely East European accent, "If you weesh."

Their work was not aimed at punch lines but at the humor arising from character.

Nichols and May's deeply satiric dialogues were really small plays that mocked popular culture and provided a much-needed puncturing of suburban illusions. They were deeply cynical about any kind of sentiment, especially love.

They had an extraordinarily brave technique. They would ask audience members to yell up lines and select two at random. They would then perform, beginning the sketch with one line and ending with the other.

By 1957, Nichols and May were working in nightclubs. They did television, radio, comedy albums, and advertisements. They appeared on Broadway in *An Evening of Nichols and May*, which opened on October 8, 1960.

They were serious about their satire. Once during a sketch, Nichols hit May across the face, and in return, she scratched her nails across his face drawing blood. In 1960, they were supposed to perform at the Emmy Awards program but eventually declined when they were not allowed to perform a sketch mocking a sponsor's product.

Nichols and May were also among the first comedians, along with people like Lenny Bruce, Mort Sahl, Shelley Berman, and, later, Woody Allen, to dare to present subtle material that appealed to the audience's intelligence. But Nichols and May were, characteristically, brave about even that. They were not afraid to mock those intellectuals who pretended to know everyone:

> Nichols: And then there's Albert Einstein's theory.
> May: Oh, you mean Al. A great dancer. Love his hair.
> Nichols: But of course he had to leave Germany because of Adolf Hitler.
> May: Oh, that Dolphie. He was a riot. I used to call him Cuddles.
> Nichols: Good God!
> May: Oh, Him. A close personal friend of mine.

Nichols and May scathingly presented the desire of the young in the culture to separate from their parents but who felt guilt about such a desire, a guilt induced with gusto by the parents. In one bit in the show and on a record (the son's name changed for the recording) a mother calls her son, who is a missile scientist: "Melvin, this is your mother. Do you remember me? . . . I don't want you to worry, Melvin, just because I had to go to the doctor again this week. Please don't worry. And don't think I don't understand why you don't call your poor, sick mother. I do. I do understand. You're too busy, that's all."

Despite their success, the routine itself became difficult. Nichols was like Lou Costello in preferring situations they both knew would work. May was more restless. In July 1961, after more than three hundred performances of their Broadway show, the team split.

But another team many compared to them emerged.

Jerry Stiller and Anne Meara focused on domestic bits. They were Nichols and May without the acid and with warmth. Their material had a new twist. Stiller was Jewish and Meara Catholic, and they used that effectively in their act.

They had met when, at an audition, Stiller heard a woman scream and run out of an office. He asked Anne Meara what was the matter, and she told him the agent had literally chased after her. Stiller went right in and confronted the agent, who, as Stiller later told the story, also chased him. They went for coffee to discuss the hard lives of struggling actors. Their relationship blossomed, and although at that time, interreligious dating and marriage was not yet widespread, they married in 1954. After performing in some straight plays, including Shakespeare, Stiller, and later Meara, went to St. Louis to join the Compass Players. By 1962, they were working as stand-ups. They soon appeared on the influential *Ed Sullivan Show*, where they eventually made thirty-six appearances.

After some early confrontational humor, they developed characters from their own lives: Hershey Horowitz and Mary Elizabeth Doyle, a Jewish man who was confused by life and his Irish sweetheart.

When they went to their agent with an idea for a Horowitz-Doyle sketch in which the couple meets through computer dating, the agent was not optimistic. He told them Ed Sullivan would never permit it to air because so much of the nation was Protestant. Sullivan courageously allowed it. In part of the sketch, they compared families:

Meara: In my family I got plenty of sisters . . . Sister Mary Monica, Sister Bernadette Marie, Sister Mary Virginia . . . Do you have any brothers and sisters?

Stiller: Three brothers . . . Buch, Bujie,
and Sol.
Meara: Buck?
Stiller: No, no, Buch, B . . . uch.
Meara: Buck?
Stiller: No, it's Bu-uch.
Meara: Bu-uck.
Stiller: No . . . Bu-uch.
Meara: Bu-uch. Oooh! I think I hurt my-
self.

The couple also discussed food. Stiller
invited her to his house for a Friday-night
traditional dinner.

Meara: I couldn't come over. It's Friday.
I can't eat meat on Friday.
Stiller: Didn't they change the rule on
that?
Meara: Sure, they changed the rule.
But my family don't go along with
it . . . Why don't you come to my
house for Sunday dinner? . . . My
mother always has a big
spread: roast stuffed pork, baked
Virginia ham. Oh! I'm sorry! You
don't have to eat any of that stuff.
I'll fix you bacon and eggs.

Eventually they agree to go to a delicatessen, where Meara suggests they have "filtered fish" until Stiller gently points out, "That's gefilte fish."

Younger Americans yearned for the freedom to love across religious and ethnic lines. Intermarriages rapidly increased starting in the 1960s, and Stiller and Meara pioneered the comic difficulties of this emerging social phenomenon. Theirs was a gentler humor than Nichols and May's had been, a humor based on the differences in relationships and, despite the conflicts, on the ultimate possibilities of harmony in an increasingly fractured country. (In real life, Anne Meara converted to the Jewish faith in 1962 after the birth of their daughter.)

There were other comedy teams that emerged from improvisational comedy. Jack Burns had once teamed up with George Carlin. Burns had been a Texas newscaster when the two began to work together on a Fort Worth radio show. They went to Hollywood where, in 1960, they served as morning disc jockeys at KDAY. Lenny Bruce, among others, admired their talents. Bruce helped them, and they soon appeared on *The Tonight Show*. After two years as a team, Burns and Carlin decided that they wanted to end the partnership, and Carlin began his own brand of comedy.

Burns made his way to Chicago where, at Second City, he met Avery Schreiber, who, after a stint in the army and work at a theater, had joined the troupe, as he recalled, sometime in 1960 or 1961.

Burns was Catholic and Schreiber Jewish, and they, like an all-male counterpart to Stiller and Meara, took over the comedic exploration of cultural differences. Burns and Schreiber even looked gloriously at odds: Burns was thin and clean-shaven, and Schreiber had heft, loads of curly hair, and an impressive mustache.

Because Burns was generally politically and socially conservative and Schreiber more of a liberal, their personal differences, filtered through an ethnic lens, provided almost dueling stand-ups, unlike Stiller and Meara who had created more accommodating characters. Burns and Schreiber were after something darker. Stiller and Meara's characters communicated understanding; Burns and Schreiber's characters remained forever locked in their own individual psyches.

Their most famous sketch, "The Cab Driver and the Conventioneer," captured their differences perfectly and, in doing so, reflected very early the emerging cultural divide that was to mark American life in the late 1960s and early 1970s.

The sketch had Burns playing a bigoted passenger in Avery Schreiber's cab. Schreiber's character was patient but slowly grew less so as Burns's ranting continued. They developed a trademark exchange. Burns would want to make sure Schreiber was listening, so he'd end a statement with a "huh?" to which Schreiber would respond "Yeah." The words would be repeated quickly, as though the two would never really be able to communicate. It all built up to a great ethnic divide:

Burns: I don't care about the color of a man's skin. I was the first guy to scream when they took *Amos 'n' Andy* off the air . . . By the way, your name on the nameplate there. You're of the Judeo-Hebraic tradition?

Schreiber: You mean I'm a Jew.

Burns: Hey. I don't go in for name-calling. But let me tell you, pound for pound Hank Greenberg was one of the greatest ballplayers who ever lived.

Schreiber: What about Sandy Koufax?

Burns: Don't tell me he's one of them too?

The impact of improvisation on all of these comedians was intense. Less obvious, perhaps, is the impact it had on the two major television comedy teams of the decade: the Smothers Brothers and Rowan and Martin.

The Smothers Brothers constructed their act in the same way improvisation comedians — and jazz musicians — did. They started with an idea and kept expanding. One would ad-lib to see what the other's reaction would be, and if it was interesting, the exchange was added to the act.

It is no accident, therefore, that Elaine May was a guest on their show in its first season. Ironically, considering the eventual fate of the show, she played a censor. The actual censors at CBS, the Department of Program Practices, cut the entire routine from the program.

The Smothers Brothers had started out wanting to lampoon the folk boom. Good-looking, well-dressed, and clean-shaven, they seemed to arrive from central casting's idea of Middle America. They were able to replicate the harmonies and melodies of the great folk artists, especially the then very popular Kingston Trio. And they were very smart. Their comedy began when Tom, introducing a song, started making up hilarious and obviously untrue stories about the piece. They played off their real relationship. Dick, for example, would say, with great consternation: "You know why I'm mad most of the time? Because it's difficult being an only child." Eventually, they came up with a trademark line uttered by a supposedly emotionally injured Tom, who would accuse Dick with the words, "Mom always liked you best." Like many other great comedy lines, this one was improvised during a performance, and the audience loved it.

The characters developed out of their fraternal feuding. Tom became the neurotic, insecure, Woody Allen–type that audiences wanted to protect; Dick, the annoyed older brother. For example, they would be singing, and in true folk fashion, Dick would yell out to his brother, "Take it, Tom." Tom, though, in very un-folk-like fashion, yelled back, "No."

The humor soon worked its way into the lyrics. The Smothers Brothers began to parody the lyrics so sacred to folk audiences. The old standby "John Henry" turned into: "When John Henry was a little baby, sittin' on his daddy's knee / His daddy picked him up, threw him on the floor and said 'This baby's done wet on me.' "

Dick was a great straight man, remaining serious, guiding his brother through the mocking remarks and then bringing him back. As Tom said of his brother's ability: "He is the drummer. He's the tempo keeper . . . A comedian can do the most absurd thing, but if the straight man reacts and the audience believes it, then they believe the comedian." Actually, their timing had to evolve. Early in their career, Tom spoke a lot in the act. But a study of the classic teams surprised him. He noticed how much Hardy spoke and how little Laurel did. He was surprised at how much more Abbott spoke than Costello. Consequently, Tom began to reduce the amount he spoke, letting the audience savor his outbursts when they came and not be overwhelmed by them.

Tom was especially accomplished in the juvenile role. While many of his comedic ancestors had performed well with similar characters, Tom realized its full potential. After all, in the team, the member who doesn't have the mature role is free to say more and get away with it, like a dummy in a ventriloquist's act. Not all of the comedy members of a team took advantage of this freedom. Tom Smothers, though, saw the opportunities to make social and political statements.

Because the Smothers Brothers had started out as satirists, because, as Tom put it, "A comedian is contrary by nature," and because Tom especially had nurtured a deep interest in politics and the emerging youth movement, it is unsurprising that the pair gravitated to a position that mocked the ongoing conflict in Vietnam, that supported the war's protesters, that looked favorably on the growing subculture of drug users, whose slang completely baffled CBS's otherwise diligent censors, and that in general championed America's youthful counterculture. Indeed, their satirical approach and the cultural milieu in which they performed were the elements that ensured their survival precisely when other teams were having a tough time.

They wanted to prove that popular entertainment could be an agent of social change. This was, of course, a central message of the folk music they gently mocked.

The Smothers Brothers revolution developed over time. *The Smothers Brothers*

Comedy Hour, their signature show, began on February 5, 1967. During the first season, they sought a middle ground; they were Ed Sullivan for the young, or as *Time* put it, they were "hippies with haircuts." They wanted real comedy, and so they didn't use the standard laughter and applause electronic "sweetening" done for other shows.

The real controversy over the show began with the second season premiere on September 10, 1967. Pete Seeger, the prominent folksinger who had been blacklisted, was the guest. Seeger wanted to sing "Waist Deep in the Big Muddy," a parable about Vietnam, with its pungent allusion to President Lyndon Johnson in the words, "And the big fool says to push on." Seeger was not allowed to appear, although he sang the complete song on a later show. All the controversy and experimentation drew young audiences.

The Smothers Brothers had found a cause, acclaim, and an audience. Tom's juvenile character (and his genuine intelligence) had located some very powerful targets to mock and a generation's culture to embrace.

From then on, Tom and his writers (who included Mason Williams, Steve Martin,

Bob Einstein — who developed the character Super Dave Osborne and who was Albert Brooks's brother — and, in the final season, Rob Reiner, a rising talent who kept pushing Tom to go even further) played a game of chicken with the CBS censors. They made raids across the borders of the acceptable to see if they would be caught and punished.

Their exchanges were extremely tame by today's standards, but in 1967 no one else on television would have this dialogue:

Tom: There's a theory of clothes and politics. There's a definite correlation. You can tell who's running the country by how much clothes people wear.

Dick: You mean some people can afford more clothes on and others less on?

Tom: (nodding) The ordinary people are the less-ons.

Dick: Then who's running the country?

Tom: The more-ons.

The show also had great fun when Pat Paulsen, one of the regulars, made a mock presidential run in the Gracie Allen tradition, though with much more satirical intent.

The show was popular, and so CBS was criticized for its attempts at censorship. There were murmurs of political pressures being put on CBS by Richard Nixon's White House. Staffers there supposedly complained of the Smothers Brothers joking while soldiers were dying in Vietnam. And CBS perhaps genuinely believed that comedy and politics didn't go well together. As Mike Dann, the former vice-president for programming at CBS put it in *Smothered*, a documentary about the controversy, "You can't have a lot of fun if you take up a lot of causes."

The network wanted the Smothers Brothers to provide early previews of each show. This was supposedly for the benefit of local network affiliates; they wanted to determine whether the show was appropriate for broadcast in their region. Such a step had never before been taken, and it increased the tension considerably.

The third season, starting in September 1968, was the most confrontational. The height of the battle focused on Harry Belafonte, who wished to sing a song that the network believed criticized the police for the violence at the recent Democratic convention in Chicago. The network pulled the complete number. But, because both sides were now at war, that wasn't enough. The network then sold the five minutes made available by Belafonte's cancellation, and a Nixon-Agnew campaign advertisement ran in its place.

The confrontations went beyond politics. The censors found fault with sexual and drug references and had a whole new problem when comedian David Steinberg came on with some mock sermons, which the network found "sacrilegious." Steinberg had started by doing a "sermon" about Moses and was astounded when a large amount of mail came in from outraged viewers. Some of the mail was anti-Semitic. Steinberg was not used to such reactions to his work. CBS officials said Steinberg could come back if he made no biblical references. Tom reacted with anger to the CBS dictum and told Steinberg to do another sermon. Steinberg's second appearance — on Easter Sunday, during the week of President Eisenhower's funeral — was about Solomon and Jonah and was made more provocative by Steinberg's famous lines: "The Gentiles, as is their wont from time to time, threw a Jew overboard . . . The New Testament scholars literally grab the Jews by the Old Testament." A gesture followed that some at CBS thought was obscene. This was the final countercultural straw for the network.

The war ended with a seeming victory by CBS when Wood sent the telegram firing the brothers. As if to underscore its disdain, CBS decided to replace the Smothers Brothers with *Hee Haw* — a rural, folksy, mom-and-apple-pie music-and-comedy show. Though the Smothers Brothers would create other television shows and continue to perform concerts and receive honors and recognition, their names would remain synonymous with youthful protest and the crushing of dissent.

Ironically, while the Smothers Brothers show was repeatedly censored at CBS, an equally outrageous show on NBC was getting big laughs and huge audiences. Despite its content, it managed to survive even as the Smothers Brothers were axed.

Dan Rowan and Dick Martin had worked hard in clubs for years, beginning in 1953. As a child, Rowan had appeared onstage with his parents, who were performers, but they died when he was eleven. He then spent four difficult years in a home for children. He was a fighter pilot during World War II and was shot down in 1943.

After his service was completed, Rowan decided to enter show business, wanting to continue the family tradition. He contacted his friend, comedian Tommy Noonan. Noonan was the comic in a team with Peter Marshall acting as the straight man. The team appeared in several films, hoping to catch the Martin and Lewis comedy wave, but they never did. After the team split, Noonan later gained notoriety for a film he did with Jayne Mansfield. Peter Marshall eventually hosted game shows, most famously *Hollywood Squares*.

When Rowan and Noonan spoke, Noonan was seeking writers for a solo act. He liked Rowan's sense of humor, but thought he needed a partner. And Noonan knew the right person: Dick Martin.

Nine days after they first met, Rowan and Martin rented tuxedoes and performed a routine originally conceived for Noonan. After a year of performing, they realized, as Burns and Allen had, that they had to reverse roles. Rowan became the straight man. They switched the order of their names on the billing to Rowan and Martin to avoid any confusion with Martin and Lewis.

Ironically, after working so hard to make it as a comedy team, and then finally hitting it big on television with *Laugh-In* (also called *Rowan and Martin's Laugh-In*), they were much less a comedy team than ringmasters or masters of ceremonies. They ran the show, but they didn't do skits together, although they did do short bits with Martin's non sequiturs or deliberately raunchy rejoinders.

Rowan: For your own good, you should pick up some weight.
Martin: Shoulda been with me last night. I picked up 118 pounds.
Rowan: I don't want to hear about it.
Martin: It was for my own good, too.

Still, the fact that they were a team was important for *Laugh-In*. The show was deliberately presented as structured lunacy because the young '60s audiences craved it, but it was crucial for that audience to find comfort, so that no matter how crazy the show became, there was always some stability and unity in the form of Rowan and Martin.

Laugh-In was both a revolution in style and content and something of a throwback when it first appeared in January 1968. It was a bit of a variety show, in that it had guests. It certainly was a comedy program. But it didn't obey any of the rules. The guests were often there only to present one-liners. The show was made up of blackouts and endless streams of jokes. *Laugh-In* owed a lot to vaudeville, Olsen and Johnson's *Hellzapoppin'*, and the Keystone Kops, mixed with the contemporary satire explored by the Smothers Brothers and the political satire *That Was the Week That Was*. The show had a stage feel to it and reveled in slapstick, most famously when Judy Carne said "Sock it to me!" and was doused with water or dropped through a trapdoor.

But the style of the show was completely new to television. Rowan and Martin grasped a true if unpleasant fact about the young audiences: They no longer had a long attention span. The one-liners of the stand-ups had replaced the longer skits of the teams. In such an attention-deprived world, comedy would have to be lightning fast. And Rowan and Martin made it so.

They, like the Smothers Brothers, had a staid appearance; Rowan and Martin were even comparatively old for the young audience. But they knew the audience's taste; indeed, the show went to number one in the ratings after just eight broadcasts. The new audience was most of all interested in exploring sex, so Rowan would deliver lines like "News of the Past. 1793. On returning to Moscow today, the Czar and Czarina declined to discuss their honeymoon. But it was noted that he called her 'Catherine the Great,' and she called him 'Ivan the Terrible.' " *Laugh-In* was the first show to use the word "pregnant" instead of the more euphemistic "expecting." The show also had thinly veiled references to drugs, such as this observation from Judy Carne: "All the kids at my school really admire the astronauts. Imagine staying that high for that long."

The show had a unique look with its psychedelic joke wall, through which regulars and guests would pop their heads to deliver one joke after another. It had an assortment of loveable, oddball characters and trademark lines, such as "You bet your sweet bippy" and "Look that up in your Funk and Wagnall's." The comic style was clever. Different characters had set routines that were repeated over and over, prompting automatic laughs. Arte Johnson, for example, played a German soldier with his tag line "Verrry interesting." Henry Gibson played a character who recited poetry. Lily Tomlin played a telephone operator, and Goldie Hawn a dumb blonde. Johnson and Ruth Buzzi developed a particularly well-liked bit about a dirty old man approaching a not very attractive older woman with a handbag. The man kept making indecent proposals on a park bench and kept getting smacked with the handbag for his efforts:

Johnson: Do you believe in the here-after?

Buzzi: Of course I do.

Johnson: Then you know what I'm here after.

The show also had political content, but much of it was relatively safe humor with lines like "George Wallace, your sheets are ready." The show's producers protected themselves in another way as well. They arranged for conservative figures of the day to appear, including Richard Nixon, no less, who uttered a mock question, "Sock it to me?" John Wayne was a guest, as was Billy Graham — who said on the show, "The family that watches *Laugh-In* together really needs to pray together."

In other words, the show was not afraid to make fun of itself, and it covered all the political bases. Rowan did have a political position, one that had evolved from his original conservatism to a Smothers-like counterculturalism. As Rowan himself put it, "We think sex is funny and war is dirty."

But Rowan also knew there were other reasons why *Laugh-In* didn't encounter the sort of censorship problems the Smothers Brothers had. The Smothers Brothers had clear targets, whereas Rowan and Martin didn't; they made fun of everyone and everything. The very diffusion robbed any particular target of both anger and a sense of being singled out. The Smothers Brothers had sent a message. Rowan and Martin delivered an array of jokes. Their age also helped. They just didn't look like they could join a youth revolution.

It is not that Rowan and Martin's producers didn't have any censorship problems; they did, though NBC tended to focus more on sexual innuendo than on politically sensitive material. In fact, the show had a censor who went over every script and was present at all the rehearsals and tapings. But the producers figured out ways around the problem. For example, Joan Baez appeared on the Smothers Brothers show and dedicated a song to her husband, David Harris, who was then in prison for draft evasion. CBS censors edited out the reason for Harris's incarceration. On *Laugh-In*, Goldie Hawn delivered a line about Baez, alluding to her arrest for participating in anti-war demonstrations: "I *love* Joan Baez. I've even got a set of her fingerprints." That got by. It was funny and it was fast.

The speed was crucial. The Smothers Brothers developed lengthy sketches, whereas Rowan and Martin delivered drive-by jokes. By the time audience members realized a political point had been made, they had to concentrate on the next joke. Two hundred jokes were delivered in the fifty-three minutes of airtime. A normal variety show had about thirty cuts, whereas *Laugh-In* had approximately two hundred and fifty.

Laugh-In survived for six years, and the Rowan and Martin partnership, which lasted for thirty years, ended amicably.

There were other teams on television such as Allen and Rossi and Wayne and Schuster, but none that had the enormous success of the Smothers Brothers or Rowan and Martin. They represent the end of their era.

The 1956 breakup of Martin and Lewis had marked the death of classic teams that were successful in all media. The firing of the Smothers Brothers was a dramatic moment symbolizing the death of the classic comedy teams that had stayed together across performances and over time. The Smothers Brothers didn't go gently, driven from fame by a yawning audience. They didn't go willingly and happily, as Dean Martin did. They were dragged off the stage, despite their soaring ratings. The corporate culture drove them away, and the wider culture kept them and other comedy teams from returning.

Ironically, the Smothers Brothers remain the last major team still performing today.

FOURTEEN

VANISHING STARS

Final Acts and
the Death of Comedy Teams

The disappearance of classic comedy teams was due, in part, to the changing nature of show business. The teams emerged and became popular in vaudeville and radio, matured and flourished in movies that showcased teams, and continued to perform in the early television variety shows — especially Ed Sullivan's. That is, comedy teams had built success over several decades and in several media. By the 1960s, however, a stand-up comedian could literally become famous overnight with one appearance on *The Tonight Show*, and this new potential for instantaneous fame drew a crowd of contenders. Moreover, it took much less time to put together a stand-up act than to get the timing right for a two-act. And most important, the environments that had traditionally nurtured comedy teams were going or gone.

The comedy clubs, which had become the training ground for comedians, were geared toward young, single, white audiences, and unsurprisingly, it was young, single, white comedians who initially succeeded. The clubs focused on a relatively small group of subjects, such as relationships. That is, clubs, meeting the needs of their audiences, reduced comedy from a very wide spectrum of subjects to a few and narrowed the variety of comedy styles, including pantomime and slapstick, to the single one of a performer standing at a microphone telling jokes. The club performers founded their work on the traditional monologuists, such as W. C. Fields and Bob Hope, not on the legacy of the comedy teams.

Additionally, although the teams had grown strong during the eras of vaudeville and radio when linguistic humor was prized, by the 1960s, this comedic heritage had largely disappeared. Americans groaned at bad puns, tolerated malapropisms only in limited numbers, and generally did not find language an interesting subject of humor, except for the creative exceptions like Norm Crosby or George Carlin. The clean language of the teams was left behind by the coarser language of the culture, especially in the comedy clubs and later on cable television.

Economics also profoundly affected the decline of team comedy. Comedy teams were paid the same amount of money as a single stand-up comedian, so there was more incentive to go it alone. After all, a team had to spend twice as much on travel, accommodations, and other expenses. John Trueson, a member of the popular 1980s comedy team Corson and Trueson and now manager of Governor's Comedy Cabaret on Long Island, has identified other potential problems with teams: "Being in a team also doubles the chances that one of the participants will possess certain self-destructive tendencies or that the participants will develop personal issues with one another. It's like anything else — the more humans you have involved, the more the chances that something will go awry. There is also potential for petty jealousies or outside interference. Logistically, you have to work around two schedules because when comics start out they always have second or 'day jobs.' "

Robert Thompson, director of the Center for the Study of Popular Television at Syracuse University, has noted another change that undermined the economic viability of teams. By the late 1960s, the management representatives of performers realized that if they were working with a team, their options for bookings were quite limited, and it made more sense for managers to contract with individual performers. Of course, these individuals could be teamed for a specific movie or show — and that would mean commissions from each performer, rather than a single commission from a team act.

Besides the changes in show business and the economic realities that weakened the viability of comedy teams, the enormous changes taking place in society in the 1960s sealed the fate of classic comedy teams.

Except for a brief period in the 1920s, American life in the twentieth century had been marked by degrees of self-sacrifice. During the Great Depression and World War II Americans needed to surrender their own desires in order to face down a national threat. After the war, with relative peace and prosperity, self-sacrifice was called for again, this time to reconstruct the country and raise the large new generation of children.

The nation needed harmony during those troubled decades of national challenges. The humor of classic comedy teams was focused on opposites — in appearance, temperament, and outlook. Team comedy emerged in part from the diametrical differences between the members of the team, between, for example, the thin, mild Stan Laurel and the overweight, more aggressive Oliver Hardy, or the suave, adult Dean Martin and the childlike, manic Jerry Lewis. Comedy teams exemplified how different personalities could, in working together, become a cohesive unit.

Comedy teams were a symbol of a cooperative society, of people working together for a common good. Comedy teams fit seamlessly into American culture through the first half of the century, but not so seamlessly in the second half when personal desires and ambitions became more acceptable.

Postwar suburban life was materially comfortable but a bit dull; its safety was a barrier to a more thrilling reality, and its gift of washing machines and shiny cars a cover for enforced conformity in school and on the job. Happiness itself became defined as adapting to the needs of institutions and the attainment of material goods.

The late 1950s and the 1960s saw the emergence of a revolt against the suburbs' troubled Eden, against the suppression of the self, against the submersion of sexual desire, against the repression of the burning quest for fame and glory, against the still stagnant social roles for women and African Americans. It was the shriek of an ego released from history's penitentiary.

People were exhausted by communal obligations, and many had the economic means to satisfy their personal desires. As pollster Daniel Yankelovich put it, "the 1960s raised the question of whether one needed to sacrifice one's own self-expressive needs if it was not economically necessary to do so." In the late '60s, Americans clearly answered that question.

The 70 million children born immediately after World War II became teenagers and young adults during the 1960s. Because of the size of their demographic bulge, all they had to do was move through the culture together to change it.

Of course, not all young people shared the same values. Their identity as a generation was shaped, at least in part, by media representations of the more vocal members of their peer group. The media, for example, were mostly focused on white, middle-class members of the generation whose changing attitudes, tastes, and values formed recognizable patterns of rebellion (such as widespread drug experimentation, changing sexual mores, and extensive protest of government policies). They were the first generation conscious of the possibility of nuclear annihilation, the first generation that grew up with television, and the first generation to grow up in such affluence.

Those baby boomers that shaped the

culture did not want to lead their parents' lives. The comedy that arose to give voice to the emerging rebellion was not a comedy fit for a team. It was a comedy that depended on a more appropriate symbol for the individual self struggling against a conformist society or meddlesome family. It was a comedy of one man or woman standing up without a partner, the lone individual, the existentially alienated, the outsider.

At first, audiences embraced the psychological insights of Shelley Berman and the daring Lenny Bruce. Later, they wanted what the writer and comedy historian Ronald L. Smith has referred to as "reality stand-up." Audiences, according to Smith, wanted comedians "sharing minor miseries that they could agree on." The increasing focus on pure reality squeezed out any need for the alternate reality created by teams.

One member of a great classic comedy team perceptively noted the comedic differences between team and individual comedy and wasn't very impressed by the change. Stan Laurel observed, "In comedy the most important person is the person you're playing to — the person you're trying to make laugh. Too many young comedians these days forget that. A lot of them are up there performing in order to make themselves feel better, when it should be the other way around. And why don't some of them even try to use a little visual humor? They stand there and talk, talk, talk — and after a while I get the feeling that the only person they're really talking to is themselves. That's sad. That means they haven't learned the very first thing a comedian must learn — it is your audience that counts, not you."

Stan Laurel died on February 23, 1965, at the age of seventy-four. The death of this quiet and dignified exemplar of team comedy, who kept his name in the phone book and responded to visitors, calls, and letters, who never performed after Oliver Hardy had died in 1957, who was so wistful about the comedy he saw overcome by new styles that he didn't particularly admire, was one more poignant symbol of an era coming to an end.

Laurel rightly identified the changes in the attitudes of comedians toward themselves and the audience. But he may not have noticed that the audience the new comedians were playing to wanted the rants, the talk, talk, talk. The comedians had surely changed, but, in part, that was simply in response to the cultural changes taking place.

Laurel's death came soon after the deaths of Chico Marx in 1961 and Harpo Marx in 1964. Groucho remained popular until his death at eighty-six in 1977. George Burns, who embarked on a movie career after Gracie's departure, lived to be one hundred and died in 1996. Bob Hope also reached his hundredth birthday. He died in 2003. These long-lived survivors, though, didn't mask the fact that the era of the comedy teams had come to an end many years earlier.

Like many deaths, the death of comedy teams came awkwardly. Team comedy succumbed to the huge new wave of stand-up comedy, but even as it was dying, new teams emerged who would try to keep its legacy alive.

However, none of the teams that tried to resuscitate classic comedy teams developed the kind of mass appeal that characterized the era of comedy teams that preceded them. For example, Cheech and Chong and Monty Python — two of the most popular teams of the post-1970 era — appealed to specialized, niche groups rather than the wider audience of the classic comedians.

The comedy of Cheech and Chong was not a confrontational, political humor. Just as the Smothers Brothers had started out by making affectionate fun of the folksinging craze, Richard "Cheech" Marin and Tommy Chong satirized the youthful drug users, who bought their records and flocked to their movies in the late 1970s and early 1980s. It was as though the younger siblings of those who came of age in the '60s had felt left out, wanted to capture the revolution for themselves, and found willing leaders in Cheech and Chong.

Their appeal for the young lay in the characters they created: two not very bright but likeable men struggling against authority imposed by the outside world. That description sounds a lot like Laurel and Hardy. But Cheech and Chong's goal in life involved a desire to be elevated not socially but herbally. The loopy, often improvised dialogue the actors provided for the characters, filled as it was with scatological humor and incessant drug references, made it difficult for their audience not to root for them. After all, like the Marx Brothers and so many other comic ancestors, they, too, simply ignored the rules and niceties of society to find in their own world a truth that eluded the rest.

Cheech and Chong had another similarity to Laurel and Hardy. Laurel and Hardy had also been both lovable and dumb, though Hardy was particularly lacking in self-awareness of his mental deficiencies. Many comedy teams that developed before Laurel and Hardy (such as Burns and Allen) and those that came after them (such as Abbott and Costello, and Martin and Lewis) consisted of one smart partner and one dumb one. This is also true of the television teams, such as the Smothers Brothers and Rowan and Martin. But Cheech and Chong reverted to the Laurel and Hardy model; they were both cheerfully and pleasantly daft.

Cheech and Chong inspired a small industry of team comedy in the last three decades of the twentieth century. Many of the temporary teams, including most significantly the Blues Brothers, but also Mike Myers and Dana Carvey in the *Wayne's World* movies, were made up of mentally challenged heroes. There were also non-dumb teams, but the predominance of the "dumb and dumber" types signaled that audiences were receptive to characters with an excuse to be crude, rude, and lewd. The characters' very dumbness provided a freedom that those in the audience didn't have in their own lives. These teams are the cinematic children of Jerry Lewis without the restraints of order provided by Dean Martin.

Cheech and Chong's gentle mocking of themselves as drug users could be seen, for example, in their first film *Up in Smoke*. The film was made for $2 million and grossed $47.5 million. Marin later perceptively noted, "We represent the frustrations of modern man. Guys who fantasize themselves in great situations they'll never have." In this, they were like comedians in all previous American generations, providing for their particular audience a way to navigate through society and through life. And the message was crucial. Just as the Marx Brothers had provided solace for immigrant audiences and a way to mock the rich and powerful without surrendering their identities, so, too, did Cheech and Chong give their young audiences in the barrios, ghettos, dorms, and elsewhere hope that they, too, could survive American culture without giving in to the system.

They wrapped that message in soft, self-deprecatory humor. At one point in the film, Cheech asks his partner, "Am I driving okay?" Chong looks around and says, "I think we're parked, man."

In *Cheech and Chong's Next Movie*, Chong, having aided his friend in stealing a garbage can full of gasoline, complains, "I'm going to be late for work again, man. That's the fifth time I've been late this week, and it's only Tuesday, man."

Marin's very expressive face, infectious laugh, and easygoing style added immeasurably to the films. His proud Chicano identity did not prevent Marin from engaging in ethnic self-mockery through his character's disdain for work and obsession with women. Actually all ethnic groups, including WASPs, are mocked in Cheech and Chong movies, and Marin's performance is both so clearly over the top and so endearing that it is difficult to see the character as perpetuating stereotypes. The character's good humor makes his actions a subtle mockery of such stereotyping.

Despite Marin's joking around, it is not clear that he is the comic and Chong the straight man. Again, like Laurel and Hardy, they both joked, they both were in costume, and they both fed lines to the other. They've often been called the Abbott and Costello of the drug age, but the comparison, at least from the point of view of comedy teams, is not quite accurate. Abbott was a straight man, a bit of a bully, and Chong is neither.

Their subsequent films, although very successful, could not capture the newness and vitality of their first picture. *Cheech and Chong's Nice Dreams*, *Things Are Tough All Over*, and *Still Smokin'* used up all the drug gags. Without new ways to present the old characters and with a changing audience, the duo was forced to change. They made *Cheech and Chong's The Coriscan Brothers*, but the film was not successful, and the team broke up after that.

Other temporary teams emerged after Cheech and Chong, some of whom used the form Hope and Crosby had made popular, but their appeal was limited. The two most prominent of the older temporary teams were Walter Matthau and Jack Lemmon, and Richard Pryor and Gene Wilder. The younger temporary teams mostly emerged from improvisational comedy.

Director Billy Wilder had been watching a football game when he saw a fullback run out of bounds and land on top of a fan. Wilder's immediate reaction was that the scene could be made into a film and immediately thought of Jack Lemmon as the poor fan. Lemmon had appeared in the Wilder comedy *Some Like It Hot* in 1959; Jerry Lewis had been offered a part in the film but turned it down because he didn't want to appear in drag for so long.

Wilder had also approached Walter Matthau to play a role in *The Fortune Cookie*. Matthau had achieved fame in 1965 when he starred, opposite Art Carney, as Oscar Madison in Neil Simon's *The Odd Couple*. Matthau was shocked when he got Wilder's script. Matthau's role as the slimy lawyer "Whiplash" Willie would make him the star of the film. The Lemmon character was the straight man, although it was Lemmon who was famous for his comedy roles. Lemmon would spend most of the film immobilized in a wheelchair.

Matthau and Lemmon knew each other at the time of filming, but Lemmon was by far the more famous actor. Matthau called him up and asked him why he had not taken the lead role. Lemmon told him that it was time for Matthau to receive the recognition he deserved. He ultimately did, winning an Oscar for best supporting actor.

As a team, Matthau and Lemmon worked well together in part because of their real-life friendship and in part because of the quality of the writing and acting. Neither Matthau nor Lemmon were really comedians; they were both comic actors. In this sense, it is conceivable, at least in some of their films, especially *Out to Sea*, that they could have switched roles.

Lemmon's put-upon character could vary. For example, in the team's second pairing, *The Odd Couple*, Lemmon played a much different and more comic role. However, Matthau's wisecracking curmudgeon was there in full force, as when he complained about Lemmon's character's penchant for tidiness: "Two single men should not have a cleaner house than my mother."

Still, both of these characters fit together well. Lemmon's character, like Bob Newhart's, was an ordinary sane person surrounded by insane characters. The character's real edge is his awareness of his predicament, which results in continual anxiety. Matthau's character is the tempter, the one believing that no impulse is so bad that it should be resisted. Such a pairing was enormously attractive for Americans caught between the moral strictures of their parents' generation and the pull of personal interest. Audience members wanted to take part in the sexual revolution but were worried about being wounded by lost love or disease. They wanted to get rich, but they didn't want to work as hard as they knew was necessary. Lemmon and Matthau were the opposing pulls on their conscience.

Lemmon and Matthau worked with Wilder again in 1974 in a not very successful remake of *The Front Page* and an even less successful film in 1981, *Buddy Buddy*. The roles seemed familiar: Lemmon as a suicidal man with love problems and Matthau as a hit man. The audience was small for the latter film in large part because the American audience had changed.

Realizing that they, too, had to change, the Lemmon-Matthau team in *Grumpy Old Men* and its sequel *Grumpier Old Men* focused on constant bickering as a comic device. It worked partially in the first film, but the two never quite captured the magic of their earlier work.

In contrast, Richard Pryor's hip, black, ruthlessly honest stage presence captured his era perfectly. Pryor had begun his comedy career in a nightclub in Peoria, and by 1963 he was successful enough to move to New York. He quickly established himself, appearing on several television shows, including Ed Sullivan's and Merv Griffin's. Pryor then moved to Los Angeles and began appearing in films. It was in 1976 that he appeared in *Silver Streak*, the first of four films he made with Gene Wilder. Ever so tentatively, Hollywood comedy began to experiment with a white and black team.

It was not a first. There were other minor black-white teams, including Tom Dreesen and Tim Reid (Reid later found national fame in *WKRP in Cincinnati*), Steve Rossi and Slappy White, and Freeman King and Murray Langston (who appeared frequently on the *Sonny and Cher Show*). In addition, the great comedian Bill Cosby had teamed up with the white actor Robert Culp in the television series *I Spy*, but that was not a comedy. Still, it proved to Hollywood that audiences were ready for a black and white team, if the team was right.

Pryor and Wilder were different from the other black and white comedy teams; they were already major stars. The two had almost had a chance to work together in 1974 when Mel Brooks attempted to cast Pryor in *Blazing Saddles*, an idea vetoed by nervous executives. Nonetheless, Wilder's successful teaming with the black actor Cleavon Little in that film was a forerunner of the tremendous success he would find with Pryor in *Silver Streak.*

Silver Streak offered a gentle exploration of racial issues; it provided a warm vision of black and white harmony, cooperation, and even deep friendship. One of the funniest scenes in the film portrays Wilder's enthusiastic but inept attempt to pass as a black man. It was, intentionally or not, a deft comic apology for the minstrel shows of the past.

Pryor's character in such a gentle film is not as angry or as smart as Pryor was in real life. The character doesn't quite get white society despite his bravado. He needs Wilder's character as a guide to white society as much as Wilder's character needs Pryor's as a guide to black life. That was the basis of the team; they desperately needed each other for survival in the other's world. Such an approach is different from traditional teams like Laurel and Hardy, the Marx Brothers, or Abbott in Costello, in which the team needed each other to survive against an outside world that was their common enemy. Pryor and Wilder were, in this limited sense, a more political team, attuned to the social context of their teaming, if hesitant to make open ideological statements about race.

Also, the film didn't focus exclusively on comedy but cleverly mixed the humor with an absorbing suspense story. This light, Hitchcock-type touch of innocents getting caught up in a crime tied to modern race relations can be seen as a smart mixing of older and newer traditions. In this sense, there was more suspense than comedy, rendering the humor more comic relief than full-bore comedy.

Furthermore, the suspense can be understood as a mask for the unmentioned racial tensions between the characters. In this interpretation, the crucial part of their task as a team is to overcome those racial tensions and find a way to cooperate. Additionally, *Silver Streak*'s blending of suspense and a temporary comedy team became a model for a group of films that mixed such suspense or violent action with two characters who joked with each other.

Pryor and Wilder were next teamed in the 1981 comedy *Stir Crazy*. Playing falsely accused jail inmates, the two have to team up in order to survive a rough new environment and ultimately escape from it. Once more, Pryor tries to make Wilder hip in order to survive in prison. Although *Stir*

Crazy is funnier than *Silver Streak*, it is much less suspenseful and is a far less successful movie. The somewhat tired idea for the movie, of an inmate with a special skill prized by the warden and used by the warden in a bet against a rival, is taken from the Burt Reynolds movie *The Longest Yard*, which had borrowed its idea from the British movie *Loneliness of the Long-Distance Runner*.

Once again, the racial elements are interesting. The protagonists are characters similar to the ones they played in *Silver Streak*. Wilder continued with his charming innocent character, a nonthreatening, open-faced, ordinary guy caught up in a world of evil beyond his control. Pryor played a character with a hip exterior just barely covering his insecurity. He was not so much dangerous as wounded. This was a black character Hollywood could sell.

But Pryor off the screen didn't seem to have any of the soft inner core of the characters he played on it. He was tough all the way through; the deep wounds of his personal life had forged a core that was not at all sweet. Indeed, the tensions he felt found their way to the set. The crew was annoyed because Pryor would arrive at noon, four hours after filming was scheduled to begin.

Although Pryor and Wilder co-starred in two more movies, *See No Evil, Hear No Evil* and *Another You*, neither approached the quality of their first two films. *Another You* was hampered by Pryor's deteriorating health and an inadequate script. After *Another You*, the two stars did not appear together again but instead faced great personal crises. Wilder worked with his extraordinarily talented wife, Gilda Radner, up until her tragic death in 1989 from ovarian cancer, and Pryor's drug-filled life caught up with him when, in 1980, he suffered third-degree burns over much of his body when he reportedly freebased cocaine.

As the temporary teams made up of movie stars faded, new temporary teams rose to take their place. These new temporary teams came primarily from the gang comedy that emerged in the 1970s. Gang comedy, primarily attracting intellectuals and the young, reached its cinematic zenith in the work of Monty Python and its television zenith on *Saturday Night Live*.

Monty Python's Flying Circus emerged from the satirical comedians who flourished both in the United States and Great Britain from roughly the mid-1950s to the late 1960s. Mort Sahl, Lenny Bruce, Shelley Berman, and Nichols and May wandered the nightclubs of America, poking at their culture and mocking the unpleasant contradictions they found. In Great Britain, however, satire emerged not from the improvisational groups or stand-up comedians but from universities, particularly Oxford and Cambridge, where groups crafted witty send-ups of their own social world. By 1962, the British Broadcasting Corporation saw the enormous popularity of these intelligent young humorists and ran David Frost's *That Was the Week That Was*, a news commentary in revue form. The show was particularly pointed in its criticism of the Conservative Party in power, and the show was soon cancelled. Frost, however, regrouped and started *The Frost Report* in 1966. It was on that show that the group of performers later known as Monty Python came together.

By then, John Cleese and Graham Chapman had already performed at the Footlights Club in Cambridge and in New York. Eric Idle had also attended Cambridge. Their work was topical in a way that Frost (and many listeners) found both exciting and relevant. Terry Jones and Michael Palin came from Oxford and brought from there a taste for absurdity. The five worked with Frost until 1969, when the BBC started a new series. For the series, Cleese contacted Terry Gilliam, an American artist with whom he had worked in New York.

Monty Python's Flying Circus was created. Graham Chapman explained the name with gracious nonsensical ease: The five of them had been referred to as a circus — not always politely. Further elucidating the name, he explained, "it's a snake which constricts, crushes and then consumes its prey. 'Flying' had a First World War sound to it, and 'Monty' would be the name of a terrifically bad theatrical agent." The new Pythons blended the Cambridge and Oxford approaches to humor but leaned most heavily toward the latter's absurdist approach.

The first show, broadcast late at night, was popular beyond anyone's expectations, and a second series began in 1970, followed by a third series in 1971–1972.

The youthful viewers of the show were the first generation that had grown up watching television. The worldwide anti-authoritarianism of the late 1960s and early 1970s fit well into the Python worldview, and so did the intense interest in the medium itself, which was simultaneously a source of humor and a key way for that generation to separate from their parents' television-free early lives. The viewers intimately understood the television rules that were being mocked. The *Flying Circus* was relentless. Phony BBC officials showed up to complain about content. Popular shows were spoofed. Opening and closing credits might pop up anywhere, at any time. The daring young men on the *Flying Circus* wanted to throw out every predictable television convention. They would use stream of consciousness monologues. Sketches might last no longer than one line. They created funny movements for a "Silly Walks" sketch. Audiences didn't know what to expect of them. They might steal telephone booths for no reason or dress up as Hell's Grannies, three older women walking down the street pushing people, or as Vikings singing a hymn to pressed meat. A Monty Python soccer team was made up exclusively of players with wooden legs. They even created a character with possibly the briefest speaking part in comedy history: the "It's Man," who would run up to the camera and say

"It's" just before the opening credits.

Their comedy was deeply satirical and profoundly anti-authoritarian — but was never weighed down by being tied to specific political personalities. Still, the Cambridge humor was evident in the biting attacks on the powerful, the Church of England, wealthy professionals, particularly lawyers, and politicians.

The Pythons were a bit of a boys club; they had trouble writing for women, and so they ended up playing older women themselves. They finally found Carol Cleveland and hired her as a stooge.

Fans began watching the shows over and over, memorizing lines.

The success led the group to take some sketches from the first two series and create the film *And Now for Something Completely Different*. They did add a small amount of connecting material, but generally kept the sketches exactly as in the original. However, the film failed to find an audience, perhaps because viewers didn't feel a need to see a refilmed television show. Cleese left, and the remaining members made six additional episodes without him. It seemed as though the Monty Python era had flickered out.

British television shows, though, were

popular on the Public Broadcast Service in the United States, and so with little fanfare, KERA-TV in Dallas put the show on during the summer of 1974. The success of the show led other PBS affiliates and some commercial stations to play it as well. By 1975, the show was being broadcast on more than 130 stations.

The Python legend blossomed with the release that year of *Monty Python and the Holy Grail*. Cleese had returned for the new film, but if it had received the same reception as *And Now for Something Completely Different*, it is likely that the Pythons would have stopped performing together, and their success and impact would have been diminished.

Their decision to set the entire film in the Middle Ages sounds odd in retrospect, considering their role as counterculture comedians. First, there were the practical problems. Transportation was by horse during that era, but financial constraints prevented the use of live animals during the filming. The resourceful Pythons, though, had a brilliant solution: The squires in the film would bang coconut shells together to mimic the beat of horses' hooves as they made galloping movements as though actually riding. Of course, the absurd element wouldn't have been possible had it not fit perfectly with Python humor. Dressed in full medieval regalia, the Monty Python players were like moderns out of place. This was a pitch-perfect metaphor for the generation, feeling estranged from the seemingly ancient world created by their parents. Monty Python had it both ways. By seeming to make fun of the conventions of life in the Middle Ages, they reduced accusations that they were mocking contemporary mores, while at the same time allowing audiences to laugh at the absurdities of social life. The lines that Cleese and Chapman wrote were very funny, but the setting, by its nature, opened up the potential for visual humor, as in the scene Crossing the Bridge of Death over the Gorge of Eternal Peril — although Cleese used a stunt double for the dangerous shot. (This was the only Python scene he didn't perform himself.) They also added humor not tied to history, such as a killer rabbit attacking the knights. The film was enormously successful.

Other movies would follow, including the controversial *Life of Brian*, released in 1979. *Brian* seemed like a sensible follow-up film to the *Holy Grail* film. The notion of a story set in biblical times once again offered some aesthetic distance to play around with satire, but biblical stories are not Arthurian legends. A lot of people were offended by what seemed to be the mockery of early Christians. Indeed, the story originated as a life of Jesus but evolved into a tale about Brian, the thirteenth apostle, who would always just miss the crucial events. He might, for example, be stuck at home with his wife's friends and show up late at the Last Supper. The Pythons liked the idea, but there was a problem with the apostle story. It inevitably would have to include scenes with Jesus, and that meant a more reverent tone and a stop to the laughs. Finally, they conceived the crucial idea that Brian's story be parallel to that of Jesus, with the premise that Brian, who is completely ordinary, would be mistaken for a holy man.

One of the film's unmistakable messages is that people should not blindly follow religious leaders. At one point, Brian (Chapman) comes to his bedroom window (totally nude after a night spent with a young woman) to address an adoring crowd gathered outside. Brian says to them, "You've all got to work it out for yourselves." The crowd screams back, "Yes, yes! We've got to work it out for ourselves." Impressed, Brian says, "Exactly." The crowd pauses, and in unison, they raise their voices. "Tell us more!" The charge of being unable to think for themselves stung some religious believers. A few southern states in the United States, some towns in the United Kingdom, and even some countries banned the film. Still, aside from the controversy, as a film, it is Monty Python's best. It has a sustained story line, very witty dialogue, excellent acting, and a distinctly barbed point of view.

The Pythons next reunited in *The Meaning of Life*, released in 1983. The film was successful, but the era had changed, and some of the Pythons themselves were anxious to move on to their own projects. Graham Chapman's early death in 1989 ensured that the many rumored future reunion projects would never happen. The Pythons decided that the team was a team or nothing. The decision was a touching assertion of the values of teamwork and a recognition that no one of the Pythons would ever be as zany or as brilliant as they were together.

The Python legacy, though, was ably carried on by new groups and such television shows as *Saturday Night Live*, *SCTV*, and *The Kids in the Hall*.

The experimental generation that fused sex, drugs, and rock 'n' roll with social rebellion needed some television to fill the void left by the departure of the Smothers Brothers. It is odd that television executives were so slow to realize this. *Saturday Night Live* came into being only because NBC needed a low-budget show after Johnny Carson told them he didn't want reruns of his show on the weekends; he wanted to show the reruns on weekdays so he could take some additional time off.

NBC hired Lorne Michaels to create that weekend show. The network knew Michaels from his work on *Laugh-In* and with Lily Tomlin. Michaels had the comic sensibility but not yet any idea for a show. He liked the work done by the improvisational troupes, and so a live show, right on the edge of programming danger, suited him well. But he also knew the enormous pitfalls of improvisation — weak lines, crosstalking, and timing difficulties. He found a solution: Get a funny script and hire talented people who could improvise if needed.

Saturday Night Live debuted on October 11, 1975, with an incredibly gifted group of young, unknown performers who made a point of connecting excesses in their personal lives to wild experimentation in their professional lives. The Not Ready for Prime Time Players included Dan Aykroyd, John Belushi, Chevy Chase, Jane Curtin, Garrett Morris, Laraine Newman, and Gilda Radner and would soon include Bill Murray.

The show brought back the topical satire of the Smothers Brothers and was more successful in its battles with censors, pushing television's comic possibilities in unchartered and previously unacceptable directions.

Cleverly, Michaels included music as part of the mix. The result did more than draw an audience; it made a connection in the audience's mind between comedians and rock stars. No fans had squealed at Mort Sahl or Shelley Berman. Now, though, the young came to regard comedians in a new, more exalted way. Comedy would never be quite the same. The irreverent SNL style would find its way to a wider group of comedians, to David Letterman, Conan O'Brien, Jon Stewart, and many more.

The veterans of *Saturday Night Live* also formed many of the most well-known temporary film comedy teams. John Belushi and Dan Aykroyd were the first of such teams and served as the model for those to come.

Belushi and Aykroyd were on one of their cross-country road trips from New York to Los Angeles, driving Aykroyd's Oldsmobile Rocket 88. They were escaping, as usual, from the rigors of *Saturday Night Live*. Flying down the highway, released from the intense pressure of weekly live television, they could be their own exuberant selves. They both enjoyed music, but Belushi, ever restless, was bored by the same old rock 'n' roll. Aykroyd was a huge fan of American blues music.

The music mixed with their search for new characters, and the Blues Brothers were born. Aykroyd and Belushi, always anxious to have fun even with their most serious passions, decided to adopt the look of late-1940s blues musicians. The comedians put on sunglasses, dark, baggy suits with ties, and porkpie hats. They looked like what they were: two white guys doing a bad imitation of John Lee Hooker in 1950. The half-serious, half-in-jest duet began by warming up audiences. Their fantastic reception led to many appearances on the show and eventually to a movie.

Belushi and Aykroyd, like the Blues

Brothers characters Jake and Elwood Blues, were finally a team, one that would be ended by Belushi's disquieting death in 1982.

The Blues Brothers was an odd mix. It was, like *Saturday Night Live*, smart enough to tie its comedic sensibility to an outstanding musical experience. In this case, guest stars James Brown, Cab Calloway, Ray Charles, and Aretha Franklin added an authenticity as well as recognized talent to the film. The Blues Brothers, on a self-described "mission from God," sought to raise money to save the Catholic orphanage in which they grew up. Such a quest gave some order to the film and simultaneously inoculated it from charges of nihilism. (Belushi and Aykroyd actually presented Chicago's mayor, Jane Byrne, with a check for $50,000 to aid orphanages.) As it was, the car chases and the simulated destruction of a mall and many of the Chicago police force's squad cars required the use of seventy-eight stunt people and led critics to dismiss the film, without understanding why it was so popular.

In many ways Belushi reflected the sensibility that made the film a huge success. Belushi's real-life anger, which was visible in his comic characters, mirrored the repressed anger of the young audience. The countercultural revolution had failed. Watergate had revealed the corruption of government. Increasingly, single parents raised those who came of age in the late '70s. Their kids' anger did not express itself as outmoded social protest so much as asocial behavior. They added cocaine to the drug culture of the '60s and early '70s generation and embraced punk's nihilism. They saw society as absurd. The comedians who spoke to them would have to match their anger and resentment.

John Belushi created that character. His threatening, manic, charmless persona left no cushion between the anger and the actor. This was different from earlier angry comedians. Bud Abbott's anger had always been tempered by a genuine affection for Lou Costello and the charm of a con man. Oliver Hardy's bluster also masked an attachment to his screen partner, and even though his character didn't see it, he let the character's incompetence add to the humor. Belushi was the straight man and the comic in one person. He wanted his characters to be angry and outrageous all the time. This, of course, was more in keeping with the stand-up comedians who bared their souls and seemed to hide no part of their personalities behind a character, who indulged in excesses and then publicly and shamelessly confessed to them.

It may fairly be asked, then, what is the place of Dan Aykroyd in such a team? Aykroyd is far more controlled than Belushi. He projects more culture and intelligence than his character might be thought to possess. This would ordinarily be useful in tempering the excesses of a comic partner, but unlike Bud Abbott or Dean Martin, Aykroyd's character is not able to control his partner. This team consists of two people with strong personalities that are not altered by interactions with each other.

At the time of Belushi's death, Aykroyd was working on screenplays for two new films, which were eventually made as *Doctor Detroit* and *Ghostbusters*. Belushi was to have co-starred in both.

There were many other movie temporary teams that emerged from *Saturday Night Live* and *SCTV*, some extremely successful and funny, such as Mike Myers and Dana Carvey. Others like John Candy and Eugene Levy were extraordinarily talented but never quite found the right movie to project their comic genius. It's possible to make a wistful argument that they would have been successful had they had the opportunity to make a few more films together. John Candy's early death is reminiscent of Belushi's in the sense that he still had so much left to give to comedy. Chris Farley's death is even more reminiscent, because his end was intimately connected to his drug use.

Farley, like Belushi, made vulgar excess the point of his humor, but unlike Belushi, Farley blunted it with an incredible innocence. They both embodied the audience's desire to consume without accepting the social restraints of their parents. Both Belushi and Farley's weight was less a sign of a jolly and funny character, as it was, say, with John Bunny or Oliver Hardy, than it was a symbol of their refusal to curtail appetites.

What was so funny about such excess? Perhaps audiences laughed because they recognized themselves, just as radio listeners during the Great Depression had laughed at Jack Benny's stinginess because they themselves had been forced by circumstance to become cheap. Belushi and Farley mirrored the shared appetites of their fans. They weren't mocking the

American taste for excess; they were embracing it.

Farley and his screen partner, David Spade, were an interesting combination for a comedy team. Spade was a small man with a big mouth, whereas Farley was huge with a kind of split personality — half filled with Belushi's anger and half filled with a Jim Carrey–like sweet dumbness. The two actors made only two film appearances together. Their first movie was *Tommy Boy*, followed by *Black Sheep*, a considerably less successful film artistically.

Farley's characters captured perfectly the psychological state of many in his young audience — at least those who thought of themselves as the discarded losers, the ones who couldn't succeed by their family's or by society's standards but who desperately wanted their approval. They saw themselves in Farley. It could also be that many in the audience identified with one of Farley's real-life problems that emerged in the characters: his self-loathing.

By contrast, John Candy, a contemporary fat comic, played characters whose sweetness was just funny. They were not tinged with emotional depth. Candy was a classic nice, fat funnyman. He had many ancestors in the comic pantheon.

The legacy of Belushi's and Farley's anger can be seen in Adam Sandler's edgy characters and in the aggressive, almost manic dumbness of Jim Carrey's characters.

These teams were its final expression outside of a few interesting efforts, such as those by Kathy Najimy and Mo Gaffney and by Penn and Teller (Penn Jillette, the tall, opinionated magician and Ray Teller, the shorter, silent helper). In the spirit of the times, Penn and Teller relied on cruel tricks for their comedy. However, they were magicians first, comics a distant second.

The Wayans brothers were, as African Americans, rare in the history of comedy teams. Because they came from a strict religious family, they had not been allowed to play with other children, and the ten siblings had to learn to amuse each other. Keenen, deeply influenced by Richard Pryor, moved to Los Angeles to enter the world of comedy. He wrote and directed *I'm Gonna Git You, Sucka* and included his brother Damon in the cast, a risky decision since Damon had recently been fired from *Saturday Night Live*. The movie led Fox Broadcasting to offer *In Living Color*, which had a mostly African American cast that included two other Wayans siblings, Shawn and Kim. Jim Carrey was one of the two white members of the cast.

In Living Color gleefully satirized a variety of stereotypes. Keenen and Damon, for example, were hawkers on the Homeboy Shopping Network selling stolen merchandise. The show did its best to offend everyone and inevitably got into trouble with censors. Damon and David Alan Grier portrayed two flamboyantly gay movie reviewers, and the show risked offending blacks with Damon playing a homeless drunk who gives tours of his temporary abode — a cardboard box.

Shawn and Marlon Wayans later developed their own situation comedy titled *The Wayans Brothers*. In 2000, they had a massive film hit, writing and starring in *Scary Movie*, a send-up of the horror genre. Keenen directed the film, which went on to become the most financially successful movie ever directed by an African American. Marlon told CBS News, "My dad's a Jehovah's Witness, so some of the humor was a little too much for him. So he had to leave halfway through and go pray for us. My mom stayed till the end, but that's because she broke her foot. She tried to hobble out, but that didn't work."

Whatever their parents' reactions, young audiences loved it.

But the Wayans were, like Belushi and Farley, several evolutionary leaps away from the pure comedy teams. They were popular because they had moved on, breaking new ground. By the end of the 1980s, the classic comedy team, with a rich heritage of abundant laughs, buoyant effects on American spirits in times of crisis, and breakthroughs in comedic form, had come to the end of a steady, sad decline and experienced a quiet but dignified death.

FIFTEEN

THE STARS RETURN

The Unexpected
Afterlife and Enduring Legacy
of Comedy Teams

After the death of comedy teams, American audiences discovered a continuing need for and love of the humor the comedy teams provided. Audiences wanted their guide to vital and sustaining friendships, communal spirit, and the simultaneous attachment to and detachment from reality. With classic teams no longer available to satisfy those needs, Americans have had to look elsewhere, to find the spirit of comedy teams in other forms.

If one surveys the field of contemporary comedy, one finds that the spirit of comedy teams lives on in a variety of inheritors. For example, the comedy team legacy can be seen on the late night shows in the pairing of a comic announcer and his sidekick. Johnny Carson and Ed McMahon, Conan O'Brien and Andy Richter, and Jimmy Kimmel and Adam Corolla, among others, depended on the tradition of team comedy for their humor.

It can be seen in buddy action films and in temporary screen pairings.

But the sturdiest and most enduring legacy of comedy teams has emerged in television situation comedies. The structure of such shows usually requires a team, as two or more of the characters are placed in some problematic situation and then need to rely on their friendship and knowledge of each other to resolve the problem.

Drawing on the situation comedy tradition that began with *Amos 'n' Andy* on radio and that continued with the pioneering television teams, contemporary sitcoms illustrate that an attachment to an ongoing group of characters provides a crucial emotional touchstone for American audiences. Audiences want something no stand-up can provide: group humor.

Not all situation comedies derive their structure from comedy teams. Many are based on a single strong central character, such as in *Hogan's Heroes*, *The Mary Tyler Moore Show*, and *Everybody Loves Raymond*, or are genuine ensemble shows where no single character predominates, such as in *Soap*, *Barney Miller*, or *Cheers*.

However, many sitcoms are overt and direct descendants of the teams. Shows like *Gilligan's Island*, *Perfect Strangers*, *Laverne and Shirley*, and *The Andy Griffith Show* depend on a classic team formula: the pairing of the straight man and the comic. Any sitcom that relies on signature lines, mutually needy characters, or volatile comic pairings, such as *The Odd Couple*, owes its existence to Laurel and Hardy.

Even a very brief mention of some of the

best situation comedies will provide a hint of the enormous legacy provided by comedy teams.

M*A*S*H, for example, was about a medical unit in the Korean conflict, struggling to save lives and maintain sanity. *M*A*S*H* was widely perceived as an anti-war show, and it certainly was a protest of sorts against the absurdities of war. Its subversiveness and anti-authoritarianism were at the heart of its appeal, but audiences also found appealing the show's humor and the way the characters functioned as a team to overcome difficulties.

Although the M*A*S*H unit was a team, Hawkeye Pierce, played by Alan Alda, was the first among equals. Indeed, increasing emphasis on Hawkeye's character is what prompted Wayne Rogers, who played Trapper John, to leave the show.

The crucial team element was most evident in the show's final episode. Colonel Potter, bidding farewell to Hawkeye and B.J. Hunnicut, played by Mike Farrell, says: "Well, boys, it would be hard to call what we've been through fun, but I'm sure glad we went through it together. You boys always managed to give me a good laugh, right when I needed it most."

Hawkeye and B.J. have the same realization:

Hawkeye: Look, I know how tough it is for you to say goodbye, so *I'll* say it. Maybe you're right, maybe we *will* see each other again, but just in case we don't, I want you to know how much you've meant to me. I'll never be able to shake you. Whenever I see a pair of big feet or a cheesy mustache, I'll think of you.

B.J.: Whenever I smell month-old socks, I'll think of *you*.

Hawkeye: Or the next time somebody nails my shoe to the floor . . .

B.J.: Or when somebody gives me a martini that tastes like lighter fluid.

Hawkeye: I'll miss you.

B.J.: I'll miss *you*. A lot. I can't imagine what this place would've been like if I hadn't found you here.

In the 1990s, two enormously successful situation comedies centered on groups of friends emerged. In one, *Seinfeld*, the four central characters were loosely connected individuals who interacted in seemingly mundane situations. In *Friends*, some of the various members of the group coupled with each other, while viewers were teased with the possibility that the others might do so in the future.

Seinfeld's immature characters gave viewers permission to not grow up. The characters needed each other because no one else could put up with them. Despite their mutual tolerance, however, they had a mutual aggressiveness. Kramer, for example, was constantly coming up with new schemes and borrowing items from Jerry without returning them. Jerry, in turn, always made fun of Kramer's schemes. This balance of mutual tolerance and mutual aggressiveness is a hallmark of team comedy, especially in Laurel and Hardy and in Abbott and Costello, teams that Jerry Seinfeld has, in particular, mentioned as having had a crucial influence on him. As with the traditional teams, it is the friendship the *Seinfeld* gang had that made them so attractive to viewers. Everyone needed and wanted such fundamentally endearing friends, even if the relationships were sometimes exasperating.

Jerry Seinfeld also relied on Burns and Allen in forging the structure of the show. Originally, at least, he wanted to fuse stand-up comedy with situation comedy.

Seinfeld's successful marriage of the two

most prominent comedic forms, stand-up and sitcom, was important because in doing so Jerry Seinfeld and writer Larry David combined the individuality of the former with the community of the latter. It was a team comedy about people who found it difficult to be part of a team.

The characters on *Friends*, like those on *Seinfeld*, are a gaggle of emotional co-dependents. Their chemistry involves much more sexual attraction than *Seinfeld*, however. Their relationships are incredibly tangled, but underlying them is a very simple formula that saw the show through ten successful years. At first, none of the characters ever seemed likely to settle in a conventional one-on-one relationship. All the plotlines were about their ever-changing interpersonal relationships. Ross can marry and divorce Rachel, Monica can date and marry Chandler, Joey can be attracted to Rachel, talk about Phoebe, and still live most of the time with Chandler (in an apartment proudly displaying a poster of Laurel and Hardy). Everything changes, but everything is the same.

Friends is a comedy about pairs who are sometimes couples and sometimes not. It is a relationship comedy like Burns and Allen or *The Bickersons* on radio and like

Lucy and Desi and *The Honeymooners* on television — but multiplied. Though the relationships on *Friends* have been updated for their time, made more fragile, more fitful and volatile, the jokes about men and women are the same.

In contrast to *Friends*, *Frasier* depends on a more direct link to male comedy teams. The Crane brothers, Frasier and Niles, both neurotic psychiatrists, are bonded by family, by profession, and by common elitist interests. They are skilled with language — the source of much of the show's humor — and their mutual aggression emerges directly out of the tradition of Abbott and Costello by way of *The Odd Couple*. The Niles and Frasier team is neatly balanced by their opposites, Martin, the father, and Daphne, who was Martin's live-in physical therapist until she married Niles. Both of them are from the working class and regularly undercut the brothers' pretensions.

Unlike many other situation comedies, *Frasier* has maintained much more of the undiluted original flavor of comedy teams, in that much of the humor is fast-paced verbal sparring. The dialogue contains lines that would have worked in the mouths of Burns and Allen:

Frasier: I know what you think about everything. When was the last time you had an unexpressed thought?

Niles: I'm having one now.

Or the Marx Brothers:

Frasier: I do not have a fat face!

Niles: Oh please, I keep wondering how long you're going to store those nuts for winter!

Or Lucy and Ethel:

Frasier: We've got a free evening. This sounds like the perfect opportunity for a couple of guys on the loose to hit a sports bar, have a couple of brewskies, maybe take in a game or two.

Niles: Right. But what shall we do?

Frasier: Dinner?

Niles: Perfect. No place fancy, I'm sure neither of us wants a heavy meal with lots of wine and expensive desserts.

Frasier: Oh, it's your turn to pay, isn't it?

Niles: You know me so well.

And that is the essence of a team —

knowing the other "so well."

It is a feeling that we will always need, and that is why we will continue to treasure the enduring contributions of comedy teams. They, after all, created characters that reflected our private dreams, suppressed longings, and most bedeviling fears. And, most importantly, as we remember their routines and their friendships, we find ourselves laughing.

ACKNOWLEDGMENTS

It was a great moment in my life when, some years ago, I realized how wonderful it was to interview people who knew more than I did about a subject. They were shockingly abundant.

Happily, in the case of this book, they were also uncommonly generous with both their time and knowledge.

In particular, I want to thank the comedians I have spoken with over the past several years. I was onstage in Beverly Hills with Shelley Berman, Shecky Greene, Jeffrey Ross, and Jerry Stiller and had a fascinating experience both backstage and participating in the talk. I had spoken to all except Jerry previously, and he was as gracious as possible in discussing his career with Anne Meara. All of them were unbelievably helpful.

Dick Smothers was extremely helpful and kind as we spoke about his role as straight man and the history of the Smothers Brothers.

Joan Rivers not only invited me on her radio show but also provided incredible insights about comedy.

I reviewed the notes, tapes, and memories of pertinent interviews I had done for previous writing. I couldn't use materials from every comedian I had spoken with previously, but there was much I have been able to use because I had talked with most about both the business and its history. Those whose interviews were helpful in this book include Steve Allen, Ed Asner, Richard Belzer, David Brenner, Sid Caesar, Norm Crosby, Estelle Getty, Buddy Hackett, Louis Nye, Soupy Sales, Avery Schreiber, Tommy Smothers, and Abe Vigoda.

There were a number of other people who provided help in interviews for earlier work. They are Judy Carter, comedy instructor and author of *The Comedy Bible*; Larry Coven, a comedy teacher and former member of Second City; the late esteemed literary critic Leslie Fiedler; Don Freeman, critic at the *San Diego Union-Tribune*; Charna Halpern, founder of ImprovOlympic and an important part of Second City history; and Stanley Ralph Ross, the creator of many television shows.

There are several people I had interviewed before to whom I returned for this book. Jeff Abraham, entertainment agent, knows an incredible amount about comedy and must be the world expert on the Ritz Brothers. Lawrence E. Mintz is the director of the Art Gliner Center for Humor Studies at the University of Maryland.

Rocky Kalish and I had spoken when I interviewed Steve Allen, and he knew so much and was so well acquainted with the history of comedy writing that I called upon him again. He was, once more, extremely valuable in providing useful tips. As an added bonus, I got to speak with Irma Kalish, one of the heroic women who pioneered the comedy-writing business. They both had many tales to tell.

Leonard Maltin is simply a phenomenon. His meticulous television work on *Entertainment Tonight*, his radio work, and his irreplaceable body of written work have justly made him among the most famous of all entertainment critics and historians. His enthusiasm for the material I write about is inspiring, and his old-fashioned kindness is too rare but extremely admirable. Leonard wrote the seminal and highly influential *Movie Comedy Teams*, among other works vital to this book. I had spoken with him previously, and somehow he found time to have another extended discussion that ranged over the entire field of comedy team history.

Ron Smith, whose research and writing in comedy are deservedly legendary, knows so much about the field that it is a pleasure to learn from him. His books are required reading for anyone interested in comedians.

Robert J. Thompson, Director of the Center for the Study of Popular Television at Syracuse University, is always a treasure house of information, and it was a useful pleasure to speak with Bob again.

Mark Dawidziak, writer, sometime comedy team performer, and television critic for the *Cleveland Plain Dealer*, was the first person I called about this book. By the time our three-hour discussion was done, Mark had guided me through the whole course of comedy team history. He was like a comedy team jukebox. I'd press a button, and out would come all this brilliant knowledge about a particular team. I deeply appreciate his supplying photographs for this book.

I then began the rigorous, subject-by-subject, exploration starting with vaudeville. I talked to my friend Ron Kaplan and his mother, Marcelle Kaplan, about family experiences.

Then, as would be a pattern for researching the whole book, I spoke to a series of writers. To learn more about vaudeville, I spoke with Marc Fields, co-author of *From the Bowery to Broadway* and relative of Lew Fields, a member of the first nationally prominent comedy team; renowned vaudeville expert Tony Slide, author of many crucial books in the field; and Rob Snyder, author of *Voice in the City,* who was especially useful on audiences.

When it came time to research radio, I called Donna Halper, friend, radio historian, and author of the wonderful and much-needed book *Invisible Stars: A Social History of Women in American Broadcasting.* Donna took the time to answer my questions, sent me valuable materials, and guided me through the era. I was also lucky enough to speak with two highly informed experts, J. Fred MacDonald and Elizabeth McLeod, who were both very insightful.

There were many experts in early film with whom I spoke formally and more briefly. I conducted formal interviews with Jeanine Basinger, author of, among many wonderful works, *Silent Stars,* and with whom I had an extended, warm, and fascinating conversation; William M. Drew, author of such books as *Speaking of Silents*; my very good friend Mike Gerien, chair of the TV/Radio/Film Department at Suffolk County Community College, who made many valuable suggestions; and Kristine Karnick, who is an expert on women in film, co-editor of *Classic Hollywood Comedy*, and with whom I spoke most usefully about the Thelma Todd/ZaSu Pitts/Patsy Kelly films and the role of women in Hollywood.

I gleaned much-needed new perspectives about Laurel and Hardy from Leo Brooks, author of the book *The Laurel and Hardy Stock Company*; John Larrabee, co-director of the invaluable Web site, http://laurelandhardycentral.com; Ali Stevenson, co-editor of the *Intra-Tent Journal*, the official publication of the Sons of the Desert, the international organization for fans of Laurel and Hardy; and David Bullard on behalf of the Berth Marks Tent in Harlem, Georgia, home of the Laurel and Hardy Museum.

For insights about the Marx Brothers, I turned to Joe Adamson, author of the classic book *Groucho, Harpo, Chico, and Sometimes Zeppo*. Joe was gracious and patient in giving me a lot of time to go over questions I had. Wes Gehring and I spoke about the Marx Brothers, Hope and Crosby's *Road* pictures, Laurel and Hardy, and much else. Wes's books on comedy provide the indispensable academic knowledge, and his writing is so clear that he makes it all enjoyable to absorb. Everyone who writes about the Marx Brothers depends on Paul Wesolowski's storehouse of knowledge. He is a one-man encyclopedia who is always willing to share, and I found his guidance very valuable. I also spoke with Lois Levine, a member of the extended Marx family, who provided very interesting insights into family life.

I knew I wanted to speak with Chris Costello after reading *Lou's on First*, her moving memoir of her father. Chris was simply wonderful as she made suggestions and enthusiastically responded to questions. Lou Costello's memory couldn't have a better guardian. I also spoke with his other surviving daughter, Patricia Costello Humphries, who was kind enough to provide her own moving memories.

David Bianculli, the television critic for the New York *Daily News* and the NPR program *Fresh Air* and the author of such books as *Teleliteracy: Taking Television Seriously*, is a great Abbott and Costello fan. We ended up talking especially about them and the Smothers Brothers, but across a range of all television teams. Unsurprisingly, David is extraordinarily knowledgeable.

Bob Furmanek, co-author of *Abbott and Costello in Hollywood*, was a model of kindness, support, and gracious help. Bob's co-author, Ron Palumbo, gave me valuable insights, especially about Bud Abbott.

Jim Mulholland, an accomplished and extraordinarily successful comedy writer himself, is the author of *The Abbott and Costello Book* and an invaluable resource not only about the comedy team but also about how jokes work.

Jim was one of several comedy writers I spoke with. All these conversations were marked by great humor. I talked with the comedy-writing legend Bob Orben, the always helpful Steve Voldseth, and Larry Wilde, author of an incredible number of valuable and funny books on comedy. Larry sent me a book and a CD of his interview with Jerry Lewis. Jordan Young, author of *The Laugh Crafters: Comedy Writing in Radio and TV's Golden Age*, emailed useful information.

Eric Lamond, grandson of Larry Fine, and currently with Comedy III Productions, was my very warm and very generous guide to the Three Stooges. He sent me a crucial book and provided help in every way possible. I also spoke with Jeff Forrester, co-author of *The Three Stooges* and Robert Kurson, author of *The Official Three Stooges Encyclopedia*, who were both very helpful. Gary Lassin, president of The Three Stooges Fan Club, provided a unique fan's point of view. Jim Neibaur, author of such books as *Movie Comedians: The Complete Guide*, graciously provided excerpts of several interviews he conducted, including one with Jules White, who directed many of the Three Stooges films.

Shawn Levy, author of *King of Comedy: The Life and Art of Jerry Lewis* and other books, gave an extremely intelligent analysis of film comedy in general and Jerry Lewis in particular. Brent Walker, co-author of *The Films of the Bowery Boys*, gave me the historical background on the Bowery Boys that I needed.

David Schwartz, Chief Curator of Film, American Museum of the Moving Image, and Art Gliner, founder of the Art Gliner Center of Humor Studies, were valuable resources about television history.

I discussed Lucille Ball and Vivian Vance with several people. Michael Karol, author of *Lucy, A to Z*, provided important insights into Lucy's popularity.

Gregg Oppenheimer, son of Jess Oppenheimer, the creator of *I Love Lucy*, had some intriguing tales. He was also kind enough to send me a copy of *Laughs, Luck . . . and Lucy*, the terrific book he co-wrote with his father.

Stephen Silverman, the author of *Funny Ladies: The Women Who Made Us Laugh*, guided me on an anecdote-filled trip through the Lucy story. His mind was packed with wonderful stories, and he was gracious enough not only to share them but also to do so in an enormously entertaining way.

Rob Edelman and Audrey Kupferberg, authors of *Meet the Mertzes*, were very clever and provided many useful suggestions in thinking about Vivian Vance and other comedians and comic actors, such as Walter Matthau.

Michael Starr, television critic at the *New York Post* and author of *Art Carney: A Biography*, was extraordinarily perceptive in his assessment of many of the television teams.

Adam Hanft was kind enough to send me an article he'd written that contributed significantly to my understanding about why comedy teams disappeared.

John Trueson, stand-up comedian and, as I mentioned in the text, former member of Corson and Trueson, and now manager of Governor's Comedy Cabaret and Restaurant on Long Island, provided invaluable insights about the economic and personal challenges faced by comedy teams.

Many other people were kind enough to email me information. They are Paul Castiglia; Chris Franco; Steve Kelly; Norm Lehfeldt; Brian McKim of SHECKY magazine.com; Don L. F. Nilsen, Executive Secretary of the International Society for Humor Studies; Frank Reighter (who runs the oldest and largest nonsports card show in the country); and David E. E. Sloane, Executive Director of the American Humor Studies Association. I'd also like to thank the many people who sold me books and other materials from various sites on the Web. I appreciate the encouragement offered by Stefan Kanfer, author of *Ball of Fire*, his wonderful biography of Lucille Ball.

Research for the book began in Los Angeles at the Museum of Radio and Television. The staff there was enormously helpful. For a previous book, Michael

Terry, head of the Jewish Division, New York Public Library, provided me access to an unpublished interview with George Burns conducted by the American Jewish Committee. The New York Library of the Performing Arts has extensive and useful files. I discovered long-forgotten bits of information, for example, in the George Burns file.

I owe an enormous personal debt of gratitude to Ned Comstock, Archivist at the Cinema/TV Collections of the University of Southern California. Indeed, I'd like to know where I can find the form to nominate Ned for archivist of the century. He was indefatigable in looking for materials in the Constance McCormick Collection and the Hal Humphrey Collection. In all, I ended up with 513 photocopied pages of material from those collections; those pages contained more than 600 newspaper articles on most of the major comedy teams.

It was a necessary but pleasurable task for me to read several hundred books and articles to find pertinent information. The material I needed was not conveniently collected, but, once again, the library staff at Suffolk County Community College was heroic in its efforts to get needed materials.

Hedi BenAicha, Campus Head Librarian and Associate Dean, is a warm friend who is a writer's dream: intelligent, enthusiastic, and always helpful. Hedi provided constant support.

Susan Rubenstein DeMasi, media librarian, always has valuable suggestions. She's the person I go to when I need to locate some ridiculously obscure film or video. Sue's deeply appreciated enthusiasm is always a help. MaryAnn Romano and Irene Rose at the Media Resources Center were also very supportive.

I also want to thank Marilyn Ventiere, who was relentless in tracking down a hard-to-find volume through interlibrary loan. Marilyn Heller very ably assisted her in this task, as did Bonita Plaue, who arranged for the various intercampus books I needed.

The members of the English Department at Suffolk County Community College are constantly wonderful. I'd like to thank Michele Aquino, Academic Chair of English, and Sandra Sprows, Assistant Academic Chair, for their indispensable support. I'd also like to thank Sandra for providing articles, for alerting me to an important Web site, and for her very important advice about the comedy tastes of her generation.

I thank all the members of the department because they are all like part of an extended family. Tony Martone was especially insightful in providing perspectives about Sid Caesar and Jackie Gleason. Lloyd Becker provided an article about Bob and Ray and excellent insights about 1960s comedy. Don Gilzinger also gave me some materials. I spoke about the book with Molly Altizer, Carol Cavallo, Jeff Coven, Maury Dean, Tony DiFranco, Doug Howard, Ed Joyce, Sam Ligon, Jim Mattimore, and Ivan Sanders. Richard Britton, then of the Communications Department, also made clever suggestions.

The departmental and building secretaries and student aides I have worked with over the years have always been extremely helpful. They are Ellen Bolier, Arnita Mason, Kathy Morrisette, Claire Scola, Kathryn Seher, and Sharon Weeks.

I also want to thank my students over the years for helping me think through many issues regarding writing. Audiences are great teachers, and my students and the audiences that have heard me lecturing have been very instructive.

Friends have been extremely helpful. I nominated Mike Fitzpatrick for sainthood in the acknowledgments of my last book, and he's only gotten better. Mike turns a journey to a lecture into an adventure in eating and bookstore hunting. My life would be unbearably poorer without his friendship. Mike's wife, Lorena, and his brother, John, are like part of my family. I deeply appreciate John's incredible support.

I've worked with Susan Lustig in a wide variety of community activities for many years, and her cheerful optimism and constant help are crucial.

Doug Rathgeb, a librarian and author, most recently, of *The Making of Rebel Without a Cause*, has been a close friend for four decades. Some people have late-night cravings for pizza or chocolate. I have those, but I also sometimes need to talk about writing. Doug is always available for those discussions, and his knowledge makes the talks perpetually fascinating.

All the people at PublicAffairs deserve a special thanks. Peter Osnos, Publisher and Chief Executive, has built an amazing and unique house, one that is congenial to authors and one that contributes enormously to the national conversation. Peter has always been especially helpful to me. I enjoy his warp-speed mind and thank him for his invaluable support.

Paul Golob, then Executive Editor at PublicAffairs, acquired the manuscript. Paul was an editor in the best sense of the word. He always applied his probing and unbelievably gifted mind to my writing with the inevitable result that the work significantly improved. But Paul did more than that. He helped shape the kind of writing that I did. This book would simply not have existed without him.

I have more good editorial fortune than one writer deserves. When Paul left, Clive Priddle joined PublicAffairs as Executive Editor. Clive's subtle wit, great enthusiasm, and brilliant mind were much needed and deeply appreciated. He provided extensive and invaluable suggestions and always did so with great professionalism and kindness.

David Patterson served as a co-editor on this book. It is always a great pleasure to work with David. I really appreciate his quick and keen sense of humor, constant and dependable support, and useful and practical advice about improving the book.

Gene Taft, Director of Publicity, seems to work around the clock. His energy and funny emails make working with him very enjoyable.

I'd also like to thank everyone else at

PublicAffairs, especially Lisa Kaufman, Marketing Director and Senior Editor, Robert Kimzey, Managing Editor, and Jaime Leifer, Publicist.

Don Gastwirth is the embodiment of an agent who believes in his clients, who responds to calls with lightning speed, who is unwavering in support, and who knows the answer to every question with an accuracy and brilliance that is dazzling. Once again with this book, Don was there. From the moment I called him with the idea for the book through its completion, he was sensitive and generous with his time and counsel.

Don's brother, Dr. Joseph L. Gastwirth, has always provided warm support and kind words.

My cousins, Toby Everett and Dr. Sheldon Scheinert, have been extremely close since childhood. They are as much great friends as relatives.

My in-laws, Harvey and Marsha Selib and Judy Marshall, have always been most helpful and kind.

My late father, Fred Epstein, would have really enjoyed this book. He always watched comedians and laughed at their antics, and he always supported my attempts at writing.

My late mother, Lillian Scheinert Epstein, gave me a love of humor, and so much more. She was always a great audience, even when my comments didn't deserve her rich laughter. Her loving kindness shaped my life.

My brother, Richard, is always my first reader. How he remembers all the movies and shows we saw as children is beyond me, but he does. His interest and support, and his unwavering enthusiasm and uncommonly good sense, were vital to the book's completion. His wife, Perla, and children, Adam and Sondra, have always listened to tales of my writing with interest.

The book's dedication to my family is an inadequate attempt to thank them. My son, Michael, and daughter, Elana, were invaluable in tracking down materials. They found an enormous number of radio shows and some hard-to-find movies. My two younger daughters, Rachel and Lisa, both made very acute and helpful editorial suggestions. They added emotional resonance and verbal precision to the text.

My wife, Sharon, is irreplaceably vital in my life. She consistently offers wise advice, bottomless support, and honesty. She also really enjoys going on trips and speaking with comedians.

It is when I hear her laughter and that of our children that I am most conscious of the great gifts that comedians have given to us all.

PHOTO PERMISSIONS

All photos except for Chapters 2 and 15 courtesy of Mark Dawidziak.

Permission for the vaudeville routine on page 265: Grateful acknowledgment is made to Leonard Maltin and *Film Fan Monthly* for permission to reprint an excerpt from *The Abbott and Costello Book* by Jim Mulholland. New York: Popular Library, 1975.

PHOTO IDENTIFICATIONS

Chapter 1
George Burns and Gracie Allen

Chapter 3
Joe Weber (right) and Lew Fields

Chapter 4
Freeman F. Gosden (left) and Charles J. Correll, creators of *Amos 'n' Andy*

Chapter 5
Stan Laurel (left) and Oliver Hardy

Chapter 6
The Marx Brothers: (left to right) Chico, Groucho, Harpo, and Zeppo

Chapter 7
Bert Wheeler (left) and Robert Woolsey

Chapter 8
Bud Abbott (left) and Lou Costello

Chapter 9
Bob Hope (left) and Bing Crosby

Chapter 10
The Three Stooges: (left to right) Moe Howard, Curly Howard, and Larry Fine

Chapter 11
Dean Martin (right) and Jerry Lewis

Chapter 12
Lucille Ball (left) and Vivian Vance

Chapter 13
(left to right) Ed Sullivan, Tom Smothers, Dick Smothers

Chapter 14
Cheech Marin (left) and Tommy Chong

REFERENCES

Research is seductive and mind-numbing, all-consuming and daunting, fun and frustrating. The research for this book included gathering and reading books and articles, visiting libraries, bookstores, museums, and archives, watching hundreds of movies and television shows, listening to radio shows, records, and CDs, prowling the Internet, buying bizarre articles at auction sites on the Web, and requesting help from special interest groups and fan clubs.

I also interviewed some very kind and smart people. Most of the interviews of the well-known comedians were done for my earlier book, *The Haunted Smile*. I conducted many additional interviews for this book and informally spoke with and received materials from scores of others.

And then, after the research, came the writing. Of course, as I wrote I came to see that I needed to do more research, and everyone I asked displayed enviable patience as I returned for follow-up questions trying to find a telling detail or piece of information.

There was one big research problem.

Many stories in print by and about the members of the comedy teams contradict other stories. Egos, the desire to get even, and the urge to design a reputation supplemented the normal human frailties of memory. Some frustrated and ungenerous writer might even accuse tellers of these stories as being in a careless relationship with truth. I don't look at it that way. I prefer to think that such tellers supposed that even if a particular event didn't happen exactly in the way they reported, it should have. I have tried my best to sort through all the stories to get at the accurate account.

Some works that I used to accomplish that task were valuable throughout the book; some were more useful for a particular chapter. I have not included discographies, filmographies, or lists of television appearances, all of which are readily available elsewhere.

GENERAL REFERENCES

Published References

Allen, Steve. *Funny People*. New York: Stein & Day, 1981.

———. *More Funny People*. New York: Stein & Day, 1982.

Burr, Lonnie. *Two for the Show: Great 20th Century Comedy Teams*. Lincoln, Neb.: i.Universe.com, 2000.

Epstein, Lawrence J. *The Haunted Smile: The Story of Jewish Comedians in America*. New York: PublicAffairs, 2001.

Franklin, Joe. *Joe Franklin's Encyclopedia of Comedians*. Secaucus, N.J.: Citadel Press, 1985.

Maltin, Leonard. *The Great Movie Comedians*. New York: Harmony, 1982.

———. *Movie Comedy Teams*. New York: New American Library, 1985.

Mast, Gerald. *The Comic Mind: Comedy and the Movies*, 2nd ed. Chicago: University of Chicago Press, 1979.

Neibaur, James L. *Movie Comedians: The Complete Guide*. Jefferson, N.C.: McFarland, 1986.

Rickman, Gregg, ed. *The Film Comedy Reader*. New York: Limelight, 2001.

Robinson, Jeffrey. *Teamwork: The Cinema's Greatest Comedy Teams*. New York: Proteus, 1982.

Siegel, Scott, and Barbara Siegel. *American*

Film Comedy. New York: Prentice-Hall, 1994.

Smith, Ronald L. *Goldmine Comedy Record Price Guide*. Iola, Wis.: Krause, 1996.

————. *Stars of Stand-Up*. New York: Sure Sellers, 1995.

————. *The Stars of Stand-up Comedy: A Biographical Encyclopedia*. New York: Garland, 1986.

————. *Who's Who in Comedy: Comedians, Comics, and Clowns from Vaudeville to Today's Stand-Ups*. New York: Facts on File, 1992.

Wilde, Larry. *The Great Comedians Talk About Comedy*. Mechanicsburg, Pa.: Executive Books, 2000.

Files

Constance McCormick Collection and Hal Humphrey Collection, Cinema-Television Library, University of Southern California.

Videos

Classic Comedy Teams. Goodtimes. 1986.

Web Sites

www.comedycollege.net (Comedy College)

1. MUSTY THEATERS AND ASBESTOS CURTAINS: THE RISE OF BURNS AND ALLEN

Interviews

Steve Allen and Rocky Kalish

Published References

Allen, Gracie, as told to Jane Kesner Morris. "Inside Me." *Woman's Home Companion Magazine*, March 1953, 40–41, 100, 102, 109, 112, 116, 119, 122–124, 126–127.

Burns, George. *All My Best Friends.* New York: Putnam, 1989.

———. *Living It Up.* New York: Putnam, 1976.

———. *One Hundred Years, One Hundred Stories.* New York: Putnam, 1996.

———. Unpublished interview. American Jewish Committee.

Gottfried, Martin. *George Burns and the*

Hundred Yard Dash. New York: Simon and Schuster, 1996.

Files

George Burns. New York Public Library, Billy Rose Collection.

2. WILD GAGS AND MURDERED ENGLISH: THE BIRTH OF COMEDY TEAMS

Interviews

Steve Allen, Mark Dawidziak, Leslie Fiedler, Marcelle Kaplan, Ron Kaplan, Anthony Slide, and Rob Snyder

Additional Material

Tony Belmont, Comedy Hall of Fame Museum and Library.

Published References

Esposito, Tony. *Golden Era of Vaudeville.*

Miami: Warner Bros., 1995.

Gilbert, Douglas. *American Vaudeville: Its Life and Times*. New York: Dover, 1963.

Laurie, Joe. *Vaudeville: From the Honky Tonks to the Palace*. New York: Holt, 1953.

Levitt, Paul M., ed. *Vaudeville Humor*. Carbondale: Southern Illinois University Press, 2002.

Slide, Anthony. *The Encyclopedia of Vaudeville*. Westport, Conn.: Greenwood, 1994.

———. *Selected Vaudeville Criticism*. Metuchen, N.J.: Scarecrow Press, 1988.

Snyder, Robert W. "The Vaudeville Circuit: A Prehistory of the Mass Audience," in *Audiencemaking: How the Media Create the Audience*, ed. James S. Ettema and D. Charles Whitney, 215–231. Thousand Oaks, Calif.: Sage, 1994.

———. *Voice of the City: Vaudeville and Popular Culture in New York*. Chicago: Ivan R. Dee, 2000.

Spitzer, Marian. *The Palace*. New York: Atheneum, 1969.

Videos

Vaudeville. American Masters, PBS, 1997.

Web Sites

www.theparamount.com (Sean McIntyre, "History of the Paramount Theatre")
www.vaudeville.org (American Vaudeville Museum)

3. AN EXPLOSION OF STARS: THE FIRST CLASSIC COMEDY TEAMS

Note: For Marx Brothers material, see references for Chapter 5.

Interviews

Steve Allen and Marc Fields

Published References

Fields, Armond, and L. Marc Fields. *From the Bowery to Broadway: Lew Fields and the Roots of American Popular Theater.* New York: Oxford, 1993.

Isman, Felix. *Weber and Fields.* New York: Boni and Liveright, 1924.

Slide, Anthony. *The Encyclopedia of Vaudeville.* Westport, Conn.: Greenwood, 1994.

―――. *Selected Vaudeville Criticism.* Metuchen, N.J.: Scarecrow Press, 1988.

Snyder, Robert W. "The Vaudeville Circuit: A Prehistory of the Mass Audience," in *Audiencemaking: How the Media Create the Audience,* ed. James S. Ettema and D. Charles Whitney, 215–231. Thousand Oaks, Calif.: Sage, 1994.

―――. *Voice of the City: Vaudeville and Popular Culture in New York.* Chicago: Ivan R. Dee, 2000.

Staples, Shirley. *Male-Female Comedy Teams in American Vaudeville, 1865–1932.* Ann Arbor, Mich.: UMI Research Press, 1984.

Zeidman, Irving. *The American Burlesque Show.* New York: Hawthorn, 1967.

4. "IN THIS COUNTRY WE'RE ONLY PERMITTED ONE HUSBAND": COMEDY TEAMS ON RADIO

Interviews

Donna Halper, J. Fred MacDonald, and Elizabeth McLeod

Published References

Andrews, Bart. *Holy Mackerel! The Amos 'n' Andy Story.* New York: Dutton, 1986.

Douglas, Susan J. *Listening In: Radio and the American Imagination.* New York: Times Books, 1999.

Dunning, John. *Tune in Yesterday: The Ultimate Encyclopedia of Old-Time Radio, 1925–1976.* Englewood Cliffs, N.J.: Prentice-Hall, 1976.

Ely, Melvin Patrick. *Adventures of Amos 'n' Andy,* 2nd ed. Charlottesville: University of Virginia Press, 2001.

Firestone, Ross, ed. *The Big Radio Comedy Program.* Chicago: Contemporary Books, 1978.

Halper, Donna L. *Invisible Stars: A Social*

History of Women in American Broadcasting. Armonk, N.Y.: M. E. Sharpe, 2001.

Harmon, Jim. *Great Radio Comedians*. Garden City, N.Y.: Doubleday, 1970.

MacDonald, J. *Fred, Don't Touch That Dial! Radio Programming in American Life, 1920–1960*. Chicago: Nelson-Hall, 1979.

Maltin, Leonard. *The Great American Broadcast: A Celebration of Radio's Golden Age*. New York: Dutton, 1997.

Nachman, Gerald. *Raised on Radio*. New York: Pantheon, 1998.

Wertheim, Arthur Frank. *Radio Comedy*. New York: Oxford University Press, 1979.

Web Sites

www.old-time.com (Old Time Radio)

www.old-time.com/halper/index (Donna Halper's History of Radio)

www.antiqueradios.com/radiocity.shtml ("Broadcast Metropolis," by Samuel Kaufman, Radio News, December 1933)

www.geocities.com/Heartland/Ranch/8546/otr.htm (Rick's OTR/Vic and Sade Page)

5. COMEDY COMES TO THE BIG SCREEN: MR. LAUREL AND MR. HARDY

Interviews

Jeanine Basinger, Leo Brooks, David Bullard, Mark Dawidziak, William F. Drew, Wes Gehring, Kristine Karnick, John Larrabee, Leonard Maltin, and Ali Stevenson

Published References

Bergman, Andrew. *We're in the Money: Depression America and Its Films.* New York: New York University Press, 1971.

Dale, Alan S. *Comedy Is a Man in Trouble: Slapstick in American Movies.* Minneapolis: University of Minnesota Press, 2000.

Durgnat, Raymond. *The Crazy Mirror: Hollywood Comedy and the American*

Image. London: Faber and Faber, 1969.

Edelson, Edward. *Funny Men of the Movies.* Garden City, N.Y.: Doubleday, 1976.

Fuller, Kathryn. *At the Picture Show: Small Town Audiences and the Creation of Movie Fan Culture.* Washington, D.C.: Smithsonian Institution Press, 1996.

Holston, Noel. "The Story of 'D'Oh!'" *Newsday.* April 27, 2003, D14.

Lahue, Kalton C., and Terry Brewer. *Kops and Custards: The Legend of Keystone Films.* Norman: University of Oklahoma Press, 1968.

Louvish, Simon. *Stan and Ollie.* New York: St. Martin's Press, 2002.

MacCann, Richard Dyer. *The Silent Comedians.* Metuchen, N.J.: Scarecrow Press, 1993.

Maltin, Leonard. *The Great Movie Shorts.* New York: Bonanza, 1972.

Maltin, Leonard, and Richard W. Bann. *Our Gang: The Life and Times of the Little Rascals.* New York: Crown, 1977.

Manchel, Frank. *The Box-Office Clowns.* New York: Franklin Watts, 1979.

McCabe, John. *Comedy World of Stan Laurel.* Anaheim, Calif.: Past Times, 1990.

————. *Laurel and Hardy.* New York: Dutton, 1975.

————. *Mr. Laurel and Mr. Hardy.* New York: New American Library, 1966.

Mitchell, Glenn. *A–Z of Silent Film Comedy.* London: B. T. Batsford, 1998.

————. *The Laurel and Hardy Encyclopedia.* London: B. T. Batsford, 1995.

Nollen, Scott Allen. *The Boys: The Cinematic World of Laurel and Hardy.* Jefferson, N.C.: McFarland, 1989.

Russo, Vito. *The Celluloid Closet: Homosexuality in the Movies,* rev. ed. New York: Perennial, 1987.

Seidman, Steve. *Comedian Comedy: A Tradition in American Film.* Ann Arbor, Mich.: UMI Research Press, 1981.

Shteir, Rachel B. "The Vaudeville Mirror." *American Theatre* 9, no. 5 (September 1992): 12–18.

Skretvedt, Randy. *Laurel and Hardy: The Magic Behind the Movies.* Beverly Hills, Calif.: Moonstone, 1987.

Videos

Cavalcade of Comedy. Produced by Bret Wood. Kino Video, 1998.

One Hundred Years of Comedy. Produced by Phillip Dye. Passport Video, 1997.

Web Sites

http://laurelandhardycentral.com/ golliwog.htm ("The Golliwog and the Lobby-Watcher," by John Larrabee)

6. "I SHOT AN ELEPHANT IN MY PAJAMAS": THE MARX BROTHERS

Interviews

Joe Adamson, Wes Gehring, Michael Gerien, Leonard Maltin, and Paul Wesolowski

Published References

Adamson, Joe. *Groucho, Harpo, Chico, and Sometimes Zeppo.* New York: Simon and Schuster, 1973.
Anobile, Richard J. *Why a Duck?* New York: Darien House, 1971.

Arce, Hector. *Groucho.* New York: Perifee, 1980.

Barson, Michael, ed. *Flywheel, Shyster, and Flywheel: The Marx Brothers' Lost Radio Show.* New York: Pantheon, 1988.

Chandler, Charlotte. *Hello, I Must Be Going: Groucho and His Friends.* Garden City, N.Y.: Doubleday, 1978.

Crichton, Kyle. *The Marx Brothers.* Garden City, N.Y.: Doubleday, 1950.

Eyles, Allen. *The Marx Brothers: Their World of Comedy,* 2nd ed. New York: A. S. Barnes, 1969.

Gehring, Wes. *The Marx Brothers: A Bio-Bibliography.* Westport, Conn.: Greenwood, 1987.

Jenkins, Henry. *What Made Pistachio Nuts?* New York: Columbia University Press, 1992.

Kanfer, Stefan. *Groucho: The Life and Times of Julius Henry Marx.* New York: Knopf, 2000.

Karnick, Kristine Brunovska, and Henry Jenkins, eds. *Classical Hollywood Comedy.* New York: Routledge, 1994.

Louvish, Simon. *Monkey Business: The Lives and Legends of the Marx Brothers.* New York: St. Martin's Press, 2000.

Marx, Arthur. *My Life with Groucho.*

Boston: G. K. Hall, 1993.

Marx, Groucho. *Groucho and Me.* New York: Da Capo, 1995.

———. *Memoirs of a Mangy Lover.* New York: Da Capo, 1997.

Marx, Harpo, with Rowland Barber. *Harpo Speaks!* New York: Limelight, 1985.

Marx, Maxine. *Growing Up with Chico.* Englewood Cliffs, N.J.: Prentice-Hall, 1980.

Mitchell, Glenn. *The Marx Brothers Encyclopedia.* London: B. T. Batsford, 1996.

Sennett, Ted. *Laughing in the Dark: Movie Comedy from Groucho to Woody.* New York: St. Martin's Press, 1992.

Zimmerman, Paul D., and Burt Goldblatt. *The Marx Brothers at the Movies.* New York: Putnam, 1968.

Files

Groucho Marx. Federal Bureau of Investigation.

Videos

Marx Brothers in a Nutshell. Produced by

Robert B. Weide. Whyaduck Productions, 1982.

The Unknown Marx Brothers. Troy, Mich.: Anchor Bay, 1996.

Web Sites

www.whyaduck.com (Why a Duck?)
www.marx-brothers.org (The Marx Brothers)

7. ANARCHY LET LOOSE: OTHER COMEDY TEAMS OF THE 1930s

Interviews

Jeff Abraham and Leonard Maltin

Published References

Jenkins, Henry. *What Made Pistachio Nuts?* New York: Columbia University Press, 1992.

Karnick, Kristine Brunovska, and Henry Jenkins, eds. *Classical Hollywood Comedy.* New York: Routledge, 1994.

Watz, Edward. *Wheeler and Woolsey*. Jefferson, N.C.: McFarland, 1994.

Winokur, Mark. *American Laughter: Immigrants, Ethnicity, and 1930s Hollywood Film Comedy*. New York: St. Martin's Press, 1996.

Web Sites

www.geocities.com/Hollywood/Derby/4720 (The Official Dorothy Lee, Wheeler and Woolsey Tribute)

8. "WHO'S ON FIRST": ABBOTT AND COSTELLO MEET THE 1940s

Interviews

David Bianculli, Chris Costello, Mark Dawidziak, Bob Furmanek, Patricia Costello Humphreys, Jim Mulholland, and Ron Palumbo

Published References

Costello, Chris, with Raymond Strait. *Lou's on First: A Biography of Lou Costello.* New York: Cooper Square Press, 2000.

Cox, Stephen, et al. *The Abbott and Costello Story*, 2nd ed. Nashville, Tenn.: Cumberland House, 1997.

Furmanek, Bob, and Ron Palumbo. *Abbott and Costello in Hollywood.* N.Y.: Perigee, 1991.

Mulholland, Jim. *The Abbott and Costello Book.* New York: Popular Library, 1977.

Thomas, Bob. *Bud and Lou.* Philadelphia: J. B. Lippincott, 1977.

Videos

The World of Abbott and Costello. Vanguard, 1964.

Abbott and Costello Meet Jerry Seinfeld. MCA Universal, 1994.

Web Sites

www.abbottandcostello.net (Abbott and

Costello Meet the Internet)

http://members.aol.com/ACQtrly (Abbott and Costello Quarterly)

www.louandbud.com (Abbott and Costello Forever)

www.lousonfirst.com (Lou's on First)

9. THE ROAD TO TEMPORARY TEAMS: HOPE AND CROSBY

Interviews

Steve Allen and Bob Orben

Published References

Hope, Bob, with Linda Hope. *Bob Hope: My Life in Jokes.* New York: Hyperion, 2003.

Hope, Bob, and Bob Thomas. *The Road to Hollywood.* Garden City, N.Y.: Doubleday, 1977.

Marx, Arthur. *The Secret Life of Bob Hope.* New York: Barricade, 1993.

Mielke, Randall G. *Road to Box Office: The Seven Film Comedies of Crosby, Hope, and Lamour.* Jefferson, N.C.:

McFarland, 1997.

Morella, Joe, Edward Z. Epstein, and Eleanor Clark. *The Amazing Careers of Bob Hope.* New Rochelle, N.Y.: Arlington, 1973.

Quirk, Lawrence J. *Bob Hope: The Road Well-Traveled.* New York: Applause, 1998.

10. LOCO BOYS MAKE GOOD: THE THREE STOOGES

Interviews

Jeff Forrester, Robert Kurson, Eric Lamond, and Gary Lassin

Additional Material

Eric Lamond and James Neibaur

Published References

Forrester, Jeff, and Tom Forrester. *The Three Stooges: The Triumphs and Tragedies of the Most Popular Comedy Team of All Time*. Los Angeles: Donaldson, 2003.

Howard, Moe. *Moe Howard and the Three Stooges*. New York: Carol, 1990.

Kurson, Robert. *The Official Three Stooges Encyclopedia*. Lincolnwood, Ill.: Contemporary Books, 1998.

Solomon, Jon. *The Complete Three Stooges*. Glendale, Calif.: Comedy III Productions, 2001.

Web Sites

www.threestooges.com (The Official Three Stooges Website)

11. "THE PLAYBOY AND THE PUTZ": MARTIN AND LEWIS

Interviews

Shawn Levy

Published References

Krutnick, Frank. *Inventing Jerry Lewis*.

Washington, D.C.: Smithsonian Institution Press, 2000.

Levy, Shawn. *King of Comedy: The Life and Art of Jerry Lewis*. New York: St. Martin's Press, 1996.

Lewis, Jerry, with Herb Gluck. *Jerry Lewis in Person*. New York: Atheneum, 1982.

Marx, Arthur. *Everybody Loves Somebody Sometime (Especially Himself): The Story of Dean Martin and Jerry Lewis*. New York: Hawthorn, 1974.

Rapf, Joanna E. "Comic Theory from a Feminist Perspective: A Look at Jerry Lewis." *Journal of Popular Culture* (Summer 1993): 101–203.

Sikov, Ed. *Laughing Hysterically: American Screen Comedy of the 1950s*. New York: Columbia University Press, 1994.

Tosches, Nick. *Dino*. New York: Dell, 1999.

Van Meter, Jonathan. *The Last Good Time*. New York: Crown, 2003.

CDs

"Jerry Lewis on Comedy." Laugh.com, 2001.

Videos

The Nightclub Years. A&E, 2001.

12. "HELLOOOO, BALL": COMEDY TEAMS OF THE 1950S

Interviews

Steve Allen, Sid Caesar, Mark Dawidziak, Rob Edelman, Don Freeman, Art Gliner, Irma Kalish, Michael Karol, Marvin Kitman, Audrey Kupferberg, Louis Nye, Gregg Oppenheimer, Stanley Ralph Ross, Soupy Sales, David Schwartz, Stephen Silverman, Michael Starr, and Brent Walker

Additional Material

Jordan Young

Published References

Adir, Karin. *Great Clowns of American Television.* Jefferson, N.C.: McFarland, 1988.

Bacon, James. *How Sweet It Is: The Jackie Gleason Story.* New York: St. Martin's Press, 1985.

Ball, Lucille. *Love, Lucy.* New York: Berkley, 1997.

Caesar, Sid, with Bill Davidson. *Where Have I Been? An Autobiography.* New York: Crown, 1982.

Caesar, Sid, with Eddy Friedfeld. *Caesar's Hours: My Life in Comedy, with Love and Laughter.* New York: PublicAffairs, 2003.

Castelluccio, Frank, and Alvin Walker. *The Other Side of Ethel Mertz: The Life Story of Vivian Vance.* New York: Boulevard Books, 2000.

Edelman, Rob, and Audrey Kupferberg. *Meet the Mertzes.* Los Angeles: Renaissance, 1999.

Edwards, Elizabeth. *I Love Lucy.* Philadelphia: Running Press, 2001.

Elliott, Bob, and Ray Goulding. *Write If You Get Work.* New York: Random House, 1975.

Hayes, David, and Brent Walker. *The Films of the Bowery Boys.* Secaucus, N.J.: Citadel, 1984.

Henry, William A., III. *The Great One.* New York: Doubleday, 1992.

Kanfer, Stefan. *Ball of Fire: The Tumultuous*

Life and Comic Art of Lucille Ball. New York: Knopf, 2003.

Karol, Michael. *Lucy, A to Z.* Writer's Showcase Press, 2002.

Marc, David. *Comic Visions: Television Comedy and American Culture,* 2nd ed. Malden, Mass.: Blackwell, 1997.

Oppenheimer, Jess, with Gregg Oppenheimer. *Laughs, Luck . . . and Lucy.* Syracuse, N.Y.: Syracuse University Press, 1996.

Poole, Gary. *TV Comedians.* New York: Grosset & Dunlap, 1979.

Putterman, Barry. *On Television and Comedy.* Jefferson, N.C.: McFarland, 1995.

Sennett, Ted. *Your Show of Shows.* New York: Macmillan, 1977.

Silverman, Stephen M. *Funny Ladies: The Women Who Made Us Laugh.* New York: Abrams, 1999.

Stand-Up Comedians on Television. New York: Abrams/Museum of Television and Radio, 1996.

Starr, Michael Seth. *Art Carney: A Biography.* New York: Applause, 2002.

Unterbrink, Mary. *Funny Women.* Jefferson, N.C.: McFarland, 1987.

Young, Jordan R. *The Laugh Crafters: Comedy Writing in Radio and TV's*

Golden Age. Beverly Hills, Calif.: Past Times, 1999.

Files

Lucille Ball. Federal Bureau of Investigation.

Videos

Caesar's Writers. Michael Hirsh Productions, 1996.

Web Sites

www.ammi.org/site/site.asp (American Museum of the Moving Image)

13. "MOM ALWAYS LIKED YOU BEST": COMEDY TEAMS OF THE 1960s

Interviews

Ed Asner, Richard Belzer, Shelley Berman, David Bianculli, David Brenner, Judy

Carter, Norm Crosby, Estelle Getty, Shecky Greene, Buddy Hackett, Charna Halpern, Lawrence Mintz, Avery Schreiber, Joan Rivers, Jeffrey Ross, Ron Smith, Dick Smothers, Tom Smothers, Jerry Stiller, Abe Vigoda, Steve Voldseth, and Larry Wilde

Published References

Adler, Bill, and Jeffrey Feinman. *Mel Brooks.* Chicago: Playboy Press, 1976.

Berger, Phil. *The Last Laugh: The World of the Stand-up Comics.* New York: Ballantine, 1975.

Erickson, Hal. *From Beautiful Downtown Burbank: A Critical History of Rowan and Martin's Laugh-In, 1968–1973.* Jefferson, N.C.: McFarland, 2000.

Hanft, Adam. "Laughing Alone." *Civilization* 7, no. 1 (February–March 2000): 27.

Hendra, Tony. *Going Too Far.* New York: Doubleday, 1987.

McCrohan, Donna. *The Second City.* New York: Perigee, 1987.

Nachman, Gerald. *Seriously Funny: The Rebel Comedians of the 1950s and*

1960s. New York: Pantheon, 2003.

Stiller, Jerry. *Married to Laughter.* New York: Simon and Schuster, 2000.

Wilde, Larry. *How the Great Comedy Writers Create Laughter.* Chicago: Nelson-Hall, 1976.

Yacowar, Maurice. *Method in Madness.* New York: St. Martin's Press, 1981.

Videos

Smothered: The Censorship Struggles of the Smothers Brothers Comedy Hour. New Video Group, 2002.

Web Sites

www.smothersbrothers.com

14. VANISHING STARS: FINAL ACTS AND THE DEATH OF COMEDY TEAMS

Interviews

Larry Coven, Rob Edelman, Audrey Kupferberg, Robert J. Thompson, and John Trueson

Additional Material

Adam Hanft

Published References

Edelman, Rob, and Audrey Kupferberg. *Matthau: A Life*. Lanham, Md.: Taylor, 2002.

Holtzman, Will. *Jack Lemmon*. New York: Pyramid, 1977.

Hunter, Allan. *Walter Matthau*. New York: St. Martin's Press, 1985.

Johnson, Kim "Howard." *The First 28 Years of Monty Python*. New York: St. Martin's Press, 1999.

Littleton, Cynthia, and Josh Spector. "Cheech and Chong Look for Another Hit." *Hollywood Reporter*, July 23, 2003, at www.cnn.com/entertainment.

Morgan, David. *Monty Python Speaks!* New York: Avon, 1999.

Perry, George. *The Life of Python*. Boston: Little, Brown, 1983.

The Pythons, with Bob McCabe. *The Py-*

thons: *Autobiography by the Pythons.* New York: St. Martin's Press/Dunne, 2003.

Shales, Tom, and James Andrew Miller. *"Live from New York": An Uncensored History of Saturday Night Live as Told by Its Stars, Writers, and Guests.* New York: Little, Brown, 2002.

Widener, Don. *Lemmon.* New York: Macmillan, 1975.

Williams, John. *If I Stop I'll Die: The Comedy and Tragedy of Richard Pryor.* New York: Thunder's Mouth Press, 1993.

Woodward, Bob. *Wired: The Short Life and Fast Times of John Belushi.* New York: Simon and Schuster, 1985.

Yankelovich, Daniel. *The Shifting Direction of America's Cultural Values.* Speech. May 29, 1998.

Videos

The Life of Python. BBC and A&E, 2000.

15. THE STARS RETURN: THE UNEXPECTED AFTERLIFE AND ENDURING LEGACY OF COMEDY TEAMS

Interviews

Mark Dawidziak, Douglas Rathgeb, and Robert J. Thompson

ABOUT THE AUTHOR

Lawrence J. Epstein is an English professor and the author of *The Haunted Smile: The Story of Jewish Comedians in America.* He frequently lectures on American popular culture and lives with his wife and family on Long Island, New York.